Adolescence in Urban India

Shagufa Kapadia

Adolescence in Urban India

Cultural Construction in a Society
in Transition

 Springer

Shagufa Kapadia
Department of Human Development
and Family Studies
The Maharaja Sayajirao University of Baroda
Vadodara, Gujarat
India

ISBN 978-81-322-3731-0   ISBN 978-81-322-3733-4   (eBook)
DOI 10.1007/978-81-322-3733-4

Library of Congress Control Number: 2017937122

Printed on acid-free paper

This Springer imprint is published by Springer Nature
The registered company is Springer (India) Pvt. Ltd.
The registered company address is: 7th Floor, Vijaya Building, 17 Barakhamba Road, New Delhi 110 001, India

For my parents
I am, because you were.
You live within me, through me.

Foreword

The task of contemporary scholarship in the area of human development is becoming increasingly complex on two counts. First, the analyses of developmental phenomena are being enriched by contextualizing them in disparate cultural traditions. Second, the real-time context of human development is undergoing phases of rapid change at macro- as well as micro levels. In particular, the revolutions in areas of information, communication, travel, and medicine are transforming the contour and texture of our lives in dramatic ways. The spatial and temporal aspects of life are being reconfigured. As a consequence, the style and substance of human engagement is changing the pattern of movement across various stages in the life span. The prevailing situation is posing peculiar stresses and uncertainties, causing unique challenges of adaptation. Therefore, surviving and growing demand constant negotiation with the emerging reality.

The present volume entitled *Adolescence in Urban India: Cultural Construction in a Society in Transition* authored by Prof. Shagufa Kapadia from Department of Human Development and Family Studies, The Maharaja Sayajirao University of Baroda, offers an impressive analysis of an important facet of social and developmental reality. By addressing the world of adolescents, it raises issues significant for a large segment of the Indian population. Health-related challenges and issues of adolescent well-being are attracting considerable attention of media, policy makers, educationists as well as common people. The risks and vulnerabilities in the lives of adolescents prominently figure in the everyday discourses in households.

The book points out that the uncertainties in the lives of adolescents relate to many issues including career, job opportunities, interpersonal relationships, and family life. Adolescents often times report interpersonal conflicts, mood disturbances, and risk behaviors. It becomes a period of crisis in which (parental) *authority* and (adolescents') *autonomy* become contested issues. The context has shifted from the erstwhile era positioned in relatively stable agrarian societies where lives were regulated with the help of powerful institutions of joint family, marriage, kinship, and religion. These institutions strongly emphasized the value of sociality and social bonds by introducing notions of debt (*Rinas*) and performing action (*Yajnas*). The significance of social obligations and responsibilities rather than individual choice happened to be the hallmark of personal and social life. These, however, provide a weaker match for the demands of the new social order characterized by a dynamic, individualized, professionalized, and secular functioning. The ensuing mind-set opts to celebrate the themes of autonomy, individuation, and disengagement. The young mind is beginning to entertain a model of selfhood in which separation from parents and segregation from the adult world may be desired.

Development is a future-oriented process, and there is general interest in pursuing a safe and secure future. The Indian people are particularly keen to see that their offspring (*santan or santati*) lead a life that is of relatively better quality. Care and protection of *kishora/kishori*, or *yuva* (youth) constitute major parental woes and concerns. This burden assumed by most parents generates a marked tension between parents and their growing children. It is most evident during the stage of adolescence when a child undergoes unparalleled transformations in physical, social, and intellectual domains. Navigating through the related changes simultaneously becomes a critical challenge for both the parents and their wards. This raises threats and vulnerabilities while dealing with emerging life challenges, particularly in the middle class whose aspirations are guided by the spirit of consumerism.

The empirical work reported by Prof. Kapadia shows that today's adolescents focus chiefly on the issues related to educational choices, career, and relationships. It implicates that rapid changes coupled with uncertainties require new grounds for decision making and criteria for opting informed choices. Today, adaptability and seeking opportunities are emphasized, but interactions with family and community are rendered complex and challenging. Professor Kapadia rightly observes that the task of parenting has to shift from the role of authority/disciplinarian to that of friend, guardian, and guide.

The explorations of human development are increasingly indicating that it takes place through several trajectories which are situated in the local and global cultural contexts. As development is embedded in the cultural context, the two function in an interdependent fashion. The cultural and traditional aspects form an integral part of social memory which plays a key role in regulating the modes of being and becoming. It is gratifying that Prof. Kapadia has explored the developmental challenges during adolescence in the Indian context with a deep cultural sensibility. Informed by key perspectives on human development, she offers a nuanced theoretical and empirical analysis of adolescent development from the vantage points of adolescents as well as parents. Her main thesis is that cultural world views and contextual contingencies interact to shape development.

The findings of research reported in this volume indicate that there are pressures for career building and developing social–emotional maturity. The qualitative analysis of images, hopes and fears, insecurities, and anxieties of adolescents has uncovered many aspects of adolescent lives. It was observed that the disagreements between adolescents and parents often occur in relation to chores, academics, finance, regulation of social activities and physical appearance, use of cell phone, friendships, and romantic interests. Adolescents like to function with their own choices, but they are often guided by social comparisons. Some parents are now acting as "managers," and adolescents are their "projects." The rising level of material and social aspirations is shaping the lives of adolescents in the period of transition, which inevitably leads to vulnerabilities. In general, the findings implicate that socialization and parenting take place in a dynamically evolving socio-cultural context marked by continuity as well as change.

Professor Kapadia has been successful in bringing out the fact that the Indian model of development considers self and family in ways different from those noted in Euro-American settings which were treated as a prototype or normative. In particular, the encompassing relational model of selfhood underscores the spiritual, moral, and religious aspects of one's being. The Indian view of self consists of a multilayered inclusive structure comprising of physical, vital, social, mental, and blissful (spiritual) levels of existence. As detailed by Prof. Kapadia, the middle classes have had extensive contact with Western education and the recent past has brought in the presence of free market and consumerism as chief architects of life concerns. Indian society is experiencing the impact of the "global" in terms of cultural disintegration and breakdown in values and practices. There is also large-scale migration of people from one state to another and to other countries. Indian society is in transition due to politico-economic changes, and socialization goals are being directed by different priorities and life goals.

I congratulate Prof. Kapadia for this excellent piece of work that enables one to appreciate the social construction of adolescence and parenting relationships in the context of urban middle class. By blending conceptual and empirical analyses, this book helps gauge problems and challenges of parenting adolescents. Needless to say that there does exist considerable diversity in the composition of adolescents based on the categories of class, caste, gender, reservation, region, etc. There is a need for more studies of this kind in different parts of India so that a comprehensive understanding may be gained; issues of vulnerability may be addressed; and the goal of positive adolescent development may be pursued. We need to invest in adolescents as they constitute a key human resource for society.

Prof. Girishwar Misra
Vice Chancellor
Mahatma Gandhi Antarrashtriya Hindi Vishwavidyalaya, Wardha, India

Preface

The genesis of this book can be traced back to my personal experiences as a young college girl or an "adolescent," a term I got more closely acquainted with in the course of my study of human development. In the second year of undergraduate study, we had a course on "Understanding One's Own Self", which focused on adolescence as a developmental stage. As the course unfolded, we engaged in the classic theories of human development such as the psychoanalytic and psychosocial theories. The recurrent theme of adolescence highlighted in these theories was that it was a stage fraught with tension, essentially emerging from the renewed pace of development across domains, and the adolescent's striving for autonomy from parents. As adolescents, we were supposed to be preoccupied with our own selves, reflecting on the central question of identity, "Who am I?"

Much as I would try, it was difficult for me to experience the many psychological developments addressed in the course, nor was I troubled by the question of identity or had experienced any special turmoil in relation to myself or felt the need to seek autonomy from my parents. In fact, much of my free time was spent with family, the pleasant memories of which have stayed with me through the years. Moreover, I was often plagued with insecurities related to my parents' health and a lurking fear of anything untoward happening to either of them.

Questions and doubts surfaced intermittently in my mind; nevertheless, given the cultural tendency to assimilate the guru's teachings, seldom did I articulate these confusions or question the relevance of the proposed theoretical perspectives. In fact, I often found myself trying to "fit in" with the model that was highlighted in the theories. Pushing the questions away however did not make them disappear and these continued to linger. Subsequently, during my master's research on understanding children in their ecological context, I got acquainted with the role of culture in development. Engagement with cross-cultural perspectives was a turning point in that it made the puzzle of adolescence easier to unravel. The Western experience of turmoil or strain in relationship with parents was not culturally mandated after all, nor was it a problem if one did not ponder over the question, "Who am I?"

The steadily growing scholarship in the study of development in cultural context offered much respite from the nagging questions on human development in general and adolescent development in particular, at the same time encouraging engagement with this developmental period. My scholarly interest in adolescence thus took root.

Vadodara, India   Shagufa Kapadia

Acknowledgements

If each of my words were a drop of water, you would see through them and glimpse what I feel: gratitude.

Octavio Paz

The journey of translating research into book has been prolonged and challenging. Affirming the African proverb, albeit in adapted form, I acknowledge, "*It takes a village...to create a book*".

I thank my sisters, who make sure that there is seldom a dull moment in my life; Reshma and Shilpa, whose candid, witty, and astute comments never fail to ensure that I stay grounded in whatever I do. Their periodic questions "*Is it the same book you are still writing? Not finished, even now...?? !!*" pushed me along... I am grateful to Prerna, in whom I have a mentor who I can reach out to anytime to sound out even the smallest or fuzziest of ideas, knowing full well that her input will give it shape and take it to the next level. Pankaj lent color to all conversations with his wise guy interjections that evoke amusement and exasperation at the same time.

My heartfelt gratitude to Gautam, whose quiet presence, unstinting support, and gentle encouragement have stood me in good stead through the multiple vagaries of life.

A big 'thank you' to Urvi, my friend, who has patiently read earlier rather dreadful drafts, and given constructive and meticulous feedback that enabled me to move to the next stages. I am especially grateful for BGMB's continual urging to "focus and write something for myself"; it has been a steady source of support and inspiration all the way through this writing journey.

My research assistants and students have contributed to different aspects of this research and writing journey—without them, neither the research nor the book would have been possible. A special thank you to Nidhi Shah for her help with the focus group discussions and the figures, and to Priya Parikh and Krupali Patel for pitching in for some interviews and taking care of the tedious, but essential elements required to round off the book project.

Parts of the research have been presented in select seminars and conferences, and the comments and suggestions in such forums have contributed to fine-tuning this work. The inputs of Joan Miller, Professor at the New School for Social Research, New York, at various stages, right from the initiation of the research on adolescence, have been most valuable in shaping this project.

I acknowledge The Maharaja Sayajirao University of Baroda for granting me sabbatical leave that enabled quiet, contemplative time, a *sine qua non* for transforming research and reflection into writing. I thank the reviewers whose critical and insightful comments have contributed significantly to the shaping of this book. I deeply appreciate the support provided by Shinjini Chatterjee from Springer publications, whose patience and periodic interventions have enabled me to bring this project to fruition. I also thank Priya Vyas for her inputs in the final stages of preparing the manuscript for publication.

My deepest gratitude goes to the adolescents and the parents—the essence of this book. They have so kindly and generously allowed me a peep into their thoughts and lives, entrusting me with earnest, insiders' perspectives. Their disclosures have enabled the unwrapping of yet a few more folds of the vibrant, intricate tapestry of adolescence as woven in the Indian society.

Contents

About the Author

Shagufa Kapadia, PhD is a Professor in the Department of Human Development and Family Studies. She is the Department Chair and Coordinator of the Center of Advanced Study (CAS) in Human Development, and Hon. Director of the Women's Studies Research Center at the Maharaja Sayajirao University of Baroda, Vadodara, India. Her research interests center on culture and human development with a focus on adolescent and youth development, parenting and socialization, and gender and women's issues. She has significant international cross-cultural research and teaching experience. She is on the review and editorial boards of the journals *Culture and Psychology, Emerging Adulthood*, and *Psychological Studies*. Prof. Kapadia has received prestigious awards and fellowships, including the Fulbright Senior Research Fellowship (2003–2004) and the Shastri Indo-Canadian Faculty Research Award (2006 and 2010). She is the India coordinator of the International Society for the Study of Behavioral Development (ISSBD) and a Founding Board Member of the International Society for the Study of Emerging Adulthood (SSEA).

List of Figures

List of Tables

Chapter 1
Culture, Context, and Development

Abstract This chapter centers on the fundamental idea that cultural worldviews and contextual contingencies interact to shape human development. Cultures are dynamic and evolve over time in response to contextual changes. This chapter begins with an overview of individual development as a function of culture–context interaction. Presented next is a discussion of the context of social change and globalization. Select theoretical frameworks that explain cultural and contextual variability in human development are then described. The next section discusses socialization and parenting as culturally embedded bidirectional phenomena. Following this, the Hindu model is presented as an Indian model of human development, family, and self, highlighting the cultural worldview, life goals, and ideal precepts and practices. The unique characteristic of the Indian self containing the spiritual and embodied forms is described, followed by the moral and religious significance of the parent–child relationship. A discussion on the socialization goals and approaches in traditional and contemporary contexts is described next. This chapter then turns to an overview of the urban middle class in contemporary India. Presented next is the conceptual framework that scaffolds the depiction of adolescence and parent–adolescent relationship presented in this book. The final section provides an account of the empirical studies discussed in this book.

Keywords Culture · Context · Globalization · Social change · Socialization · Parenting · Indian · Hindu · Family · Middle class · Adolescence

Individual Development: A Culture–Context Interaction

"One mind, many mentalities: universalism without the uniformity," the dictum put forth by Richard Shweder eloquently and evocatively encapsulates the complex phenomenon of culture–context–development interface. Culture and psyche, mentalities and practices are intimately associated, and socially produce and reproduce each other. Culture constitutes shared meanings and practices, whereas contexts are multiple and often contested. Individuals are embedded in multiple interacting

© Springer (India) Pvt. Ltd. 2017
S. Kapadia, *Adolescence in Urban India*,
DOI 10.1007/978-81-322-3733-4_1

1

layers of context, influencing each other in a multidirectional and dynamic manner (Shweder et al. 2006, p. 723). Context and person, culture and psyche make each other up (Shweder 1990) or co-construct each other (Valsiner 1994).

Human development thus evolves along universal and variable developmental pathways. The variations are a function of different cultural and contextual factors that interact to determine the worldview, the goals of development, the ways of being, the nature of self, and the nature of beliefs, practices, and behaviors. Early anthropological research (Srinivas 1960; Whiting and Whiting 1975) demonstrated that individual development unfolds within an intricately integrated context of political, economic, ecological, religious, and other forces at play. Through their extensive anthropological explorations across cultures, well known as The Six Cultures Study, the Whitings highlighted the significance of cultural learning environments for childrearing and child development (Whiting 1963). They used the metaphor of theater to contend that the drama of childrearing and child development plays out on a family and household stage, in a cultural community, which is the theater. This occurs in the backdrop of outside forces—history, ecology (New 2010). Likewise, Srinivas's (1960) contribution is significant in rooting the understanding of human behavior in the Indian reality, based on the idea that individuals can be best understood in the contexts where they live and work, playing multiple social and cultural roles. He challenged the dominant Brahmin paradigm for understanding Indian society and drew attention to caste as fluid and dynamic (not static and unchanging as was the colonial view), involving regional dimensions, and an important principle of social stratification of the Indian society. Models interweaving culture and context in the study of human development have drawn from and built upon such early frameworks to further extend and explicate the concept of development-in-context (Berry 1994; Bronfenbrenner 1979; Greenfield 2009; Super and Harkness 1986).

The discipline of cultural psychology contends that "…relatively few components of the human mental equipment are so inherently constrained, hardwired, or fundamental that their pathway is fixed in advance and cannot be transformed or altered through cultural participation" (Shweder et al. 2006, p. 719). Culture offers both symbolic and behavioral inheritance. Symbolic inheritance refers to notions such as "parents must be obeyed," and behavioral inheritance comprises routinized or institutionalized practices, for instance, "touching feet of parents as a mark of respect." "Culture (is viewed) as a socially interactive process of construction comprising two main components: shared activity (cultural practices) and shared meaning (cultural interpretation). Both components of cultural processes are cumulative in nature since they occur between, as well as within, generations. Meanings and activities not only accumulate but also transform over both developmental time—across a single life cycle, and historical time—between generations" (Greenfield et al. 2003, p. 462). Different sociocultural constructions have evolved over time, across societies. "… these various constructions are an inherent feature of particular ways of life, embedded as they are in various institutions, societal structures, rituals, and so on" (Gergen 1994 cited in Gergen 2011, p. 205).

The notions and concepts that we imbibe from our culture shape our interpretations of the world and of development.

The idea that individual development takes place within social phenomena at the household, community, and macrosocietal levels is thus well-accepted. All societies of the world prescribe developmental pathways within certain ecological-cultural or ecocultural contexts. The pathways and endpoints of development are intricately embedded in cultural worldviews and processes. Based in biology, the processes comprise cultural practices or shared activity and cultural interpretations or shared meaning, which transform across developmental and sociohistorical time (Greenfield et al. 2003).

Culture requires an environmental context, and in turn, culture influences every context inhabited by human beings (Dasen 2003). Context and culture thus interact to co-construct human development. Cultural continuity is evident in how cultures retain core values and norms. However, cultures are not static but constantly changing; hence, cultural adaptation is a sustaining phenomenon (Valsiner 2000). Cultures unfold and evolve over time with active participation of its people, and although the core values may sustain, their representations and meanings are likely to undergo change (Tripathi 2013). Equally, individuals play an active role in constructing culture and influencing context. The unidirectional culture transmission model renders individuals as passive recipients in their acceptance of cultural messages; for instance, children's psychological functioning is said to be shaped by parents and teachers. The bi- or multidirectional transfer model on the contrary contends that individuals actively reconstruct cultural messages. Messages communicated by the older generation are analyzed and reassembled in newer forms. Cultural transformation is thus a continuous process (Valsiner 2000) as evinced in social change. The following section addresses the context of social change and globalization.

The Context of Social Change and Globalization

The idea of the inevitability of change needs to be accepted and interwoven in any study of culture and human development. According to the developmental-contextual view, development occurs in a multilevel context, and the nature of changes in this context leads to development. Individual development constitutes a major component of social context and social change, respectively. It is influenced by changes in multiple contexts including the immediate contexts such as family, the interactions between these, and changes in the society at large, which is social change (Lerner 2002; Lerner et al. 2002).

Social change is defined as change in the typical characteristics of a society, such as the economic system, social institutions, cultural products, laws, norms, values, and symbols (Calhoun 1992 cited in Pinquart and Silbereisen 2004). The changes that occur at the macrolevel are mediated through the microsystems. Social change may be gradual, for example, increasing population of elderly in some societies, or it may be sudden, for example, the breakdown of the communist system in Eastern Europe. Compared to sudden social change, gradual social change is often difficult to discern. Gradual social change may occur across generations, for example, preference for smaller families, or it may occur within one generation, for example, differences in and values related to options that were available to one's parents and grandparents compared to oneself. In gradual social change, the old options are still available and "resource-poor" individuals may perhaps follow old developmental pathways, whereas "resource-rich" individuals may adopt the new paths. Further, gradual social change is likely to be facilitated by resources such as unconventionality of thinking and behaving, and tolerance for ambiguity (Pinquart and Silbereisen 2004, p. 295).

In the present times, globalization, an element of distal social change (Silbereisen and Chen 2010), is a major phenomenon that is prompting significant changes in the lives of people across the world. The world over societies are experiencing an interaction of local and global, a collective of cross-cultural relations, dynamic in character. Globalization is a multidimensional phenomenon (Diaz and Zerkel 2012). Notwithstanding the myriad definitions of globalization, it is commonly acknowledged that "… the process of globalization involves extensive and often imposed contact among people from different cultures, nations, and empires with subsequent social, cultural, economic, and political interdependencies and consequences" (Marsella 2012, p. 456). New contact zones are being created across cultural boundaries. These include ethnoscapes (e.g., immigrants, tourists, guest workers); technoscapes (global configuration of mechanical and information technology); mediascapes (newspapers, television stations, film production studios); financescapes (currency markets, commodity speculations); and ideoscapes (e.g., ideas about freedom, rights, welfare) (Appadurai 1990). Each of these facilitates multiple and wide ranging interactions and influences. Cultural contact is not a new phenomenon; however, the unique feature of globalization is the exceptional development of telecommunication and transportation, resulting in immediate contact and impact (Marsella 2012), as well as increase in economic and financial interdependence (Arnett 2002). The momentous transformations in communication technology and transportation brought on by globalization have rendered the world a "global village." A unique feature of these processes of economic interconnection and cross-national cultural influences is the speed at which these connections happen and the extent of reach to even the most remote parts of the world (Scholte 2000 cited in Diaz and Zerkel 2012). Common features of globalization include the increase in intensity and frequency of contact with the global culture of free markets and consumerism, greater reach and influence of globalization in urban areas, challenges arising from adapting the global culture to the local culture, and perception of globalization as a source of opportunities and problems (Arnett 2002).

The influences of globalization are often imposed, directly or indirectly, for instance, when penetration of Western values challenges the traditional ways. In general, globalization brings about changes with potential positive or negative outcomes. Examples of positive changes include increased quality of life, social mobility, exposure to new ideas and customs, new opportunities, acquaintance with alternative beliefs and values, new technologies (Internet), and changes in gender status and opportunities, whereas potential negative outcomes may include cultural disintegration, breakdown in traditional values and customs, new social dysfunctions such as generational conflicts and family disintegration, decreased predictability and control, cultural homogenization, out-migration, English language penetration, and new social dysfunctions and disorders. It is important to acknowledge that the impact of global forces is mediated by the context and setting and is likely to vary by country as well as by region within a country (Marsella 2012), and by socioeconomic class.

Globalization and political processes constitute the distal elements of social change. The demands of the macro context are often discrepant from the ideological base of a society, which compels individuals to engage actively in deriving a balance between old and new ways. An example is the rapid economic change in China and its consequences on the shift in family socialization from a general orientation of parent dependence to one where the child is encouraged for autonomy and initiative in exploring opportunities. Individuals' adaptation to social change involves institutional filtering (e.g., gender, stages of life span) and resources (e.g., human, social, economic). These in turn determine how one copes with the social change (e.g., active attempts to resolve demands, seeking help and support) and the resultant psychosocial outcomes such as well-being, satisfaction, mental health, lifestyles, career paths, and close relationships (Silbereisen and Chen 2010). In the context of fast-paced social change as being experienced in societies across the world, the traditional forms may not be compatible with the new demands and hence necessitate change in attitudes, goals, and practices of socialization (Chen and Chen 2010).

Adaptation is an ongoing process, wherein cultural values are adapted to and hence influenced by the sociodemographic environment. At the family level, adaptations are required on part of parents as they raise the new generation, and at the same time, the new generation plays an active role in adapting to the changing conditions (Greenfield 2009). A contextual view of human development thus becomes relevant in the present times of massive socioeconomic transformation, especially for a better understanding of how social change affects intergenerational relationships. Examples are changes in relationship quality in terms of support, emotional closeness, and intergenerational solidarity; continuity or discontinuity of intergenerational relationships over time; similarities and differences in values; and mutual perceptions between generations (Trommsdorff 2006).

The following section presents an overview of select theoretical models and frameworks that address cultural and contextual variability in development, including the construction of self.

Models of Cultural and Contextual Influences on Human Development

Cultural worldviews and contextual factors shape the development and lives of individuals. This section describes select theoretical models that integrate culture and context, as well as different models of self to explain cultural variability in human development.

Ecological Framework

Bronfenbrenner's ecological systems theory, also called development-in-context or human ecology theory, identifies five environmental systems with which an individual interacts: micro-, meso-, exo-, macro-, and chronosystems. Each system offers a diversity of options and sources of growth over time. The micro system "…is the complex of relations between the developing person and environment in an immediate setting containing that person (e.g., home, school, workplace, etc.)" (Bronfenbrenner 1977, p. 514). The mesosystem comprises "the interaction among major settings containing the developing person at a particular time in his or her life"; it is a system of microsystems (Bronfenbrenner 1977, p. 514). An exosystem is "an extension of the mesosystem embracing other specific social structures, both formal and informal, that do not themselves contain the developing person but impinge upon or encompass the immediate settings in which that person is found, and thereby influence, delimit, or even determine, what goes on there. Major institutions of the society constitute this structure … (such as) the world of work, neighborhood, the mass media, agencies of the government…and informal social networks" (Bronfenbrenner 1977, p. 515). The macrosystem is the overarching institutional patterns of a culture or subculture such as social, economic, legal, educational, and political systems. The chronosystem consists of environmental events and transitions that occur through the child's life, including any sociohistorical events (Bronfenbrenner 1994). There is a reciprocity and constant interaction within the factors of each system and between systems. Furthermore, within and between each system are bidirectional influences; that is, relationships have impact in two directions, both away from the individual and toward the individual. An integrated expansion of the model is the person–process–context–time model and the interactions between these (Bronfenbrenner and Morris 2006).

Ecological Model of Deprivation

Drawing from the Ecological Systems Framework, Sinha (1982) put forth an ecological model of deprivation, which can be applied to understanding the ecology of various socioeconomic groups in India. This model conceptualizes the child's ecology in terms of two concentric layers. The upper more visible layer constitutes home, school, and peer group and comprises three dimensions, namely physical space and material, social roles and relationships of the child, and activities. The supporting layer constitutes the geographical and physical environment as well as the institutional setting in terms of social class, caste, and the general amenities available to the child. The visible and surrounding factors often combine and interact with each other and shape economic pursuits, way of life and also socialization processes and interpersonal relationships, and in turn the development of the individual.

Ecocultural Model

One of the most popular theoretical approaches to study culture–development–behavior interaction is the ecocultural approach (Berry 1994; Weisner 2002) which views development as an adaptation to the physical and economic conditions of the environment, positioning individual psychological functioning in a sociocultural context (Dasen 2003). The specific economic and environmental conditions create different social structures from which different developmental pathways evolve. Ecocultural pathways are the most influential in shaping development processes and outcomes. The ecocultural approach to studying cultural and psychological phenomena is based on the view that groups and individuals develop their customary and individual behaviors as adaptations to the demands of their particular ecosystem. The approach also considers sociopolitical influences on the population from outside the local habitat (e.g., acculturation, via schooling, religion) as important sources of social and psychological development. These two sets of external influences alter the basic cultural and psychological features of people (Berry 2013).

Independent and Interdependent Developmental Pathways

Greenfield et al. (2003) have proposed a framework of independent and interdependent developmental pathways in Western and non-Western societies, respectively. The framework draws from the theoretical perspectives of the ecocultural, sociohistorical, and values approach to consider the overlapping influences of the material conditions of the environment, the social factors including the cultural activities and practices over time, and the ideals or meanings inside individual psyche. The values approach maintains that different cultural values give rise to different idealized developmental pathways of independence and interdependence. In an independent pathway, social obligations are individually negotiated and individual rights are maximized, whereas in an interdependent pathway, social obligations take precedence over individual choice. Each pathway supports culturally relevant goals, which give rise to implicit or explicit ideas and beliefs regarding the nature of an ideal child and related socialization practices.

The ecocultural model informs the notion that developmental pathways are differentially adapted to different types of physical and economic conditions in societies. In small face-to-face communities with subsistence economies, the interdependent pathway of development is better adapted, whereas in large urban fast-changing societies with a commercial economy, the independent pathway is a better adaptive response. In the former societies, there is a vertical transmission of parental ethnotheories from one generation to the next; in the latter, however, negotiation of parental ideas occurs horizontally within generations. Western industrialized societies (e.g., German, European-American) and factors such as high socioeconomic status (SES) and formal education are inclined toward the cultural ideal of independence, whereas non-Western societies (e.g., India, China, Japan) favor the interdependent ideal (Greenfield et al. 2003). The sociohistorical approach draws from the values approach and recognizes that socialization practices or cultural learning is constructed in specific situations, with the active involvement of the child. Value orientations generate specific socializing practices and interactional routines that shape cultural learning along a certain developmental pathway. It is relevant to bear in mind that there are variations in the nature of independent or interdependent orientations even within Western and non-Western societies. Hence, we need to caution against applying the same characteristics to all Western or non-Western (East Asian and South Asian) societies, in the interest of recognizing distinctive cultural outlooks (Miller et al. in press).

The above theoretical models highlight the intricacies of the culture–context–development interactions. Also relevant in understanding this dynamic is the ways in which the concept of self is construed in multiple ways in different cultures. Individuals and their social worlds are mutually constituted, with each shaping the other. Like culture, self is dynamic and amenable to cultural change (Markus and Kitayama 2010).

Models of Self

Individuals and their social worlds are mutually constituted, with each shaping the other. The dynamic character of culture is revealed in the ongoing invention and change of sociocultural ideas, practices, products, economic factors, and ecological factors. Like culture, self is dynamic and changes with cultural change. The genesis of self is located either in economic and ecological factors or in philosophy and religion (Markus and Kitayama 2010). The different yet overlapping cultural models of self are discussed below.

Independent and interdependent self-construal. Notwithstanding the idea of multiple selves as being universally available, cultures differ in their foundational schemas of self as independent or interdependent (Markus and Kitayama 1991).

The independent self emphasizes the inherent distinctness of individuals, and the normative imperative is to become independent from others and express one's unique attributes. Cultural goals and tasks are constructed along this framework. The interdependent self evolves in interaction with others; it is connected or related to others. Correspondingly, cultural goals and tasks emphasize harmonious interdependence, encourage fitting in with others, taking their perspective, being aware of others' expectations, and adjusting to others.

Autonomous-related self. Rooted in the contextual-developmental orientation, the model of the autonomous-related self puts forth the idea that autonomy and relatedness are basic human needs in all societies and govern self, self-other relations, and social behaviors. Privileging one over the other depends upon the cultural blueprint of human development in a society as well as the socioeconomic context. Autonomy comprises two dimensions: One is agency, which means the capacity to act on one's own, and the other is interpersonal distance, which refers to more or less relatedness and separation between selves. In the individualist view, autonomy and relatedness are posed as conflicting. Relatedness is viewed as incompatible with autonomy, and in fact, separateness (especially from parents) is considered necessary for the development of autonomy. The autonomous-related model presents an alternate conception in which self is moored onto the construal of autonomy as agency with volition, which is distinct from relatedness. The two can coexist in that an individual's position on the interpersonal distance dimension may not affect one's standing on the agency dimension. In departure from the portrayal of autonomy and relatedness as conflicting and thereby unlikely to coexist, in most societies a combination of the two needs is more prevalent. The autonomous-related self develops in the model of family psychological interdependence in which intergenerational material interdependence weakens, thereby enabling autonomy to enter into socialization. At the same time, psychological interdependence continues to be valued, and hence, the goal of connectedness rather than separateness remains significant (Kagitcibasi 2005, 2013).

Coexisting multiple models of self. This model is based on the premise that multiple and divergent aspects of self coexist and co-occur within and between cultures (Mascolo et al. 2004). The model addresses specific differences in the construction of individuality and social connectedness. Four models of self-conceptions are advanced: independent, interdependent, relational, and encompassing that may exist concurrently in any society, with some models prevailing more than others do. The independent self represents self as distinct and separate from others. The interdependent self is similar to the "we-self" and refers to shared experiences wherein one defines self in relation to others with blurred boundaries between self and other (Markus and Kitayama 1991). The relational self views self in terms of dispositions and actions in dialogical relation with others. The selves may be distinct, but are interrelated, and "self" and "other" act with reference to each other; it includes self-relating-to-other and other-relating-to-self descriptions. The encompassing sense of self views self as being embedded in a relationship, mostly hierarchical, in which one is obligated to or responsible for the other. Further, four relational orientations are identified to signify the direction of action and experience, between self and other. Within-self descriptions consist of action and experience that occur within the self and not directed at another person (e.g., I feel anxious). Mutuality consists of reciprocal joint actions between persons (e.g., we care about each other). Other-relating-to-self refers to representations of actions and experiences of other people that are directed toward self (e.g., she likes me), and self-relating-to-other denotes actions and experiences in self that are about or directed toward others (e.g., I like her) (Mascolo et al. 2004).

Models of Social Change

Model of family change. Kagitcibasi's (1996) model of family change presents the links between changing socioeconomic context and family systems including cultural values, family interactions and socialization across societies, and its implications in defining the self as autonomous, related, or autonomous-related. This model derives from the developmental-contextual perspective, taking into consideration the global pattern of socioeconomic development and urbanization. The family is situated within the social and cultural context and is viewed as a system. The key elements are generational dependencies, the value attributed to children, and the family relationships. Three prototypical models of family change are identified. The *family model of total interdependence* is largely prevalent in traditional rural agrarian societies, where intergenerational interdependence is a requisite for family livelihood. The child contributes to the family well-being during childhood as well as later on by way of providing old age security to the parents. In this model, the independence of the child is viewed as focus on self-interest rather than the family and hence not encouraged. The *family model of independence* is largely characteristic of the Western middle class nuclear family. Intergenerational independence is valued, and childrearing is oriented toward autonomy. Individuation-separation is considered a requisite for healthy human development. The *family model of emotional/psychological interdependence* is different from the two prototypical models of independence and interdependence. It is more prevalent in developed urban areas of the majority non-western world. It is a synthesized model with independence in the material realm together with interdependence in the psychological realm. With decrease in material interdependencies, autonomy finds space and is not considered as a threat to the family as emotional interdependence continues to be valued. In this model, even amid socioeconomic change, the principal orientation of interdependence is sustained, albeit with some accommodation of individual autonomy. The autonomous-related self develops in this model of family change (Kagitcibasi 1996, 2005, 2007).

Theory of social change and human development. Greenfield (2009) has proposed a theory linking social change and human development that relates socioeconomic status (SES) to culture in explaining the shifting pathways of human development. From the assumption of culture as dynamic and cultural change as the norm, the theory shows how sociodemographic ecologies alter cultural values and in turn learning environments. The theory anchors onto the sociodemographic changes sweeping all societies of the world to bring about transformations from rural residence, informal education, subsistence economy, and low-technology environments to urban residence, formal schooling, commerce, and high-technology environments. Two models are proposed: *Gemeinschaft* ("community" or folk society) and *Gesellschaft* (urban society) to refer to the two ecologies, respectively, and how the developmental pathways and in turn socialization goals adapt to the ecological environment. *Gemeinschaft* follows the interdependent developmental pathway, and *Gesellschaft*, the independent pathway. The theory emphasizes the processes rather than outcomes of change in pathways of human development; it addresses within group variability making it possible to highlight both similarities and differences among ethnic groups based on shared and different sociodemographic characteristics. An example would be the emerging urban middle classes in India as sharing similarities because of shared socioeconomic (SES) status. The theory identifies the relationship between SES and culture and sees SES as influencing cultural values. As ecologies shift to *Gesellschaft* structure, developmental trajectories become better adapted to these conditions, with both parents and children actively adapting to the environmental changes. Parents adapt their childrearing to fit with the changed structure and its demands. In other words, movement toward urbanization and economic development is likely to alter socialization from a collectivist interdependent orientation to an individualist independent orientation.

Cosmologies and Worldviews

In addition to or perhaps interwoven in cultural adaptations, are two other aspects that are relevant in understanding the culture-development interface. These include cosmologies or religions and values. Cosmologies or religions are worldviews shared by a large segment of a society and are resistant to cultural change or likely to coexist with newer perspectives. Cosmologies help people make sense of the universe and the place of humans in it. For example, according to the Judeo-Christian worldview, nature is to be controlled and dominated, whereas in Hinduism, humans are considered as part of nature. Cosmologies shape value systems, parental ethnotheories and childrearing practices. The value systems are linked to a society's moral and ethical guidelines that in turn determine behavioral standards (Dasen 2003). Cosmologies or religions fall in the realm of indigenous psychologies and have significant scientific potential and psychological relevance as these offer ideas, theories, and explanations regarding human development that may be discrepant with the mainstream Western perspectives. For instance,

Hinduism has provided different systems of philosophy involving theoretical analyses of the human personality and various therapeutic techniques designed to help individuals cope with the difficulties of human life and reach higher levels of development (Chakkarath 2013).

In general then, cultural and biological adaptations, cosmology, religion and values, ecological context, and the sociopolitical context mediate human development (Dasen 2003). The changes that occur in these contexts filter down to the family and in turn to the growing individual, either directly or indirectly. Family socialization precepts and practices reflect an amalgamation of these aspects.

Socialization and Parenting: Culturally Embedded Bidirectional Phenomena

Culture along with contextual contingencies shape the goals of socialization and give meaning to socialization practices (Bugental and Grusec 2006), which in turn influence children's development, characteristics, and lives. Multiple agencies are involved in socialization, especially in the present context of globalization. Yet, in most societies, family is the nucleus of socialization and parents continue to function as the primary agents of socialization responsible for transmission of cultural values.

Parenting is determined by the following factors: (a) intrapersonal and intrapsychic characteristics of parents (biological forces, personality, age, and stage of life); (b) actual or perceived characteristics of children (health status, gender, developmental age); and (c) contextual characteristics (family structure, social network, socioeconomic status) (Bornstein 2006). Parenting is embedded in the ecological and cultural contexts that shape and determine socialization goals and practices. The ecological-contextual framework situates parenting in a network of interacting systems. Parent–child relationship is at the center, situated in and embedded in the mesosystem (e.g., workplace and mass media), exosystem (e.g., extended family, peers, school), and macrosystem (e.g., social class). Culture as the overarching system shapes the immediate contexts and short- and long-term goals (Bornstein and Cheah 2006).

Parenting comprises universals; however, the degree and form of parenting cognition and practices vary across cultures. A universal, for example, is child-directed speech in the sense of adults adjusting their speech to young children, which is observed commonly across cultures. On the other hand, the same parenting cognition or practice may function differently across cultures. For example, authoritative parenting is observed to have positive outcomes in European-American societies, whereas in African-American and Chinese families, the authoritarian style leads to positive outcomes. There is considerable cultural variation in parent–child relations during adolescence. Acquiring autonomy is important in Western contexts, while interdependence is the defining feature in non-Western societies. Fulfillment of one's roles and duties in hierarchical relationships is regarded as a significant marker of maturity. Thus, cultures provide models of parenting and parents in turn organize their caregiving according to the cultural belief systems, encouraging behavior that is in accordance with these and discouraging that which may run counter. Culture thus expresses and perpetuates through parenting, thereby making parents the primary agents of cultural transmission (Bornstein 2006, 2012).

Although parents play a key role in transmission of cultural values, the mode is by no means unidirectional from one generation to the next, wherein the recipients are largely passive in the process. The bidirectional model of cultural transmission is significant as it is based on the premise that all participants, parents and children alike, are actively involved in transforming cultural messages, thereby co-constructing culture, in other words contributing to cultural change (Valsiner 2000). This process may be even more active in the contemporary globalizing context. For instance, adolescents the world over are most influenced by the myriad forces of globalization and cross-culture influences. They are especially active in embracing the revolutionary advancements in communication technology, which often renders them more knowledgeable than the older generation. The dynamics of parent–adolescent relationship in the contemporary fast-changing context thus involve an interesting negotiation of cultural values and behaviors. Further, the bidirectional view instructs that in understanding parenting, parent–child interactions, and relationships, the perspectives of both parents and children are relevant.

Parent–child relationships are lifelong relationships based on continued interconnected experiences and involve both resources and constraints that mediate need fulfillment. The nature of the relationship changes across the lifespan of the child and parent. During childhood and adolescence, the relationship is built around hierarchy and hence has an asymmetric character (Trommsdorff 2006). Parental authority is a significant element constituting parenting and parent–child relationship. In accordance with the notion of parenting as a bidirectional phenomenon, it is relevant to view parental authority as dynamic and relational, produced in the process of parent–child interactions in a given socioeconomic context. Authority is translated according to social class background, parenting philosophies and approaches, as well as typical roles and behavioral patterns of parents and children (Kuhar and Reiter 2013). Overall, cultural values and contextual contingencies mediate parental authority.

The following section discusses the Indian-Hindu model of development, the Indian family context, and the nature of self.

An Indian Model of Human Development, Family, and Self

Societies across the world have different worldviews, and these shape the ideal model of development. Models of development represent a range from those that anchor on to the individual, the social world, or the spiritual world. These models define development across life span including the central goals and tasks at each stage.

In accordance with the cultural psychological perspective, religion could be regarded as an entity that contributes significantly in presenting worldviews or cultural models constituting symbolic and behavioral inheritance that are in turn embodied into social and psychological domains. In fact, religion has been regarded as a cultural system (Geertz 1993; Shweder 1990). All religions provide guidelines related to the meanings of self and a good life in a given context and recommend a corollary set of practices. Religion operates at individual and communal levels and involves shared beliefs and practices that all group members are expected to follow, thereby connecting self to others. It also plays the role of a socializing agent. In the Indian society, religion is a significant feature of everyday life. Across centuries, multiple religions (including subsects) such as Hinduism, Jainism, Buddhism, Christianity, Islam, and Zoroastrianism have thrived in India. All religions are interpreted as having a similar spiritual core. Regardless of the occurrence of discrimination and communal strife, generally there is a shared coexistence as also a tendency to partake in multiple religious worship and practices. Religions are characterized by commonalities and differences (Kapur and Misra in press). For instance, the "middle path" (*madhyam marg, madhyamika*) is endorsed in Hinduism and Buddhism. Another example is the concept of *dharma* which is endorsed in Hinduism, Sikhism, Jainism, and Buddhism and regarded as the foundation of a good life, yet the specific meanings of *dharma* differ. In Jainism for example, *ahimsa* forms the core of *dharma*, whereas Sikhs use the term to connote moral duty (Madan 1989).

Given that indigenous concepts are often embedded in religious worldview, the latter is ideally positioned to offer culture sensitive perspectives on human development. Notwithstanding the religious plurality of India, it is relevant to note that the Hindu tradition is an important constituent of the Indian culture with 79.80% of the national population and 82.13% of the urban Gujarat population identifying themselves as Hindu (Census of India 2011). "The term 'Hinduism' refers to innumerable sects, mainly on the Indian subcontinent, that follow different ideas but share some central convictions which are derived from a vast corpus of writings (with the *Vedas* and the *Upanishads* at the core)." The term *sanatana dharma* which means "eternal rules" or code of conduct, and not religion in the Western sense of the term, is used to denote Hinduism. The Hindu view has been empirically confirmed to influence values and attitudes (Chakkarath 2005, pp. 35–36).

The author acknowledges the concurrent existence of multiple religious ideologies in Indian society; nevertheless, the Indian depiction of human development presented anchors on to the Hindu worldview. It is relevant to note that the participants in the empirical studies discussed in the book have identified themselves as Hindus. It is hence assumed that they will be guided largely (although perhaps not completely or consistently or uniformly) by a Hindu "mentality (what people know, think, feel, want, value and hence choose to do)" à la cultural psychology (Shweder 1990, p. 725).

The Hindu worldview offers a template, which helps individuals make sense of their lives (Kakar 1981). It is however important to note that this template is the ideal prescription which people are expected to follow, and the actual manifestations may not occur (Sinha 1988) or occur in variable ways. The two primary themes in the Hindu worldview and life stages: individual-in-social-world and *moksha* (transcendence from worldly life) focusing on social adaptation and spiritual self-realization, respectively, reflect the emphasis on both individualism and collectivism. Individuals prioritize one or the other theme as they progress along the *ashramas* or life stages. In departure from Western models that situate developmental change in the individual, the Hindu model of life span development is essentially organized around the theme of "individual-in-social-relations" (Saraswathi et al. 2011, p. 287).

In line with the popular classification of societies along the individualism–collectivism (I/C) continuum (Triandis and Brislin 1984), the Indian society has been construed as collectivist, which is a misleading interpretation. Based on empirical research that tapped three types of responses—individualist, collectivist, and mixed, across a range of everyday personal and social situations, Sinha and Tripathi (2003) found an overwhelmingly high incidence of a mixed orientation. The I/C classification as a descriptive category is inappropriate and inadequate to capture the complexities of the Indian society where contrasting values are observed to coexist. The nature of Indian self is essentially contextual and expressed in accordance with the exigencies of a situation. An example is the *Ayurveda* system that is founded on the principle that both positive and negative elements are present in the body at the same time and balancing these is necessary for well-being. Contextualization is the dominant ideal in the Indian society and is reflected across relationships and situations (Ramanujan 1990), which facilitates the coexistence of contradictions. An action is judged in a specific context of roles and relationships. For an Indian, collectivism consists of the factors of family integrity and interdependence. Here too, a mix is preferred, for instance, the younger generation's preference for a more individualist model of a nuclear family, with the collective advantages of the extended family. The individualist orientation is manifested in the heterogeneity and choice of beliefs and practices deemed acceptable in (Hindu) religious worship. *Karma*—the powerful Hindu ethic—also bears an individualist orientation in the sense that it is determined by the individual's own conduct and behavior in the present and past life, suggesting thereby the notion that an individual is the master of one's own destiny. Individualism and collectivism thus coexist, and this is amply demonstrated in thought and behavior. Characteristic of the Indian psych is "...a kind of coexistence of disparate elements without any synthesis" (Sinha 1988, p. 43). "The Indian form of collectivism (is thus one that) contains strands of individualism" (Sinha and Tripathi 2003, p. 207). The constant inputs in balancing opposites or contradictions urge the average Indian to take the "middle path"—*Madhyam Marg* (Sinha and Tripathi 2003). The narrative of folk stories offers multiple examples of the middle path, and parents too consider this a necessary value in a collectivist society. The propensity toward the middle path is reinforced by the hierarchical structure of the Indian society. Younger individuals are socialized to avoid conflict and unpleasantness with elders (parent, teachers). Empirical observations show that the *madhyam marg* is perceived as a solution and an option in conflict situations. The *madhyam marg* thus becomes a default way of thinking as it helps to remove stress and conflict from family and even workspace. It is perceived as a means to maintain harmony in relationship. Rather than choosing between two contradictions, for example, being part of a group and yet distinct or respecting elders and taking one's own decision, an individual resorts to the *madhyam marg* as a more viable option. This is more rewarding as it precludes the necessity of choosing between two extremes, retains goodwill, and expands space for negotiation in relationships (Panda 2013).

Grahasthya Ashrama or the stage of householder assumes much significance in the Hindu life span model; marriage, having children, and supporting a family are the primary tasks of this life stage (Chakkarath 2005). Familism or family solidarity is a core value in the Indian society, and the major task of an individual is to fit into the social network of the family, which operates on a continuous basis to nurture relationships, interdependencies, and shared goals (Misra 1995). Family cohesion and family loyalty, harmony, unity, and mutual dependence are of much value. The family collective assumes higher value than individuality. The hierarchical nature of the social structure is clearly visible in family context. Age and gender are the defining elements of hierarchy, and expectations of behavior for each individual in the hierarchy are reciprocally organized. The younger members or "subordinates" in the hierarchy are expected to show deference and loyalty to the "superiors" who in turn offer nurturance and concern and are responsible for the subordinates, with all working toward the primary goal of the well-being of the family (Roland 1988). Gender is another organizing principle, and across social class, males are considered more superior than females. Although significant changes are observed in contemporary Indian society, the gender factor continues to express itself across many domains. One's *dharma* is also shaped along the specific frameworks of hierarchical relationships (e.g., parent–child; husband–wife). Hierarchical relationships within the family are characterized by strong emotional connectedness, interdependence, reciprocity, and mutual responsiveness (Saraswathi 2005). In general, the core pan-Indian values are constructed around the themes of context sensitivity, hierarchy of age and gender, family solidarity rather than individualism, negotiation rather than confrontation, and intuitive knowledge rather than empirical proof (Anandalakshmy 2013; Panda and Gupta 2004). The construction of the Indian self evolves in congruence with these dimensions.

The Indian self reflects a multiplicity of the autonomous and socially embedded selves that are governed by the life stage and behavioral context. Roland (1988) has conceptualized the self in terms of three overarching dimensions—the familial self, the individual self, and the spiritual self as well as the expanding self. The familial self is comprised of a basic inner psychological organization that is conducive to hierarchical relationships within family and community; it is experienced as the "we self." The individualized self emphasizes the "I self" and thrives in a society where autonomy is encouraged. The spiritual self constitutes the inner spiritual reality that is a basic assumption in the Hindu culture. It is expressed through a complex structure of rituals and meditation, Gods and Goddesses, and is virtually organic to the Hindu culture.

In essence, the Indian self contains the spiritual aspect and the embodied form. The spiritual self or *atman* is considered the real self, with the central guiding philosophy being to transcend the embodied or worldly self to fully experience the spiritual self and attain *moksha* (salvation). Over time, an individual is expected to detach oneself from worldly relationship bonds and obligations and try to reach a state of personal autonomy in the spiritual sphere through individualization from family attachments, while retaining social interdependence (Mascolo et al. 2004; Saraswathi 2005). At the same time, the Indian social and moral philosophy emphasizes social relations that are enacted within the framework of duty and hierarchy—two significant elements of the Indian cultural system. The extended family is hierarchically structured by kinship position and gender. Duties are defined by an individual's position in one's extended family, class or caste, and state, with duties toward the family taking precedence (Mascolo et al. 2004). With regard to self, whereas at the motivational level, the primary focus is on self-fulfillment and independence of relationships and community, the behavioral level depicts a dependent and in-group orientation (Chakkarath 2005).

The evolution of the Indian self occurs in tandem with the life stages with social embeddedness privileged until middle age and self-actualization favored during the last two life stages. The first two stages of life, *Brahmacharya* and *Grahasthya Ashramas*, primarily focus on the familial self, which operates within a web of hierarchical relationships with well-defined expectations and norms of behavior (Roland 1988). The empirical notion of personal autonomy thus defers to familism during these life stages. It is relevant to note that notwithstanding the web of social relations and responsibilities and in contrast to the hierarchical-collectivist notion that individuality is devalued in the Indian society, with increasing age and progression in stages there is an increase in personal freedom. Mines (1988) has demonstrated the transition from interdependence to independence through his ethnographic research with emerging adult, middle adult, and older individuals in India. During the early life stages that involve greater social responsibility, there is greater compliance and conformity to hierarchy, and personal goals are generally set aside. However, once the major social responsibilities are met (e.g., getting married, having children), personal freedom and autonomy in terms of control over decision making affecting one's life and a sense of responsibility for one's actions increase. The emphasis on compliance to social demands thus shifts across life stages, and the older one gets, the greater is the flexibility in abiding by cultural norms.

Parent–Child Relationship: Sacred of All Family Relationships

In the Indian culture, family is not just a matter of convention, rather it is assumed to have "natural foundations" (Badrinath 2003, p. 131). The stage of *grahasthya* (household, family) is of utmost significance in the life of an individual as it offers the opportunity to develop strong interpersonal connections and interdependencies, that form the essence of the Indian view of human development. The core Indian values of respect for hierarchy, desire to be embedded in an in-group, and familism (Sinha 1988; Kakar and Kakar 2007) are actively demonstrated in the family context. Duties and obligations are the guiding force in defining family relationships with the well-crafted kinship system rendering further elaboration of the same.

Among all the relationships in the family, the parent–child relationship is much eulogized, occupying the central position in the network of hierarchical relationships that an individual experiences across the life span. Authority has a traditional-moral basis and is an integral part of an individual's *dharma*, especially in the parent–child relationship. Correspondingly, the child's birth order determines to a large extent his or her position and role in the family, and values such as obedience and filial piety are upheld (Sinha 1983). The child as the person in the subordinate position is expected to show respect and obedience and attempt to anticipate the wish of the superior or act unquestioningly on the superior's orders, that is, the parent. The parent in turn offers nurturance and emotional rewards such as praise and affection. Guilt and emotional rewards are common means to enforce authority (Kakar 2001; Kakar and Kakar 2007).

Parenting thus assumes deep moral and religious significance in the Indian-Hindu cultural ethos. "No matter what the character or circumstance of a father or a mother may be, their children owe to them certain duties. Similarly, parents owe to their children certain duties. Protection, loving care, a disciplined upbringing and honest advice, are the duties of parents toward children. Obedience, holding them in honor, and looking after them in old age are the duties of children toward them" (Badrinath 2003, p. 124). This observation aptly expresses the conception and the reciprocal duties involved in the parent–child relationship.

Socialization Goals and Approaches in the Indian-Hindu Worldview

The Indian-Hindu worldview shapes socialization in the Indian society, and this is reflected largely in everyday practices and ideas of life and living. Individuals are enculturated into an ethos that reinforces "we-ness" (p. 236), affective exchange, and empathic sensitivity, and being in constant presence of parents and other elders enhances this orientation (Roland 1988). Care and concern for family members, parents especially, and subordinating one's "individual" wishes for the collective good of the family are themes that are interwoven from early childhood. Parenting is regarded as a sacred duty, a *dharma*, and parents are responsible for inculcating good *samskaras* in their child, which is also evident in the traditional conceptualization of the child. Misri (1985) has conceptualized the Indian child along three axes. The first axis considers the child as a divine gift created through parents— human/divine axis; second, the child is considered as a collective being in relation to family and community as well as a unique individual based on her or his *karma* —individual/collective axis; and third, the child enters the world with *gunas* (qualities or attributes) which are altered through *samskaras* that turn the child into a social being—the inalterable/transformative axis. The child is thus conceptualized with coexisting contradictions, which need to be sorted out through socialization.

Children are considered as a gift from God, and childhood is regarded as a time for indulgence with the primary role of parents being *palna–posna* (Kakar 1981) which means nurturing and protecting the child, a notion that is reflected in parental ethnotheories and childrearing practices. Children are considered as not being capable of volitional regulation of actions, and hence, the role of caregivers becomes important. From early on, children are socialized to function within a network of relationships that expands as one moves from one stage to another. Respect for elders as ones who are authoritative and nurturing and who could be relied on for all kinds of support is a primary theme in child socialization (Saraswathi and Pai 1997). In their research on parental ethnotheories in India, Saraswathi and Ganapathy (2002) delineate parental conceptions of a good and ideal child as one who has good *samskaras*, which essentially constitutes social values such as being respectful of and obedient to parents and other elders, being truthful, modest, humble, trustworthy, compassionate and tolerant, socially conforming, and religious. The overall guiding principles of socialization that emerge are social embeddedness, adult–child continuity, and interpersonal respect and affection, which continue into adolescence and adulthood.

Gender differentials in socialization manifest across age and domain. Gender roles are taught and learnt in a complex web of relationships that are embedded in the wider context of kinship. Patriarchy is firmly ingrained in the Indian society, and the Hindu rituals and practices contribute to the structuring of women as gendered subjects. Special value is accorded to a son, which is amply observed in folk stories, proverbs as well as everyday conversations. Son preference is associated with continuation of the family lineage and his role in carrying out the last rites of parents, thereby ensuring the well-being of their souls. The daughter is seen as a temporary member of the household and preoccupation with her marriage is pervasive. The onset of puberty renders immense vulnerability to the girl, as her sexuality is to be fiercely protected; restrictions on mobility hence become necessary. Feminine identity in demeanor, speech, dress, and behavior is reinforced, and training for feminine tasks is deliberate, with distinctions between masculine and feminine work communicated from early childhood. The predominant sentiment is to train the girl for an unfamiliar setting, which renders a certain ambiguity to the socialization process. Mixed messages are conveyed with regard to loyalty to the natal home, and the imperative to be absorbed completely in the marital home. Girls thus grow up with tentativeness about their sense of self (Dube 1988; Kakar and Kakar 2007).

Socialization in Contemporary India: A Society in Flux

Information and communication technology coupled with economic liberalization has unleashed a "quiet revolution" (Appadurai 1990, p. 4) and the Indian society is an enthusiastic participant in this phenomenon. The forces of globalization are impinging vigorously upon the Indian society, persuading Indians to straddle multiple worlds. The growing middle classes in urban and rural areas are at the forefront of this revolution (Sharma 2003). The transformations are reflected in the physical landscape, people's increasing sense of connectedness with the global community, the materialist and consumerist attitudes, especially of the middle class (Varma 2007), and a general striving toward improving one's quality of life. Overall, there is a growing enthusiasm to stride forward on the path of change, one that is characterized by dynamic interactions between the modern and the traditional. As Sharma (2003) observes, this new Indianness or "transitional identity" is enabling people to be "authentically Indian yet thoroughly modern" (p. 4).

Social and economic transformations are evident across geographical areas, with the most visible impact on education, involvement of mothers in children's pedagogical routines, and inculcation of values such as competition and independence. At the same time, the emphasis on following social rules of respect and deference to older persons and the training to assume responsibility continues, along with expressed concerns regarding the possibility that traditional values may be compromised. Differential gender-based priorities in values are evident. Boys are expected to be independent and capable of making one's decisions; although similar values are emphasized for girls, they are also expected to manage household chores and realize the value of money (Sharma 2003, 2011).

Contemporary families are increasingly displaying a childcentric ethos and child-centeredness features prominently in parents' description of a good parent (Saraswathi and Ganapathy 2002). Sachdeva and Misra's (2005, 2008) study on the cultural construction of parenting across three urban communities (Bengali, Punjabi, Marwari) has highlighted some key changes in parenting in contemporary urban Indian society. The process of parenting is becoming more conscious and proactive with parents seeking information from new sources (e.g., Internet), emphasis on encouraging and molding children for educational and career achievements, and preference for English medium schools as these are associated with status and perceived to better prepare the child for the increasingly competitive world. With decreasing family size, parents focus more attention on children and are keen to fulfill their every wish and give children what they (parents) as children may have missed. Running in tandem, however, are traditional gender-specific attitudes and practices. Although parents accept that girls because of their nurturing orientation would care for parents even after marriage, their vulnerability continues to be of concern.

At the same time, Seymour (2010) in her ethnographic research in Orissa has observed that there exist contestations in age and gender hierarchies, and these are reflected in marital relations and intergenerational relations. Alterations in childrearing ideology and practices are observed and children are prepared to become more self-reliant to deal with the changing world. Families show greater inclination to accommodate to new forms such as a more collaborative process in children's marriage partner selection and acceptance of a partner that the son may have chosen. In addition, parents (in-laws) and families demonstrate openness in adjusting their expectations to situations wherein daughters-in-law are employed. The younger parents on their part appreciate the advantages of childcare that an extended family arrangement provides. Whereas girls' socialization along traditional norms continues, they are simultaneously encouraged for educational achievement. Parents and grandparents who themselves did not get the opportunity to go to school are supportive of their daughters' education. In comparison with earlier times, this also offers a more prolonged adolescence and the opportunity to develop a distinct identity.

Families differ in their perspectives on adopting patriarchal strictures. In urban middle class families, the experience of gender discrimination may be relatively less, and girls grow up experiencing the feeling of being cared for and treated equally like their brothers. School and university education for girls is encouraged, not only in the interest of developing autonomy, but also because education will enhance her value in the marriage market and enable her to contribute to the marital home, thereby increasing her status in the family. Middle class parents are also becoming aware of the need to enable girls to be independent so as to better deal with any disruption in the marital relationship. It is becoming increasingly common for parents to encourage the girl to become educated and pursue a career, and at the same time, gender-specific socialization continues. The latter comes to the fore markedly around puberty during which training in service and self-denial as preparation for the girl's future role as daughter-in-law and wife is emphasized. Restrictions on freedom of movement surface at this time, along with checks on the girl's dressing and recreational activities. Girls protest against the restrictions that parents impose, especially beginning adolescence. Parents and adults justify these restrictions by invoking the risks that abound in the social context. The girl is hence made acutely conscious of her vulnerability, and how the onus to protect her sexuality and in turn the family *izzat* (honor) rests on her behavior and reputation (Kakar and Kakar 2007). This outlook is observed across social class, albeit with some flexibility in educated middle class families.

Although such factors are contributing to increase in women's independence and autonomy, gender imbalance continues to prevail. Cultural continuity in socialization is evident in that most parental expectations revolved around a social orientation with less emphasis on individual features. The Indian cultural model of development that prioritizes increasing embeddedness in family roles and relationships, especially for women, intervenes in women's achievement of autonomy.

The traditional deeply entrenched reasons for wanting to have a son such as carrying forward family lineage and performance of religious rituals and rites persist. Simultaneously, in their desire to create a "good fit" with the changing context, parents are blending known traditional cultural precepts and practices with newly emerging ones. The tension between stability and change creates ambiguity in parents' outlook resulting in an approach-avoidance conflict, manifested in a "cold feet syndrome." On the one hand, parents wish to change with the times, yet on the other hand, they experience self-doubt and confusion, questioning their own decisions (Saraswathi and Pai 1997, p. 91).

The flux of change is thus not only presenting myriad opportunities but also confusions about appropriate approaches to child socialization. In what ways are the macro changes mediating the tension between traditional and modern beliefs and practices is a critical issue. Such issues are more likely to surface in urban middle class settings. In this regard, a question that merits attention is the notion and characterization of middle class in the contemporary Indian society. The following section presents an overview of the salient characteristics of the urban middle class in India.

The Urban Indian Middle Class

The Indian society is a veritable potpourri of paradoxes. Cambridge Economist Joan Robinson has aptly observed, "Whatever you can rightly say about India, the opposite is also true" (Sen 2005). It is thus rather difficult if not impossible, to draw a portrayal of a single social class in India. The middle class population in India is internally diverse in terms of socioeconomic standing, caste, religion, and region (Fernandes 2016). Hence, what can be derived at best is a representation in broad strokes of characteristics shared by the urban middle class.

India is on the move. The economic reforms have led to an unprecedented growth course, offering multiple significant opportunities to its people. An additional positive feature is that India is on the right side of the demographic dividend in that it is a young country and hence bears immense potential for development. The country is urbanizing rapidly, and according to the McKinsey Global Institute report (2010), in 2008, 340 million people lived in urban areas and this population is expected to rise to 590 million by the year 2030. Gujarat is one among five states that will have majority of its population living in cities instead of villages.

Much that is happening in contemporary India can be attributed to the rapidly infiltrating myriad social, economic, and technological changes, and the urban middle class is in the thick of it. The post-liberalization period witnessed increased access to economic opportunities, and material and social assets, and in turn a growing segment of "middle class'. India's middle class is on the rise, and by 2025, this segment is expected to constitute 41% of India's projected population (Southworth and Lingamfelter 2008). The middle class is regarded as best positioned to attract and embrace the changes brought in by globalization. The term middle class is profuse in media and everyday conversations, and increasing numbers of Indians are describing themselves as "middle class," indicating that they are "in the middle," neither rich or poor. Many communities now have access to the amenities of middle class lifestyle. The reality however is that middle class comprises a gamut of economic statuses, lifestyles, and values (Donner and De Neve 2011, p. 3).

The term "middle class" is frequently used in present-day India. Presenting oneself as middle class (neither poor nor rich) is thus a growing phenomenon. So who constitutes the Indian middle class? Middle class is by no means a homogenous category, and based on income, education and occupation this group is often subclassified into "upper," "lower," and "those in-between" (Jodhka and Prakash 2016, p. xxi). Given the complexity of measuring social class, it is difficult to outline the characteristics of the Indian middle class, and debates and discussions around this topic abound. Donner and De Neve (2011) deliberately use the term "middle classes" as "even the most cursory glance at contemporary India reveals that the communities and individuals described as being middle class, in fact, differ widely not only in terms of economic position and consumption practices but also in terms of status and values" (p. 3).

Post-liberalization, the Indian middle class has come to be associated with consumption practices, lifestyles and white-collar jobs. Education and credentials are important. There are however internal differences in consumption patterns among upper middle, middle and lower-middle classes. For instance, the upper middle is seen to prefer brand related goods, whereas the middle and lower classes engage in household-level purchases or buy an item that may be indicative of a middle class status. The middle class identity derives not only from lifestyle markers, but also from claims of cultural and moral superiority (Fernandes 2016). Multiple elements such as income, cultural affinities and values, lifestyles, education status, and service sector employment are involved in defining middle class. With regard to income, which is a leading variable in social class definitions, if one-third is left over after discretionary expenditure then that qualifies for inclusion in the middle class (Debroy 2009).

Broadly, the middle class has been defined as households that are between the poor and the extremely rich (The Hindu 2014). It is the segment with the largest purchasing power, in turn inviting attention not only of the country's government but also of global markets. On their part, the middle classes have become more aware of newer arenas of economic development and the urge to move up the consumer ladder is stronger than ever. Consumption has in fact become a source of identity, and values such as merit, efficiency, and competition are attributed much significance. "The contemporary Indian middle class…celebrates the market as the ultimate panacea for all the problems" (Jodhka and Prakash 2016, p. 163). Luxury personal and household items have now become necessities and symbolize social status. Such acquisitions are hence viewed as an ability to spend freely, not as materialism (Radhakrishnan 2011).

A survey tracking the aspirations and anxieties of Indians between January and May 2014 found that 49% of the respondents believed their families to be middle class. Although the share of the urban respondents was higher (56%), the share of rural respondents was also notably high (46%). Further, the higher the level of education, the greater is the likelihood of an individual defining self as middle class and yet even those with 10th standard education claimed to be middle class. The survey also reported that those who identified self as middle class were more upbeat about their present status and future prospects with regard to their children and their own improved status over a generation (Kapur and Vaishnav 2014). Across 13 societies, a defining feature of middle class was a steady job, fewer children, and greater expenditure on education and health of children (Banerjee and Duflo 2007).

It is relevant to note that although the present middle class is referred largely in terms of economic status, it is also a social identity, which encompasses region, religion, language, and caste diversities (Jodhka and Prakash 2016). Donner and De Neve (2011) observe that from the nineteenth century, middle class lifestyles began to become more homogenous, because of reform movements as well as interaction with institutions such as school, legal system, workplace, and urban infrastructure. Today there exists a general understanding of what constitutes middle class in India. Some shared features include stake in the educational system, with upwardly mobile families eager to invest into children's education, and dependence on public sector services. Further, in the post-liberalization context, "middleclassness" (p. 10) comprises continuities as well as transformations related to family values, codes of morality, and gender roles.

In general, we can say that a member of the middle class is one who is on the road to upward mobility and aspiration, exuding an air of optimism and striding ahead with confidence in pursuit of a "good life." Education is a much-valued commodity and is believed to be the route to prosperity. Keeping abreast of the palpable communication revolution, almost every member of the middle class has a mobile phone. More women from the middle class are opting for higher education and taking up jobs. Notwithstanding the immense diversity that characterizes the Indian society, there are certain pan-Indian characteristics that are mostly applicable to the middle class. These include opportunities for education, job mobility, access to radio, television and films, instant connectivity over telephones and mobiles, and a strong popular culture spanning language and region (Varma 2007). In departure from earlier values of tradition and austerity, the key drivers for the growing "new" middle class are consumerism, upward mobility, and the need to be part of the global world.

Gender is firmly intertwined in middle class identities. Although women are taking advantage of the increasing opportunities for education and career, yet the striving for a balance between home and work persists. Women continue to be responsible for preservation of tradition and tend to regard career as secondary to marriage and family life (Radhakrishnan 2012). Thus, although the lifestyle of this class is associated with modernity, traditional gendered notions continue to be reproduced.

Notwithstanding the complexity involved in putting forth an explicit definition of Indian middle class, there is considerable agreement regarding its consistently growing population, which has also contributed to a shift in the image of India from a land of snake charmers to a significant player in the global economy. The "aspirational middle class" is a term that is increasingly used in current political discourse (Jodhka and Prakash 2016, p. 195). Donner and De Neve (2011) attribute a hegemonic role to the contemporary Indian middle class. The Indian middle class has become increasingly insular, and the perks of middle class lifestyle are reserved for a privileged few. For instance, features such as access to quality education, new employment opportunities, and new "gated" urban residential complexes set the middle classes apart from the rest (Jodhka and Prakash 2016; Varma 2007).

The portrayal of adolescents in the book is situated in this broad urban middle class context in contemporary India. The following section presents the conceptual framework of the construction of adolescence and parent–adolescent relationship presented in this book.

Conceptual Framework of the Sociocultural Construction of Adolescence

Guided by the theoretical frameworks and perspectives discussed in this chapter, the understanding of adolescence and parent–adolescent relationship presented in this book is situated in the following conceptual framework (see Fig. 1.1).

Cultures and contexts interact to offer options and alternatives and impose boundaries and constraints that shape human development. Societies of the world are ensconced in cultural worldviews that shape values, beliefs, and behaviors, and prescribe developmental pathways of independence or interdependence, with the latter privileged in the Indian culture. Each culture presents precepts and practices that are embedded in social structures and everyday lives of families and individuals. Cultures and contexts are also dynamic and change over time. Adaptation of individual and family thus involves reconciling these two sources of robust and resilient influences. The spate of social change in the present context of globalization is unprecedented. The myriad sociodemographic changes are compelling active engagement with contextual factors and hold immense potential to influence cultural and familial values through direct and indirect means. The dynamic involved in this process necessitates balancing tradition with contemporary, familiar with novel, creating thereby a tapestry reflecting cultural continuity and change. This framework forms the backdrop of the sociocultural construction of adolescence in urban India presented in the book. The impact of globalization is most perceptible in the "modernizing" educated families from the middle and upper social class; it is this class that is well-poised to embrace the dramatic socioeconomic changes. It is also in this group that the distinctness of adolescence as a stage is increasingly visible. On the one hand, the middle class epitomizes all that is "truly Indian," and on the other hand, it is this very group that appears to absorb many of the persuasive Western influences. The result is a "culture of transience" (p. 13) where parents and adolescents find themselves in a "double bind", (p. 14) caught between the traditional agrarian ethos and the industrial, Western ethos (Garg and Parikh 1995).

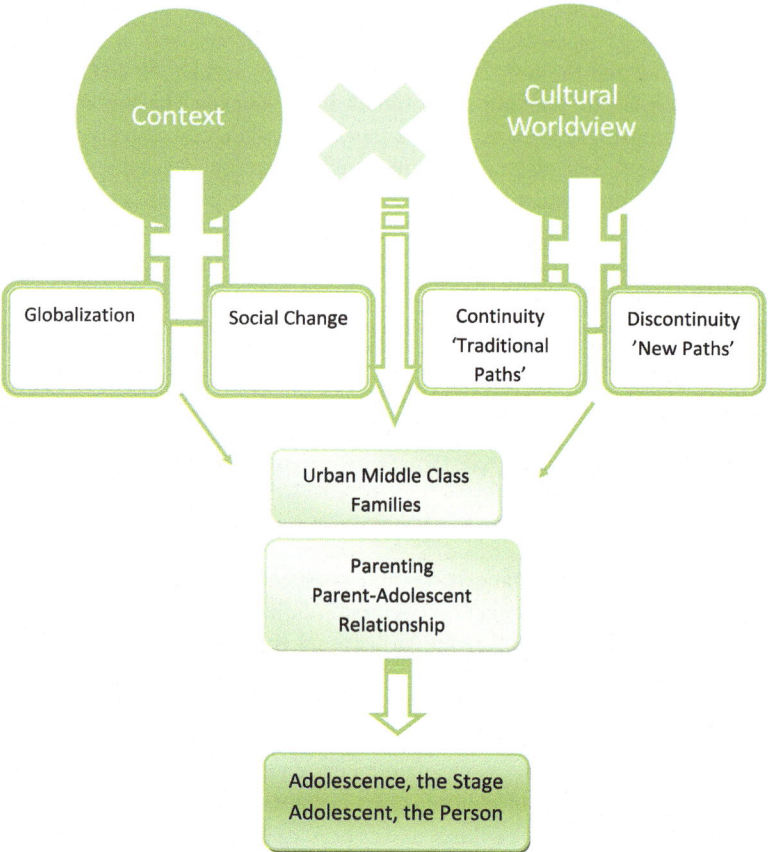

Fig. 1.1 Sociocultural construction of adolescence in urban India: A conceptual framework

The shifting contours of the larger social and economic context are thus necessitating adaptation on part of parents and adolescents. Adolescents are more vulnerable as they are in the process of transitioning from childhood to adulthood, have a higher tendency to engage in extra-familial worlds, are more open to novelty, and show greater interest and engagement with global media including the Internet. Parents are responsible for transmission of cultural values and at the same time are keen to ensure that they socialize their adolescent child for the kind of competence that will enable a good fit with the rapidly changing context. Parental socialization inputs thus need to encompass past, present, and even futuristic perspectives. The situation is complicated as, on the one hand, parents are influenced by the values instilled in them by their own parents and, on the other hand, they need to derive their own adaptations to the evolving lifestyle (Keller 2007).

As socialization is intrinsically future oriented, its process and outcomes should change when the conditions faced by the next generation are different from those that the parents experienced (Greenfield 1999). Issues of change and continuity thus become relevant in such a context, as also the multidimensional and bidirectional nature of the changes. Although forward looking, Indian urban middle class parents are at the same time apprehensive about the "modern, Western" influences that may alienate their adolescents from their culture and family. Adolescents on their part are in the process of making sense of how new elements may map on to familiar terrain. By virtue of their age and stage, adolescents are more amenable to change in favor of global ideas. In congruence with the bidirectional model of parenting (Valsiner 2000) and the view of socialization as an interactive process (Dasen 2003), both parents and adolescents actively engage in adaptations that are better suited to traverse a path of development that constitutes continuing cultural elements as well as forces that urge toward adaptation and change. Even though such demands may be experienced in every generation, the exceptional pace of change renders the situation more challenging.

Negotiating newfound ideas with traditional convictions is presenting a vital challenge to parents and adolescents in India. The scenario is one which requires adaptation on part of the parent and the adolescent, and accentuates the need to create "new" ways and means to navigate the myriad influences. The situation hence is likely to create space for discrepant perspectives leading to interpersonal disagreements. Often both adolescent and parent are rendered confused and vulnerable—a reminder of Jeffery Arnett's proposition of the plausibility of "storm and stress" among adolescents from traditional societies, arising essentially from the process of coping with a rapidly changing context (Arnett 1999).

The dynamics of navigating the changing context in the midst of the pull of cultural traditions has significant implications on how the phase of adolescence is interpreted as well as the dynamics of the parent–adolescent relationship. Critical questions that merit consideration are: How is adolescence constructed in the contemporary urban Indian society? What elements of the traditional cultural worldview are retained and what "new" elements are integrated in parents' and adolescents' ideas, aspirations, and expectations during this life stage? What are the defining tenets and features of the parent–adolescent relationship? I examine these central questions in this book.

About the Empirical Studies

The research discussed in this book comprises a series of studies with adolescents and parents from urban educated upper middle class families in Baroda city. The two central research themes are as follows: (1) social construction of adolescence and (2) parenting adolescents and adolescent—parent relationships.

Research Context and Design

The research is situated in the urban upper middle class context in Baroda city. The participants comprised adolescents 13–21 years, and their parents. The data that are discussed in this book however pertain mainly to adolescents 16–18 years. A mixed-methods design integrating quantitative and qualitative methods was used across the series of studies.

The quantitative survey was structured, with open-ended questions related to description and significance of the phase, ideal and typical qualities of girls and boys, expectations of adolescents and parents from each other, and topics of interpersonal disagreements including frequency and intensity of occurrence. The survey instrument contained questions in English as well as the local language Gujarati to ensure comprehension. The adolescent participants for the survey were identified through schools and a small proportion of participants were identified through coaching classes (a usual practice for high school students in Baroda). The school students were administered the survey in school, whereas parents completed it at home. The researchers were present at all times to address any clarifications that the participants may need.

The qualitative interviews with adolescents and parents probed further the questions in the survey, and included topics such as satisfactions and dissatisfactions in the parent–adolescent relationship, major concerns of this stage, dreams and wishes, insecurities and anxieties, notions of success, and projection of self into the future. The subject of interpersonal disagreements both hypothetical and real life and the process of resolving these were addressed in greater depth with adolescents. The themes for the hypothetical vignettes were identified from the survey data and indicate the immediate and long-term concerns of adolescents. These are choice of an academic stream, activities with friends, and marriage partner selection. Although marriage may not be an active immediate concern for urban middle class adolescents at this time, romantic interests, relationships, and thoughts of marriage begin to surface during this period, and it is not uncommon for adolescents to discuss these matters among themselves and sometimes with parents as well. Real-life disagreements pertained to actual situations that adolescents had experienced in the past six months. For both types of disagreements, in-depth probing was done on how the situation was dealt with, the extent to which adolescents and parents (as perceived by adolescents) accommodated to the situation, and the reasoning used for the same.

Interviews with parents addressed aspects similar to those discussed with the adolescents and, in addition, also integrated topics such as challenges in raising an adolescent child in the present context, gender differentials, effective parenting practices, and comparisons with one's own adolescence. All the interviews were conducted in the local language Gujarati and taped with prior consent from the participants. Adolescents and a few parents were inclined to talk in a mix of Gujarati and English languages. The Focus Group Discussions (FGDs) with adolescents reiterated questions related to the description and major concerns of the stage and delved into the aspect of parental authority, insecurities and anxieties, and opinions regarding the relative inputs of self and parents in decisions pertaining to academic subject and career choice, girl–boy friendships, marriage, social comparisons, gender, and privacy matters.

I also conducted personal interviews with two local school counselors as key informants. School counselors are a valuable source of information on issues of adolescents—what bothers them on an everyday and long-term basis, how are such issues perceived, and what are their perceptions of their parents' stance on issues of concern. The counselors who have shared their experiences and perspectives are from a psychology background with counseling experience ranging from 5 to 15 years. Appendixes A to D contain the assessment measures used across the different studies. Intercoder reliability for both quantitative and qualitative data analyses was determined using the following formula:

Reliability = number of agreements/total number of agreements + disagreements (Miles and Huberman 1994, p. 64).

The quantitative data were analyzed descriptively in terms of frequencies and percentages of responses pertaining to the themes: importance of the stage, qualities liked and disliked, ideal and typical characteristics, expectations from each other, and topics of disagreements, with their frequency and intensity. The qualitative interviews were transcribed and translated into English, taking care to preserve the original meaning of the responses by retaining the verbatim comments. A two-stage coding process was followed. The first stage involved open coding wherein descriptive phrases such as "parents know what is good for me" were highlighted. Axial coding was then used to organize the open codes into meaningful categories. Finally, the recurrent categories were interpreted into overarching themes (DeSantis and Ugarriza 2000). For the rating scale items in the interview (e.g., degree of accommodation, relative importance of considerations involved), means, standard deviations, and t-tests were computed to know the degree of accommodation, the relative importance given to different reasons that guided the resolution process, and age and gender comparisons.

Table 1.1 provides an overview of the research themes, the participants, the assessment measures, and the analysis done across the different studies.

Researcher's Positioning

In doing the research with adolescents and parents, I positioned myself primarily as a university teacher and researcher who is interested in understanding Indian adolescents. My students and research assistants posed as such. Being a college teacher enhanced my credibility as a researcher, thereby contributing to the validity of the participants' responses. This was especially important for the parents who were mostly eager to talk about their adolescents. That I belong to Baroda and have attained most of my school and college education from Baroda was an advantage. My locus standi as an urban middle class Barodian helped in identifying

Table 1.1 Research themes, participants, assessment measures, and analysis

Series of studies	Themes	Participants	Assessment measures	Type of analysis
Study 1 Phase I	Social construction of adolescence, parenting adolescents	561 early 13–15 years (n = 99) and mid-adolescent 16–18 years (n = 88) girls and boys and their parents. Parents n = 198 of early adolescents; n = 176 of mid-adolescents	Survey—Questionnaire	Quantitative: Frequencies and percentages
Phase II	Parent–adolescent relationship and interpersonal disagreements	120 adolescent girls and boys, 16–18 years	Interview—Semi-structured interview schedule and rating scale items including real-life disagreements	Qualitative: Thematic analysis Quantitative: Means and SDs (for rating scale items)
Study 2	Social construction of adolescence, parenting adolescents and parent–adolescent relationship, and interpersonal disagreements	60 adolescent girls and boys, 18–21 years	Interview—Semi-structured interview schedule including hypothetical vignettes	Qualitative: Thematic analysis
Study 3	Parent–adolescent relationship and interpersonal disagreements	60 adolescent girls and boys, 18–21 years	Interview—Semi-structured interview schedule including hypothetical vignettes	Qualitative: Thematic analysis
Study 4	Social construction of adolescence, parenting adolescents	20 adolescent girls and boys, and mothers	Interview—Semi-structured interview schedule	Qualitative: Thematic analysis
Study 5	Social construction of adolescence	Adolescent girls and boys, 13–15 years and 16–18 years	Focus Group discussions (3)	Qualitative: Thematic analysis
Study 6	Issues and concerns of adolescents and parents	20 adolescent girls and boys 16–18 years; and their mothers; 2 School Counselors	Interview guideline	Qualitative: Thematic analysis

participants and created a sense of shared experience and trust. I was thus an "insider" of sorts, and at the same time an "outsider," the latter by virtue of my profession and role in this venture. A crucial advantage was my comfort and familiarity with the city, its culture and lifestyle. Furthermore, being a Gujarati myself facilitated the interview process in terms of ease in understanding and using colloquial conversational language. Mothers in particular were willing and rather articulate in voicing their concerns related to their adolescents. In the course of the interview, a few mothers expressed their perplexity regarding the adolescent's behavior and in a lighter vein shared that perhaps them rather than the adolescent needed counseling.

With adolescents, an initial tentativeness and curiosity soon gave way to sincere and unguarded sharing and discussion, especially during interview questions related to the disagreements that they may have with their parents, and the issues and concerns that they experience in the course of everyday living. Adolescents, girls more than boys, shared their views generously and candidly, an indication of the increasing ability for self-expression. Sometimes, I sensed a stance wherein they would try to cross-check my opinion on a certain matter or even look for endorsement as it were, on how they may have dealt with an issue or their view on a certain matter. Unwittingly, I became their confidante, either because they perceived me as a neutral outsider or perhaps due to my being a professor of human development and hence potentially more knowledgeable about such issues. A heartening aspect across all the interactions was the positive feedback that the adolescents and parents shared at the end of the interview. The interview process appeared to serve as a catharsis and an opportunity to articulate satisfactions, concerns and anxieties in a neutral space.

Profile of Participants

The adolescents, all high school students, belong to educated and economically well-off middle class Hindu Gujarati nuclear families in Baroda city. All of them were studying in English medium schools. Almost all of them have a two-wheeler and a cell phone—two indispensable possessions. Much of their leisure time is spent in multiplexes, shopping malls and coffee shops. Girls and boys racing ahead on their two-wheelers (presumably to make it to tuition class on time or to catch a movie or to keep an appointment with a friend) is a familiar sight on Baroda streets, even late evenings. In terms of clothing, there is preference for modern Western styles, and at the same time, the Indo-Western fusion style (example, wearing a *kurta* over jeans) is popular. A similar pattern is observed in the language used in everyday conversations, which comprises a mix of Gujarati and English—popularly known as Indian English or "*Hinglish*." Young people are mostly seen in designated places and spaces such as fast food joints and coffee shops. In general, young individuals in Baroda enjoy considerable freedom and mobility, in comparison with

their counterparts in other states. The image of Baroda being a safe city is perhaps a
facilitating factor in this regard.

Parents of adolescents are mostly graduates, and a few are postgraduates.
Mothers for the most part are homemakers, while a few are employed in government or private firms. Majority of the fathers have their own business or are
professionals such as engineers or doctors. Some others are employed in government and private firms where they hold high positions such as senior managers or
directors.

Presentation of the Studies

Together the series of studies offer an integrated perspective about the sociocultural
construction of adolescence, parenting adolescents, and adolescent-parent relationship in the urban upper middle class context in Baroda. The data are integrated
and presented along the following major conceptual themes:

1. *Social Construction of Adolescence, the Stage and Adolescent, the Person*

The depiction of the social construction of adolescence comprises the following
domains: terms or phrases used to define adolescence, common characteristics and
perceptions of a typical and ideal adolescent girl and boy, the importance and
challenges of this phase including the insecurities and worries as well as dreams and
aspirations.

2. *Parenting Adolescents and Adolescent–Parent Relationship*

Parenting adolescents and parent–adolescent relationship covers aspects related to
the description of parent by the adolescent and parent, expectations of adolescent
and   parent   from   each   other,   satisfactions   and   dissatisfactions   in   the
adolescent-parent relationship, topics and resolution process of hypothetical and
real interpersonal disputes, the core elements guiding the parent–adolescent relationship as well as the issues, concerns, and tensions experienced.

This book is about adolescence, the stage and adolescent, the person, in the
context of family, focusing on relationship with parents. Based on the trends
derived from research with adolescents and parents over a decade, supported by
perspectives from contemporary literature, the book presents the contents and
contours of adolescence in an urban middle class context in contemporary India.
Conceding the incongruity of the predominantly Western portrayal of adolescence
with the Indian cultural worldview, it presents a culturally rooted understanding of
adolescence, thereby contributing to scholarly knowledge regarding this significant
stage of human development. The book weaves in a contextual perspective to offer
a contemporary understanding of parenting adolescents. It illustrates the changes
that parents themselves are making to create an "adaptive fit" in order to derive a
balance between the demands of the changing context and the traditional tenets and
goals of socialization. The Western depiction of individuation and disengagement

as the central developmental task of adolescence and the corollary depiction of adolescent development as fraught with tension and dispute, ensuing from the push and pull for autonomy from parents, is questioned. An alternate culture sensitive understanding of parent–adolescent relationship is presented that not only departs from the Western representation, but also offers a nuanced understanding of adolescents in a fast-changing urban society. Highlighted as well are aspects that have remained mostly unexplored, for example, adolescent capacity for empathy and perspective taking, and emerging issues of autonomy in a primarily relational culture. At a broader level, the work also contributes to an understanding of globalizing influences on human development, questioning the assumption of globalization leading to a universal endpoint of individualism.

More specifically, the book presents the following:

- Culturally and contextually sensitive portrayal of adolescence.
- Typology of parenting adolescents in the contemporary Indian urban middle class context.
- Culturally sensitive framework of parent–adolescent relationship that emphasizes interplay of cultural continuity and change.

Layout of the Book

In the chapters that follow, I present a culture- and context-sensitive portrayal of adolescents in the urban Indian middle class setting and discuss the dynamic of parent–adolescent relationship as it unfolds in the contemporary context, highlighting the defining features of the relationship. The present chapter has highlighted the interactive influence of culture and context on human development including the theoretical frameworks that have guided the research. The Indian-Hindu model of development, family, and self is presented, followed by an account of the changes observed in contemporary India. In the next section, the chapter has provided a depiction of the urban middle class in contemporary Indian society. The conceptual framework of the research is then presented. The final section provides an account of the series of empirical studies underpinning the book.

Chapter 2 transitions to adolescence as a sociocultural construction. It begins with a peep into the evolution of adolescence as a subject of scholarly interest. The predominant description of this stage in Western societies is delineated, followed by an overview of the cross-cultural variability of adolescence. The chapter also discusses the phenomenon of adolescent-parent disagreement as a mirror reflecting the nature of the relationship. Highlighted are globalization and social change influences on adolescents and the implications on parenting and parent–adolescent relationship. The conceptualization of adolescence in the traditional Indian-Hindu worldview and the contemporary Indian context is then presented. Next, the chapter offers a depiction of the urban middle class in Baroda, Gujarat, that forms the context of the book.

With Chaps. 3, 4, and 5, the book enters the realm of the research findings. Chapter 3 addresses the question: How is adolescence, the stage and adolescent, the person constructed in the urban Indian middle class context? It depicts the views of adolescents and parents regarding the stage of adolescence, highlighting the salient features and socialization goals, together culminating into a description of the contents and contours of the adolescent self. In Chap. 4, I probe into the phenomenon of parenting and parent–adolescent relationship exploring the following questions: What kind of parenting is favored in the present scenario of flux of social change? How is the changing context affecting the traditional hierarchical structure of parent–adolescent relationship? How do the dimensions of parental authority, adolescent autonomy, and interpersonal differences unfold, and what are the defining features of the parent–adolescent relationship? Chapter 5 discusses the challenges and risks of globalization as these intervene in the everyday lives of adolescents and parents. It addresses matters that matter to adolescents on daily and long-term basis, how such issues are perceived, and the adolescent's perspective on how parents deal with the same. Overall, it brings to the fore the insecurities and anxieties that adolescents and parents experience across select domains.

In the final Chap. 6, I recapitulate the central themes in the social construction of adolescence and parent–adolescent relationship in the urban upper middle class context and offer reflections and implications of the emerging cultural depiction of adolescence in contemporary Indian society. Issues such as cultural resilience and change, the direction of social change in India, the need to provide "space" for adolescents and for parents as well, to voice and share their concerns, and implications for enhancing family relationships and fostering self-growth as elements that are critical for positive youth development are discussed.

References

Anandalakshmy, S. (2013). Through the lens of culture: Studies on childhood and education in India. In G. Misra (Vol. Ed.), XIII (3), *Psychology and psychoanalysis* (pp. 191–218). In D. P. Chattopadhyaya (Gen. Ed.), *History of science, philosophy and culture in Indian civilization*. New Delhi: Center for Studies in Civilization.

Appadurai, A. (1990). Disjuncture and differences in the global cultural economy. In M. Featherstone (Ed.), *Global culture: Nationalism, globalization, and modernity* (pp. 295–310). London: Sage.

Arnett, J. J. (1999). Adolescent storm and stress, reconsidered. *American Psychologist, 54*(5), 317–326. doi:10.1037/0003-066x.54.5.317.

Arnett, J. J. (2002). The psychology of globalization. *American Psychologist, 57*(10), 774. http://doi.org/10.1037//0003-066X.57.10.774.

Badrinath, C. (2003). The householder, grhastha, in the Mahabharata. In M. Pernau, I. Ahmed, & H. Reifeld (Eds.), *Family and gender: Changing values in Germany and India* (pp. 113–139). New Delhi: Sage.

Banerjee, A. V., & Duflo, E. (2007). The economic lives of the poor. *The Journal of Economic Perspectives, 21*(1), 141–167.

Berry, J. W. (1994). Acculturation and psychological adaptation. In A. M. Bouvry, F. J. R. van de Vijver, & P. Schmitz (Eds.), *Journeys into cross-cultural psychology* (pp. 129–141). Lisse, Netherlands: Swets & Zeitlinger.

Berry, J. (2013, May 30). *Theory and method in cross-cultural and intercultural psychology.* International Symposium on Arab Youth Paper I. University of Windsor, Ontario. Retrieved from http://scholar.uwindsor.ca/arabyouthsymp/conference_presentations/presentations2/1.

Bornstein, M. H. (2012). Cultural approaches to parenting. *Parenting, 12*(2–3), 212–221.

Bornstein, M. H., & Cheah, C. S. (2006). The place of "culture and parenting" in the ecological contextual perspective on developmental science. In K. H. Rubin & O. B. Chung (Eds.), *Parenting beliefs, behaviors, and parent-child relations: A cross-cultural perspective* (pp. 3–33). New York: Psychology Press.

Bornstein, M. H. (2006). Parenting science and practice. In W. Damon & R. M. Lerner (Chief Eds.), K. Ann Renninger & I. Sigel (Vol. Eds.), *Handbook of child psychology, Vol. 4: Child psychology in practice* (6th ed., pp. 893–949). New York: Wiley.

Bronfenbrenner, U. (1977). Toward an experimental ecology of human development. *American Psychologist, 32*(7), 513–531.

Bronfenbrenner, U. (1979). *The ecology of human development: Experiments by nature and design.* Cambridge: Harvard University Press.

Bronfenbrenner, U. (1994). Ecological models of human development. *Readings on the Development of Children, 2,* 37–43. http://www.psy.cmu.edu/~siegler/35bronfebrenner94.pdf.

Bronfenbrenner, U., & Morris, P. (2006). The bioecological model of human development. In R. M. Lerner (Ed.), *Theoretical models of human development, Vol 1.* In W. Damon & R. M. Lerner (Vol. Eds.), *Handbook of child psychology* (6th ed., pp. 793–828). Hoboken, NJ: Wiley. doi:10.1002/9780470147658.chpsy0114.

Bugental, D. B., & Grusec, J. E. (2006). Socialization processes. In W. Damon and R. M. Lerner (Chief Ed.) & N. Eisenberg (Vol. Ed.), *Handbook of child psychology, Vol. 3: Social, emotional and personality development* (6th ed., pp. 366–428). New York: Wiley,

Census of India (2011). Ministry of Home Affairs, Government of India. Retrieved from http://www.census2011.co.in/religion.php;   http://www.census2011.co.in/data/religion/state/24-gujarat.html.

Chakkarath, P. (2005). What can Western psychology learn from indigenous psychologies? Lessons from Hindu psychology. In W. Friedlmeier, P. Chakkarath, & B. Schwarz (Eds.), *Culture and human development: The importance of cross-cultural research to the social sciences* (pp. 31–51). New York: Psychology Press.

Chakkarath, P. (2013). Indian thoughts on human psychological development. In G. Misra (Vol. ed.), XIII (3), *Psychology and psychoanalysis* (pp. 167–190). In D. P. Chattopadhyaya (Gen. Ed.), *History of science, philosophy and culture in Indian civilization.* New Delhi: Center for Studies in Civilization.

Chen, X., & Chen, H. (2010). Children's socio-emotional functioning and adjustment in the changing Chinese society. In R. K. Silbereisen & X. Chen (Eds.), *Social change and human development: Concept and results* (pp. 209–226). New Delhi: Sage.

Dasen, P. R. (2003). Theoretical frameworks in cross-cultural developmental psychology: An attempt at integration. In T. S. Saraswathi (Ed.), *Cross-cultural perspectives in human development* (pp. 128–165). New Delhi: Sage.

Debroy, B. (2009, March 24). Who are the middle class in India? *Indian Express.*

DeSantis, L., & Ugarriza, D. N. (2000). The concept of theme as used in qualitative nursing research. *Western Journal of Nursing Research, 22*(3), 351–372.

Diaz, J., & Zirkel, S. (2012). Globalization, psychology, and social issues research: An introduction and conceptual framework. *Journal of Social Issues, 68*(3), 439–453.

Donner, H., & De Neve, G. (2011). Introduction. In H. Donner (Ed.), *Being middle class in India: A way of life* (pp. 1–22). New York: Routledge.

Dube, L. (1988). On the construction of gender: Hindu girls in patrilineal India. *Economic and Political Weekly, 23*(18), WS11-WS19.

Fernandes, L. (2016). India's middle classes in contemporary India. In K. A. Jacobsen (Ed.), *Routledge handbook of contemporary India* (pp. 232–242). London: Routledge.

Garg, P. K., & Parikh, I. J. (1995). *Crossroads of culture: A study in the culture of transience*. New Delhi: Sage.

Geertz, C. (1993). Religion as a cultural system. In G. Clifford, (Ed.), *The interpretation of cultures: Selected essays* (pp. 87–125). London: Fontana Press.

Gergen, K. (2011). The self as social construction. *Psychological Studies, 56*(1), 108. doi:10.1007/s12646-011-0066-1.

Greenfield, P. M. (1999). Cultural change and human development. *New Directions for Child and Adolescent Development, 83,* 37–59.

Greenfield, P. M. (2009). Linking social change and developmental change: Shifting pathways of human development. *Developmental Psychology, 45*(2), 401.

Greenfield, P. M, Keller, H. Fuligni, A., & Maynard, A. (2003). Cultural pathways through universal development. *Annual Review of Psychology,* 54, 461–490.

Jodhka, S. S., & Prakash, A. (2016). *The Indian middle class*. Delhi: Oxford University Press.

Kagitcibasi, C. (1996). *Family and human development across cultures: A view from the other side*. Hillsdale, NJ: Lawrence Erlbaum.

Kagitcibasi, C. (2005). Autonomy and relatedness in cultural context implications for self and family. *Journal of Cross-Cultural Psychology, 36*(4), 403–422.

Kagitcibasi, C. (2007). *Family, self and human development across cultures: Theory and application* (2nd ed.). New Jersey: Psychology Press.

Kagitcibasi, C. (2013). Adolescent autonomy-relatedness and the family in cultural context: What is optimal? *Journal of Research on Adolescence, 23*(2), 223–235.

Kakar, S. (1981). *The inner world: A psychoanalytic study of childhood in India.* (2nd ed.). New Delhi: Oxford University Press.

Kakar, S. (2001). The themes of authority in social relations in India. In A. K. Dalal & G. Misra (Eds.), *New directions in Indian psychology, Vol. 1: Social psychology* (pp. 132–140). New Delhi: Sage.

Kakar, S., & Kakar, K. (2007). *The Indians: Portrait of a people*. New Delhi: Penguin.

Kapur, P. & Misra, G. (in press). Religious behavior: Psycho-social perspectives. In G. Misra (Ed.), *ICSSR research survey and explorations in psychology*—Part II. Oxford University Press.

Kapur, D., & Vaishnav, M. (2014, December 9). Being middle class in India. *The Hindu*. Retrieved from http://www.thehindu.com/opinion/op-ed/being-middle-class-in-india/article6673580.ece.

Keller, H. (2007). *Cultures of infancy*. Mahwah, NJ: Erlbaum.

Kuhar, M., & Reiter, H. (2013). Toward a concept of parental authority in adolescence. *CEPS Journal: Center for Educational Policy Studies Journal, 3*(2), 135–155.

Lerner, R. M., Rothbaum, F., Boulos, S., & Castellino, D. R. (2002). Developmental systems perspective on parenting. In M. H. Bornstein (Ed.), *Handbook of parenting, Vol. 2: Biology and ecology of parenting* (pp. 315–344). NJ: Lawrence Erlbaum.

Lerner, R. M. (2002). *Concepts and theories of human development* (3rd ed.). Mahwah, NJ: Lawrence Erlbaum. Retrieved from http://search.ebscohost.com/login.aspx?direct=true&AuthType=ip,cookie,url,cpid,uid&custid=s8863137&db=cat00024a&AN=vmc.b18015827&site=eds-live&scope=site&authtype=ip,uid.

Madan, T. N. (1989). Religion in India. *Daedalus*, 118 (4), 114–146.

Markus, H. R., & Kitayama, S. (2010). Cultures and selves: A cycle of mutual constitution. *Perspectives on Psychological Science, 5*(4), 420–430.

Markus, H., & Kitayama, S. (1991). Culture and the self: Implications for cognition, emotion and motivation. *Psychological Review, 98*(2), 224–253.

Marsella, A. J. (2012). Psychology and globalization: Understanding a complex relationship. *Journal of Social Issues, 68*(3), 454–472. doi:10.1037/e653772011-001.

Mascolo, M. F., Misra, G., & Rapisardi, C. (2004). Individual and relational conceptions of self in India and the United States. *New Directions for Child and Adolescent Development, 104,* 9–26.

McKinsey Global Institute. (2010). *India's urban awakening: Building inclusive cities, sustaining economic growth.* Retrieved from http://www.mckinsey.com/global-themes/urbanization/urban-awakening-in-india.

Miles, M. B., & Huberman, A. M. (1994). *Qualitative data analysis.* CA: Sage.

Miller, J., Akiyama, H., & Kapadia, S. (unpublished manuscript). Cultural variation in communal vs. exchange norms: Implications for social support. *Journal of Personality and Social Psychology.*

Mines, M. (1988). Conceptualizing the person: Hierarchical society and individual autonomy in India. *American Anthropologist, 90*(3), 568–579.

Misra, G. (1995). Reflection on continuity and change in the Indian family system. *Trends in Social Science Research, II*(1), 27–31.

Misri, U. (1985). Child and childhood: A conceptual construction. *Contributions to Indian Sociology, 19,* 115–132.

New, R. S. (2010). Cross-cultural research on children's development: Deep roots and new branches. *Journal of Cross-Cultural Psychology, 41*(4), 522–533.

Panda, A., & Gupta, R. (2004). Mapping cultural diversity within India: A meta-analysis of some recent studies. *Global Business Review, 5*(1), 27–49.

Panda, M. (2013). *Madhyam Marg:* How it constitutes Indian mind? *Psychology and Developing Societies, 25*(1), 77–107.

Pinquart, M., & Silbereisen, R. (2004). Human development in times of social change: Theoretical considerations and research needs. *International Journal of Behavioral Development,* 28(4), 289–298. doi:http://doi.org/10.1080/01650250344000406.

Radhakrishnan, S. (2011). *Appropriately Indian: Gender and culture in a new transnational context.* Delhi: Orient BlackSwan.

Ramanujan, A. K. (1990). Is there an Indian way of thinking? An informal essay. In M. Marriott (Ed.), *India through Hindu categories* (pp. 41–58). New Delhi: Sage.

Roland, A. (1988). *In search of self in India and Japan: Toward a cross-cultural psychology.* Princeton, NJ, US: Princeton University Press.

Sachdeva, N., & Misra, G. (2005). Theoretical perspective on parenting: An overview. In M. Bhargava & S. Aurora (Eds.), *Dynamics of parental behavior* (pp. 9–27). Agra: H.P. Bhargava Book House.

Sachdeva, N., & Misra, G. (2008). The changing images of parenting in the three subcultures of India. *Journal of the Indian Academy of Applied Psychology, 34,* 16–23.

Saraswathi, T. S. (2005). Hindu worldview in the development of selfways: The "Atman" as the real self. *New Directions for Child and Adolescent Development, 109,* 43–50. doi:10.1002/cd. 136.

Saraswathi, T. S., & Pai, S. (1997). Socialization in the Indian context. In D. Sinha & H. S. R. Kao (eds.), *Asian perspectives on psychology* (pp. 74–92). New Delhi: Sage.

Saraswathi, T. S., & Ganapathy, H. (2002). Indian parents' ethnographies as reflections of the Hindu scheme of child and human development. In. H. Keller, Y. H. Poortinga, & A. Scholmerich (Eds.), *Between culture and biology: Perspectives on ontogenetic development* (pp. 79–88). Cambridge: Cambridge University Press. doi:http://dx.doi.org/10.1017/CB09780511489853.

Saraswathi, T. S., Mistry, J., & Dutta, R. (2011). Reconceptualizing lifespan development through a Hindu perspective. In L. A. Jensen. (2011). *Bridging cultural and developmental approaches to psychology: New syntheses in theory, research, and policy* (pp. 276–299). Oxford University Press, USA.

Sen, A. (2005, November 18). Contrary India. *The Economist.* The World in 2006.

Seymour, S. (2010). Environmental change, family adaptations and child development: Longitudinal research in India. *Journal of Cross-Cultural Psychology, 41*(4), 578–591.

Sharma, D. (2003). *Childhood, family and socio-cultural changes in India: Reinterpreting the inner world.* New Delhi: Oxford University Press.

Sharma, D. (2011). Values, families and human development: In Indian context. In G. Misra (Ed.), *Handbook of psychology* (pp. 193–204). New Delhi: Oxford University Press.

Shweder, R. A. (1990). Cultural psychology: What is it? In J. W. Stigler, R. A. Shweder, & G. Herdt (Eds.), *Cultural psychology: Essays in comparative human development*. New York: Cambridge University Press.

Shweder, R., Goodnow, J., Hatano, G., Levine, R., Markus, H., & Miller, P. (2006). The cultural psychology of development: One mind many mentalities. In W. Damon, & R. M. Lerner (Vol. Ed.), *Handbook of child psychology, Vol. 1: Theoretical models of human development* (6th ed., pp. 716–792). New York: Wiley.

Silbereisen, R. K., & Chen, X. (2010). *Social change and human development: Concept and results*. London: Sage.

Sinha, D., & Tripathi, R. C. (2003). Individualism in a collectivist culture: A case of coexistence of opposites. In T. S. Saraswathi (Ed.), *Cross-cultural perspectives in human development: Theory, research and applications* (pp. 192–210). New Delhi: Sage.

Southworth, B., & Lingamfelter, B. (2008). Great expectations: The rise of the Indian middle class. *The Chazen Web Journal of International Business*. Retrieved from https://www8.gsb.columbia.edu/researcharchive/articles/3021.

Sinha, D. (1982, November). Toward an ecological framework of deprivation. In D. Sinha, R. C. Tripathi, & G. Misra (Eds.), *Deprivation: Its social roots and psychological consequences* (pp. 25–35). New Delhi: Concept.

Sinha, D|. (1983). *Some recent changes in the Indian family and their implications for socialization*. Reports and studies (for the study of development); UNESCO Document No. SS.83/WS/42.

Sinha, D. (1988). Basic Indian values and behavior dispositions in the context of national development: An appraisal. In D. Sinha & H. S. Kao (Eds.), *Socialvalues and development: Asian perspectives* (pp. 31–55). New Delhi: Sage.

Srinivas, M. N. (Ed.). (1960). *India's villages*. Bombay: Asia Publishing House.

Super, C. M., & Harkness, S. (1986). The developmental niche: A conceptualization at the interface of child and culture. *International Journal of Behavioral Development, 9*, 545–569.

Triandis, H. C., & Brislin, R. W. (1984). Cross-cultural psychology. *American Psychologist, 39* (9), 1006–1016.

Tripathi, R. C. (2013). Special thematic issue on Indian cultural concepts. *Psychology and Developing Societies*, 25(1), vii–xiii. doi: 10.1177/0971333613477308 http://pds.sagepub.com.

Trommsdorff, G. (2006). Parent-child relations over the lifespan: A cross-cultural perspective. In K. H. Rubin & O. B. Chung (Eds.), *Parenting beliefs, behaviors, and parent-child relations: A cross-cultural perspective* (pp. 143–183). New York: Psychology Press. Retrieved from http://search.ebscohost.com/login.aspx?direct=true&AuthType=ip,cookie,url,cpid,uid&custid=s8863137&db=edsbl&AN=CN059297830&site=eds-live&scope=site&authtype=ip,uid.

Valsiner, J. (1994). Bidirectional cultural transmission and constructive sociogenesis. *Sociogenesis reexamined* (pp. 47–70). New York: Springer.

Valsiner, J. (2000). *Culture and human development: An introduction*. London: Sage.

Varma, P. K. (2007). *The great Indian middle class*. New Delhi: Penguin.

Weisner, T. S. (2002). Ecocultural pathways, family values, and parenting. *Parenting, 2*(3), 325–334. doi:10.1207/s15327922par0203_06.

Whiting, B. B. (Ed.). (1963). *Six cultures: Studies of child rearing*. New York: Wiley.

Whiting, B. B., & Whiting, J. W. M. (1975). *Children of six cultures: A psycho-cultural analysis*. Cambridge, MA: Harvard University Press.

Chapter 2
Adolescence: A Sociocultural Construction

Abstract Adolescence is a sociocultural construction that evolves within the culture-context-development framework. This chapter begins with a glimpse into the evolution of adolescence as a subject of scholarly interest. Next, the Western perspective of adolescence is described. The next section gives an overview of the cross-cultural variability in adolescence, illustrating different meanings and interpretations of this developmental stage across cultures. After this, a discussion of adolescent socialization focusing on parent–adolescent relationship to highlight key aspects of autonomy, authority, and interpersonal disagreements is presented. The next section depicts adolescents in the context of social change and globalization. How adolescence is constructed in the Indian-Hindu worldview and in the contemporary Indian context is then discussed, followed by a depiction of the urban middle class in Baroda (Vadodara), Gujarat.

Keywords Adolescence · Sociocultural construction · Cross-cultural variability · Globalization · Indian · Hindu · Middle class · Baroda · Vadodara

A Glimpse into Adolescence as a Subject of Scholarly Interest

The term adolescence is derived from the Latin term *adolescere* which means to grow into maturity (Muss and Porton 1990). The scientific study of adolescence in the West can be traced back to a century when G. Stanley Hall published his two-volume work "Adolescence," its powerful and lingering take away being the epithet *"storm and stress."* For several decades, Western scholarship on adolescence has anchored on to this premise, with classic theories of human development such as Freud's psychoanalytic theory and Erikson's psychosocial theory lending support to this construction. The idea of adolescence as a period of crisis hence sustained, highlighting issues such as emotional turmoil, striving for autonomy, and search for identity. In consonance with the predominance of Western perspectives in much of social science and the lack of adequate culturally relevant scholarly

© Springer (India) Pvt. Ltd. 2017
S. Kapadia, *Adolescence in Urban India*,
DOI 10.1007/978-81-322-3733-4_2

resources related to non-Western or Indian perspectives, this view of adolescence was regarded as uniform and universal, applicable to adolescents all over the world. The notion of culture as the source or even a crucial mediator in the interpretation and lived realities of adolescence was largely absent.

The genesis of the engagement of culture in the study of adolescence lies in the discipline of cultural anthropology. Margaret Mead's book Coming of Age in Samoa (1928) focused on adolescence and raised significant challenges to the "received" perspectives on this developmental period, for example, continuous rather than abrupt growth pattern and little differentiation between the worlds of child and adult, which were in sharp contrast to the Western societies. Since Mead's work, there was only intermittent anthropological interest in adolescence (Schlegel 2011). Nevertheless, it contributed toward the inclusion of culture in understanding adolescence. The advent of cross-cultural psychology gave further impetus to cultural differences and universalities in adolescence, whereas cultural psychology honed in to accord culture a central place in the study of human development and behavior. The notion of adolescence as a cultural construction thus came to be accepted. In accordance with the present-day scientific imperative of understanding human development as embedded in the interaction between culture and context, adolescence too is increasingly studied within a contextual perspective. In general, a contextual framework, focusing on continuity and plasticity in human development, for example, Lerner's developmental-contextual framework is highlighted, along with focus on mini theories and an applied developmental science perspective (Steinberg and Morris 2001). In a departure from the deficit or problem-oriented perspective, which considers young people as problems to be managed, the Positive Youth Development (PYD) framework views young people as resources to be developed (Roth and Brooks-Gunn 2003). The approach focuses on indicators of optimal functioning and thriving, and emphasizes the concept and role of agency to highlight adolescent capacity to influence one's own development. Youth are considered as conscious agents who are developing knowledge, skills, and values to deal with the complexities of the changing world (Lerner 2006; Larson and Tran 2014). The study of diversity and ethnic groups has also received considerable attention in the last decade (Lerner and Steinberg 2004).

In India, interest in scientific study of adolescence ran somewhat parallel to the indigenization movement in psychology, which took cognizance of the Western dominance, questioned the "received" perspectives, and made conscious attempts to unravel culturally rooted understanding of human development (Sinha 1986). Seminal research such as socialization of children in a weavers' community in Varanasi (Anandalakshmy and Bajaj 1981) and socialization of children in rural and urban poverty contexts in Gujarat (Saraswathi and Dutta 1988) set the stage for understanding childhood and adolescence in the ecological and cultural contexts. The studies represent a significant contribution to the understanding of adolescent development in the ecological context and highlight the cultural variations in the socialization goals and practices, including gender differences. Subsequently, research and writings on adolescence focused on the myth versus reality of adolescence in India (Saraswathi 1999) and offered indigenous descriptions of how this phase is understood and lived, including the intracultural variability, especially with reference to social class and gender (Verma and Saraswathi 2002; Larson et al. 2001). Saraswathi (1999) raised relevant questions regarding the existence of adolescence as a distinct stage in India, highlighting the need to take cognizance of social class and gender differences, and concluded that the distinctness of the stage is more readily observed in upper social class contexts. Factors such as increasing interaction with modern ways of living, exposure to alternative lifestyles, extended years in formal education, delay in choice and entry into a job or career, and delayed age at marriage are leading to the emergence of adolescence as a discrete developmental period.

Notwithstanding the valuable contributions of these works, understanding adolescence or for that matter, understanding any phase or domain of human development remains a challenging endeavor in a vastly diverse society such as India. Whereas much is now known about this interesting developmental period, more is yet to be unraveled, many perspectives yet to be shared.

Setting aside the issue of the existence of adolescence as a distinct stage in India or in other societies, the fact is that almost all societies distinguish between young people and adults. However, the "cultural structuring" of the adolescent period differs across societies, for example, the developmental milestones and the social roles, settings, and activities that shape the "content" of adolescence (Crockett 1997, p. 24). For instance, in Western societies adolescence is viewed as a period of prolonged preparation for adulthood, involving institutional segregations from adult worlds. It has a distinctive character, and although this conception is being questioned, the general perception is that adolescence is a stage fraught with upheaval. The next sections present the conception of adolescence in Western societies, followed by a discussion of the cross-cultural variability in the meaning and interpretation of this developmental period.

The Western Perspective on Adolescence

As described in the previous chapter, societies across the world operate along two idealized cultural-developmental pathways, independent and interdependent. Conceptions of self and socialization goals across societies, experiences, and practices are conceptualized along these two orientations. The two pathways endorse different sets of values. "The two value systems are merely ideal paradigms that get instantiated in a multiplicity of concrete and historically differentiated cultural contexts" (Greenfield et al. 2003, p. 468). Personal choice and individual rights are emphasized in the independent developmental pathway, with much value placed on independence and autonomy. Whereas in societies characterized by the interdependent pathway, social obligations and responsibilities rather than individual choice are highlighted, with preference given to relatedness (Greenfield et al. 2003).

For long years, Western Euro-American societies that follow the independent developmental pathway have endorsed the notion that during adolescence the individual must begin the process of separation from parents, also involving institutional segregation from adult worlds. Adolescence has a distinctive character and the general perception is that this stage is fraught with upheaval. The primary developmental task of the Western adolescent has been the achievement of autonomy, individuation, and disengagement from parents with tension between autonomy and dependence as its expected corollary. G. Stanley Hall's well-known axiom "*sturm und drung*" or storm and stress is partly rooted in this idea, as also in the frequency of mood disruptions and propensity for reckless and anti-social behavior among adolescents. According to this depiction adolescents, universally and inevitably, experience some emotional and behavioral upheaval on the way to adulthood (Arnett 2006).

Arnett (1999) has discussed the interpretation of the notion of adolescence as a difficult period. The difficulty is interpreted along three elements: (1) Conflicts with parents arising from resistance to adult authority: Parent–adolescent conflict is accepted as a normal event during adolescence and is also posed as facilitating the development of individuation and autonomy. High conflict, however, is likely to have disruptive effects on adolescent development. (2) Mood disruptions: More than other periods of development, mood swings are observed to occur more during adolescence. (3) Risk behavior including reckless, norm-breaking behavior is common among majority of adolescents. These difficulties not only affect adolescents themselves, but equally those around them, parents in particular. Hence, the overall perception of this stage being fraught with difficulties appears to bear credence. At the same time, the positive feature of this period as bearing the potential for immense growth needs to be acknowledged, as also the individual differences within culture and variability across cultures.

According to Valsiner (2000), it is pertinent to note that this conception of adolescence is a nineteenth century cultural-historical construction put forth to represent European and North American societies essentially focusing on school discipline and obedience of young workers in factories. The focus on social control during this stage was advanced in relation to bringing about behavioral conformity in boys by inculcating a school spirit and loyalty. Further, the psychology textbook portrayal of adolescence as troublesome and idealistic is a "socioideological" perspective of adults who portray adolescents as "difficult" and hence focus on how they (teachers or parents) may cope with adolescents rather than how adolescents could cope with their lives. Adolescence is thus primarily interpreted as a crisis period. Even though the rapid biological maturation is likely to create turmoil in the adolescent, it may not reflect in the social realm. Parents and adults, rather than the adolescents themselves, highlight the crisis of adolescence. The period is a developmental transition not only for adolescents, but also for parents who are called upon to deal with the event or process of their child turning into an adult, which presents the risk of parental loss of control over the child. The issue of parental control comes to the fore in societies where "successful parenting" is a (self-centered) cultural task that is important for the self-identity of an adult. In societies where parental control is a natural part of everyday life, however, the transition to adulthood may be of little special concern. Also relevant is the observation that Western psychology has assumed the guise of a "worried parent" (what is wrong with the adolescent attitude) and meted out a stigmatizing view of adolescence as "troublesome," "naïve," and "idealistic" (p. 272). This outlook has served to support and reinforce the stance on how to cope with adolescents.

It is little known that G. Stanley Hall acknowledged the influence of culture in adolescents' expression and experience of storm and stress and contended that this upheaval was more likely to occur in the USA than in societies with more conservative traditions (Arnett 1999). Although the universality and predictability of the storm and stress assertion have been increasingly questioned, its influence on the study of adolescence lingers even today, especially in the Western world. This is perhaps because the developmental task of individuation and separation is embedded in the ideal of the independent "self" and the need to establish a distinct identity. The importance of the stage of adolescence for establishing autonomy and identity is well recognized in the West and adolescence is considered as the period when relationships with parents are redefined and renegotiated, and conflict is inevitable. The ideal parent–adolescent relationship is deemed less hierarchical and deemphasizes parental authority. Peer influences are considered the strongest during this stage. Autonomy, a cherished developmental task needs to be constantly negotiated and is a contentious issue (Arnett 2002). The predominant Western view thus projects adolescents as striving for autonomy and independence from parents and desiring more relatedness with peers (Albert et al. 2004).

For people in non-Western societies, this depiction would appear largely at odds with their lived realities. The next section offers an overview of adolescence in a cross-cultural context.

Cross-Cultural Variability in Adolescence

Adolescence is a cultural universal in that the onset of puberty is a biological marker of transition from childhood to adulthood. Social adolescence, however, is a product of cultural beliefs and expectations, thereby introducing variability in the meaning and interpretation of the phase across cultures. "Culture is not just another variable in the mix: The formal and informal socialization practices that transmit culture to adolescents are essential factors in making them what they are" (Schlegel and Barry 1991, p. 287). The unequivocal recognition of the cultural intricacies of human development and the recent cross-cultural project on World of Youth (Brown et al. 2002) have drawn renewed attention to the need to study and understand adolescence as a culturally shaped phase of human development.

Historically, anthropology, a field with culture at its core, has contributed significantly to the study of adolescence highlighting the cultural influences. Margaret Mead's project in Samoa (Mead 1928) was a forerunner followed by seminal works such as the Harvard Adolescent Project and the Adolescent Socialization Project in the mid-to late 1970s (Schlegel and Hewlett 2011). Such projects have illuminated the cultural influences on adolescence, deliberate and informal, transacted through family, school, religious bodies, as well as neighborhoods, peers, and the media. The Adolescent Socialization Project revealed the universality of the stage in terms of a socially demarcated period across the 186 non-Western societies compared. It addressed aspects such as the adolescent's sense of self, relationships with parents and with peers, and the ways in which different cultures prepare adolescents for sex, marriage, and adult work. Sex differences were highlighted in that across societies the adolescence of boys is different and usually longer than that of girls (Schlegel and Barry 1991). In general, ethnographical accounts of adolescence have revealed that across cultures there are some common issues of adolescence, for example, looking forward to adulthood while still dependent; unmated sexual responsiveness; and greater involvement with peers. Cultural differences, however, occur in the interpretation and experience of these issues. Developmental transition from childhood to adulthood is a universal phenomenon, which is marked by culture-specific differences in the structure and content. Cultural structuring shapes adolescence in terms of the developmental milestones, practices that render distinctness to the period, and social roles and activities. Menarche is a significant developmental marker in agrarian societies where large numbers of children are desired and hence fertility is much valued. In an industrialized society, however, rather than puberty the emphasis may be on completion of schooling, which is seen as necessary to develop social and technical competence. In many societies, marriage is considered as a developmental marker in the sense that it signifies the end of adolescence and beginning of adulthood. The distinctness of adolescence as a stage of development also differs across cultures (Crockett 1997).

To define and explain adolescence as a cultural construct, a simple exercise to start would be to look at some of the terms used to refer to an adolescent in different societies and the connotations of such terms. The word "*teenager*" in America brings to mind images of "...recklessness, rebellion, irresponsibility, and conflict..." (Brown and Larson 2002, p. 6). In Africa, adolescence is viewed as a "way station" between childhood social apprenticeship and integration into adult social life. The formal Arabic term "*murahaqa*" signifies puberty and hence has sexual overtones. It means "to reach" or "to overtake," or in human development terms "to grow to the age of sexual maturity" (p. 210). Other terms used in common Arabic parlance are "*fata*" and "*fatat*" (14–17 years) for boys and girls, respectively, which denote the status of being unmarried and on the way to adulthood. The terms "*shabb/shabba*" (13 years-late 20s) are used to define a growing person and signify a sense of responsibility and obligation toward significant others (Booth 2002). In Japan, the period between childhood and adulthood has been given different names and meanings. The terms "*seishonen*" and "*seinen*," typically describe the younger generation; whereas the terms "*seinenki*" or "*jyudai*" are used to describe the period of adolescence. Similar ambiguities in definition are also observed in the Chinese society. The terms commonly used in these countries represent the youth at large, stage of puberty, generational status within family or the legal rights and responsibilities of the person. Hence, there is no single term that offers an unambiguous description of adolescence. As a result of the diffused terminology, the general practice is to refer to an individual as "middle school student" or "high school student" (Stevenson and Zusho 2002), thereby indicating the importance accorded to academics in Japan and China.

Many societies have rites of passage comprising rituals and ceremonies that may be small and private or community based, to mark puberty and entry into adolescence. Rituals and ceremonies occur in traditional, less complex societies compared to more complex modern societies, and if there are any in the latter, these are mostly for boys. In many cultures, sexuality and fertility are important themes of initiation ceremonies, primarily for girls. For boys, the ceremonies symbolize responsibility, whereas for girls the themes represent both responsibility and fertility. As a rule, gender is a major organizing principle of rituals and across societies ceremonies are gender differentiated in that there are separate rituals for boys and girls (Schlegel and Barry 2015). Some examples of traditional rituals are conducting a pseudo marriage ceremony when girls reach puberty in Kerala, South India (Verma 2000), wearing half sari in Andhra Pradesh, South India after a girl attains puberty (Dube 1998), and circumcision of 10–12 year old boys in Kaguru tribe in Eastern Africa (Gardiner et al. 1998). The harsh nature of some rituals represents adult supervision and authority as the adolescent begins to contribute to the family. Boys need to learn to be men and girls women, hence adolescents in these societies are observed to spend more time with adults. Whether or not rituals are performed, adolescents in traditional societies transition into a new life stage in which responsibilities increase and serious preparation for adult roles begins. In modern societies, such as the US, for example, rituals and ceremonies are absent. The transition from childhood to adulthood is gradual and marked by various events such as wearing particular clothing or taking ballroom dancing, depending upon individual choice (Schlegel and Barry 2015).

The cross-cultural differences in adolescence are dealt in considerable detail in projects such as The World's Youth (Brown et al. 2002). Presented here are some random broad strokes from the book, especially pertaining to family. The African society projects an adolescent that is the product of the indigenous as well as the exogenous. The indigenous conception views the stage as a distinct period of development during which there is definitive preparation for adult status. Parental expectations (in accordance with gender and age of the adolescent) are the cornerstone of family relationships. Parental authority is viewed as being in adolescents' own interest and hence as a parental right (Nsamenang 2002). In China and Japan, the traditional perspective considers family as most significant. Youth engage in regular communication with parents and have a favorable perception of the relationship. Yet, with the changes that the two societies are undergoing, for example, the effects of the one-child policy in China and decrease in family size in Japan, adolescents are becoming more self-centered. The social interdependence is thus giving way to greater emphasis on individualism (Stevenson and Zusho 2002). Southeast Asian societies (e.g., Indonesia, Philippines) place great value on family solidarity and social relationships, which has sustained despite social change. Family ties, sacrifices for the family, and dependence on the family are accepted, and work to reduce stress that may accompany the growth process (Maria 2002). In Arab societies, adolescence is viewed as a process of learning responsibility and agency in a web of relationships. Family connectivity and group primacy are upheld, and children are socialized to bear lifelong responsibility for the family; the self is experienced in connection with others. Gender roles are firmly in place. Males are assigned the task of control and responsibility for their female kin, and the female members in turn accept male kin as their protectors and perform tasks in their service. The patriarchal system is resilient, sons are more valued than daughters, and family structure is strongly hierarchical (in Saudi Arabia) (Booth 2002). Latin American countries have witnessed significant social and economic changes in the last two decades. Important markers that denote the end of adolescence and entry into adulthood include leaving home, living with partner, and forming a family. Adolescents continue to live with their parents, often for economic reasons, and do not really become independent until they are married (Welti 2002).

The diverse terms used to denote the phase of adolescence, the different rites of passage across different cultures, and the different priorities and tasks emphasized thus give us an indication of the indigenous meanings attached to adolescence in different cultural contexts. Adolescence is thus lived and experienced differently in Western and non-Western societies. Cultural variability in adolescence is indisputable, presenting a tapestry of varied hues that comprise diverse patterns across the world, not only between, but also within cultures. The cultural outlooks are interwoven and reflected in socialization in the family and mediate the parent–adolescent relationship.

Adolescent Socialization in Cross-Cultural Context

Socialization precepts and practices evolve from and reflect the cultural worldview and are also responsive to changes in the sociodemographic context. Adolescent socialization involves conscious focus on inculcating culturally appropriate behaviors, beliefs, values, and attitudes, with the goal of preparing adolescents for adult roles. The adolescent is trying to meet the changing demands of adult socialization, and simultaneously experiencing rapid developmental changes in physical, psychological, and socioemotional domains. Developmental changes during adolescence are associated with the idea of decreasing dependence on parents and increasing adoption of adult-like roles, albeit in harmony with cultural models of human development. Cultural outlooks permeate family interactions and relationships. The following section discusses the key elements of the parent–adolescent relationship in a cross-cultural context.

Parent–Adolescent Relationship in Cross-Cultural Context: Authority, Autonomy, and Differences

The socialization process unfolds in the context of parent–adolescent relationship, which is embedded in the cultural and socioeconomic contexts. Western, Euro-American societies adopt the independent developmental model, emphasizing an individualistic orientation and the need to establish a unique identity, distinct from parents. In concurrence with this perspective, autonomy in terms of separation from parents is the key developmental task during adolescence. Research with parent–adolescent dyads in Western societies has shown that parents are more concerned about authority and adolescents are preoccupied with seeking autonomy from parents (Jensen and Dost-Gozkan 2015). The achievement of autonomy is regarded as a crucial psychosocial developmental issue, and appropriate parental support for autonomy is associated with positive developmental outcomes (Zimmer-Gembeck and Collins 2003). A more recent perspective, however, departs from the long prevalent predominant view in Western societies that adolescents are preoccupied with seeking independence from family, and instead contends that complete autonomy from parents has adverse effect on adolescent development. What is advocated instead is a judicious balance between autonomy and relatedness such that adolescents develop independence within a supportive family context (Greenfield et al. 2003). Autonomy development is increasingly conceptualized less in terms of distancing from parental influence and more in terms of parents' input in encouraging age-appropriate autonomy within a warm and supportive family climate, with close ties with parents (Soenens et al. 2007). This notion is endorsed by several developmental researchers who have emphasized that development of autonomy does not necessitate severing ties with parents (e.g., Grotevant and Cooper 1986; McElhaney and Allen in press; Steinberg and Silverberg 1986; Yeh et al. 2009; Zimmer-Gembeck and Collins 2003). A balance between separation and connectedness contributes to psychological maturity in adolescents in terms of self-awareness, sensitivity to others, and capacity for managing new situations (Bekker and Van Assen 2006).

In East Asian societies (China, Japan), interdependence is predominant and parent–child relationship is characterized by connectedness. Parents are perceived as authority figures symbolizing wisdom. Parent–child relationship is built around the elements of duty, respect, obligation, obedience, and compliance with parents' wish (Trommsdorf and Kornadt 2003). Evidently, relatedness rather than autonomy is much valued in non-Western societies. The relevance of autonomy as a key developmental task during adolescence has thus been questioned in the context of non-Western societies. At the same time, it is acknowledged that preparation for adult roles entails developing some degree of autonomy, and hence it is a period when relationships with parents may need to be redefined. Both autonomy and relatedness are basic human needs across societies. The combination of these two needs manifests as the autonomous-related self that is described in Chap. 1. This self-construal offers the possibility to satisfy both basic needs and is hence considered optimal for development (Kagitcibasi 1996, 2013).

In this same vein, cross-cultural research has highlighted the relevance of autonomy in non-Western societies, albeit in different forms and with different timelines. Globalization is likely to create greater discrepancy in parents' and adolescents' views on cultural values of autonomy and authority, and hence these issues acquire prominence (Jensen et al. 2011). In association with cultural values and norms, variations, both within and between cultures are prevalent in notions pertaining to the particular form of autonomy that may be regarded as appropriate and how much autonomy is considered optimal (Zimmer-Gembeck and Collins 2003). In interdependent societies comprising hierarchical social structures and respect to authority, the notion of autonomy is likely to be interpreted differently from Western contexts. Empirical research has consistently demonstrated the differentials in adolescent autonomy between Euro-American and non-Western populations. For example, in comparison with Euro-American adolescents, non-Western adolescents (Filipino and Mexican) tend to de-emphasize autonomy, show greater deference to parental authority, and are reluctant to openly disagree with parents. They also have later expectations for autonomy than their European counterparts (Fuligni 1998).

Cross-cultural research has explored and put forth different models of autonomy that may be more congruent in interdependent cultures. Accordingly, distinctions are made with reference to the nature of autonomy that may be encouraged in different cultures. For instance, Soenens et al. (2007) have presented the concepts of parental promotion of independence (PI) and parental promotion of volitional functioning (PVF). PI emphasizes an individualized view of how adolescents relate to their own parents and to other adults. The concept involves encouragement of self-reliance in decision making regarding behaviors and values, and the development of independence at the expense of connection with parents. PVF refers to behaviors that support adolescents to rely increasingly on their own decision making and that encourage the internalization of culturally important values. Zimmer-Gembeck et al. (2011) have put forth yet another dimension of autonomy termed as "voice." Based on the premise that autonomy thrives in positive social relationships, the authors consider the capacity to articulate one's opinions, needs, and feelings in interactions with others (parents or partners in intimate relationships) as one component of autonomy. Yet another model of autonomy advanced in the context of non-western societies (e.g., Taiwan, China) is the dual representation of autonomy as individuating autonomy (IA) and relating autonomy (RA), with the possibility of co-existence of both within an individual. The model views autonomy as constituting cognitive, functional, and emotional capacities that contribute to volitional capacity, a key constituent of autonomy. Individuating autonomy involves volitional capacity to act against social constraints and to achieve a distinct identity, whereas relating autonomy refers to volitional capacity that is expressed in favor of harmony of self-in-relation to others, the quality of interpersonal relationships, and self-transcendence. IA focuses on volitional achievement of personal goals and individuality; RA involves reflection and consideration of opinions of significant others into one's own self-identity, however, it is different from conformity and compliance. The two forms are posited as intertwined capacities and an individual may use both, thereby satisfying needs of individuality and connectedness (Yeh et al. 2007). Along similar lines, Miller (2003) has argued for a distinction between personal and social autonomy. Personal agency is linked with acting in a self-directed manner, whereas social agency is related to acting on the basis of social requirements and expectations and is likely to be more prevalent in interdependent cultures.

An issue closely related to the cultural meaning and significance of autonomy is that of parental support in this regard. Given the primacy of autonomy in Western contexts, parental support for autonomy development has been associated with positive developmental outcomes for adolescents (e.g., Soenens et al. 2007). In non-Western contexts, however, the notion and domains of support for autonomy are likely to be different. Marbell (2014) discusses four components of autonomy support for adolescents that may be applicable in non-Western contexts. These are as follows: (1) Perspective taking, which refers to taking children's point of view and empathizing with their thoughts and feelings, thereby promoting children's feelings of being heard and hence more likely to agree with the parents' views. (2) Provision of choice, involves providing children with choice, and hence reducing feelings of being coerced, and instead promotes a sense of agency. (3) Allowance of decision making refers to including children's inputs in the decision-making process, as opposed to a unilateral decision by parents, although this may run counter to values such as deference to parental authority. (4) Allowance of open exchange, involve parents allowing children to express their views, thereby facilitating the feeling of being heard. It is relevant to note, however, that some of these components may not be effective in interdependent cultures if these are viewed as promoting independence (rather than volitional functioning) as the former is likely to conflict with the cultural values of respect for hierarchy and connectedness.

Along with the sociocultural context, socioeconomic background also bears upon the extent to which autonomy and relatedness are emphasized and encouraged, and what form of autonomy is dominant. Variations in socialization goals and practices are likely to occur within a society, for example, among different socioeconomic groups and on account of social change (Greenfield et al. 2003). For example, cross-cultural research across different sociocultural and socioeconomic contexts (Germany, USA, Cameroon, and India) has revealed that mothers from urban middle class contexts consider autonomous goals as more significant than do mothers in rural settings. It is likely that autonomy may be perceived as a more useful competence in an urban educated middle class setting, and hence its value as a socialization goal (Kärtner et al. 2007). Similarly, Chinese parents are observed to modify their socialization goals and practices related to socioemotional development to achieve success in the rapidly changing economic and social contexts. Shyness has been a traditionally valued quality in the Chinese society, which is rather incompatible with a market-oriented society that lays emphasis on individual initiative and competitiveness. Consequently, parents are encouraged to expand their childrearing goals to include development of autonomy and independence (e.g., expression of personal opinion, self-confidence) which will bring success in an increasingly competitive environment (Chen and Chen 2010).

Intricately related to adolescent autonomy is the notion of parental authority. Parenting and parent–child relationship may be viewed along the continuum of authority-autonomy. Cultural values influence the meaning of authority and introduce variation in the ways in which parents and adolescents perceive it. Cultures that value interdependence tend to place greater emphasis on parental authority and control than cultures that value independence. Asian-American parents are likely to use authoritarian parenting focusing on obedience and conformity more than Euro-American parents. For example, in keeping with the Confucian ideology in the Chinese society, childrearing practices are based on indigenous concepts that denote "to train" and "to govern and to love". Parents are highly involved in their children's lives and show much care and concern. Parental authority and control are thus interpreted as reflecting parents' care, concern, and involvement in children, with such practices viewed as instrumental in preventing child misbehavior (Chao 1994, 2000). A similar pattern was revealed in a study comparing maternal and adolescent attachment in India and Germany, wherein Indian mothers manifested a balance of acceptance and control in their parenting styles. Further, Indian adolescents interpreted parental control and care as care and protection, which was contrary to German adolescents who viewed it as overprotection and constraint. Hence, unlike in Western societies, parental control and warmth are seen to be related, with authority and control bearing a positive connotation (Albert et al. 2004).

Besides cultural values, socioeconomic background also influences the interpretation of parental authority and control. High-risk settings such as dangerous neighborhoods are characterized by stricter control and lesser autonomy, which is not viewed as psychologically controlling; whereas strictness in low-risk settings is viewed as psychologically controlling (McElhaney and Allen in press). Implementation and legitimization of parental authority require active participation of the child and involves mutual acknowledgement of expectations (Kuhar and Reiter 2013). Further, as discussed in Chap. 1, authority is enacted in an interactional, bidirectional context. Hence, the perspective of the child is necessary to understand the dynamics of parenting and parent–child relationship.

The phenomena of adolescent autonomy and parental authority, and the cultural differentials therein come to the fore especially in the context of interpersonal disagreements. For example, adolescents with higher individuating autonomy are found to be more inclined to express disagreements with parents, thereby leading to greater frequency of interpersonal conflict (Yeh et al. 2007). The next section discusses cultural variability in the interpretation and resolution styles of interpersonal disagreements.

Interpersonal Disagreements: An Inevitable Phenomenon

The tension between the adolescent's demand for autonomy and the parent's assertion of authority resulting in heightened parent–adolescent disagreements in Western contexts is well documented (e.g., Goossens 2006; Smetana 1988). The Western perspective contends that such events are instrumental in the adolescent's achievement of the developmental task of autonomy and individuation through disengagement from parents and family. In Western societies, parent–adolescent conflict is regarded as a precursor to individuation and separation which is a salient goal during adolescence. Cross-cultural research has nevertheless demonstrated the ubiquity of adolescent-parent disagreements (e.g., Schlegel and Barry 1991). Further, the ways in which conflicts are resolved reveals parents' approach to adolescent autonomy. Direct expression of conflict is more common in cultures that value individual autonomy, while in cultures that value relational harmony, conflict is avoided through strategies such as compliance, negotiation, or withdrawal (Markus and Lin 1999). In non-Western collectivist societies that emphasize connection and subordination, adolescent-parent conflicts are likely to occur as the autonomy that is expected during adulthood conflicts with the cultural orientation of connection and subordination (Schlegel 2011). Conflicts are also likely to arise from adolescents' greater inclination toward futuristic global norms and values as sources of identity, which may run counter to traditional parental identities and expectations (Nsamenang 2011). Cross-cultural research has reported similarities in the themes of parent–adolescent disagreements. Disagreements occur on everyday mundane and petty issues (Fuligni 1998; Yau and Smetana 1996, 2003) such as daily home chores, physical appearance, schoolwork, interactions with friends, siblings, and other family members (Kapadia and Miller 2005).

Although disagreements with parents characterize adolescents' lives in all societies with much commonality in the topics of disagreements, cultural differences are observed in the interpretation and resolution of the same. According to Markus and Lin (1999) cultures stressing individual autonomy accept open contradiction and expression of one's point of view to understand disagreements better. In non-Western societies where the period of adolescence is short and youth are given adult responsibilities or privileges sooner, conflict may not be relevant in the same way (Schlegel and Barry 1991). In most non-Western societies, the ideal of human development is oriented more toward interdependence and connection, and the socialization goals are shaped correspondingly. For example, Latin and Chinese societies emphasize family solidarity and parental authority and value traits such as obedience and respect for elders (Fuligni and Zhang 2004; Harkness and Super 2002; Markus and Lin 1999; Phinney et al. 2000). In such contexts, adolescents are found to emphasize negotiation with parents rather than self-assertion in situations of conflict.

Much research has compared differences and similarities in parent–adolescent relationships, disagreements and their subsequent resolution on the basis of the individualist versus collectivist orientation. For example, Phinney et al. (2005)

analyzed the influence of cultural values in the resolution of hypothetical parent–adolescent disagreements among European-American, Mexican-American, Armenian-American and Korean-American families. Although the reasoning of young individuals across all groups indicated both autonomy and relatedness, the European-Americans were more self-oriented and assertive, whereas adolescents from the ethnic minority groups were more other-oriented and made reference to family respect and closeness. Similarly, a study that investigated the beliefs, expectations, and relationships with parents in the context of autonomy granting by parents among adolescents from Mexican, Chinese, Filipino, and European backgrounds residing in America revealed that adolescents from non-European backgrounds did not openly contradict parents in case of a disagreement (Fuligni 1998).

It is known that cultures with collectivist orientations apply cooperative and harmonious styles of resolving disagreements, and focus on reducing any arising tension, whereas cultures with individualist orientation resolve disagreements through open expression of views. The process of resolution reveals how adolescent autonomy is interpreted and dealt with (Collins and Steinberg 2006). Along with sociocultural outlook, the socioeconomic context also intervenes in the process of resolution of disagreements and perhaps the outcome as well. For instance, in the family model of psychological interdependence that may generally prevail in cultures that privilege relatedness, and in which material dependencies may weaken but psychological interdependencies are sustained, the socialization goals and approaches are likely to be directed toward either reducing conflict or render the process less disruptive and more in the interest of maintaining relationship harmony (Kagitcibasi 1996).

In accordance with the changing sociodemographic context, families are required to adapt their socialization goals and practices. The functional or adaptive bases of socialization are significant in understanding why certain patterns prevail in certain contexts, and how these may change to adapt to the fluctuating context. Along these lines, a large cross-cultural 30-nation study on family values, roles, and networks revealed that socioeconomic development rendered family roles and values less traditional, increased autonomy, and diluted hierarchy. This was especially observed in the context of nuclear families. Young respondents in particular rejected the authoritarian model of the father, signifying emerging autonomy in more developed educated settings in less affluent countries (Georgas et al. 2006). A macro contextual perspective is thus essential to understand adolescence, especially in the present context of rapid change. Traditionally valued goals may need to be reviewed and revised in consonance with changing contexts. Models of social change discussed in the previous chapter have considered the interactive influence of culture and context on family socialization (Greenfield et al. 2003; Kagitcibasi 1996). The social structural changes result in changing lifestyles, which in turn impact family relationships. Thus, both parents and adolescents are required to form new attitudes and behaviors that will be most conducive to meet the changing contextual demands (Kagitcibasi and Yalin 2015). Shades of such a model are observed in the Indian society, which, like other societies in the Majority World (a term coined by Kagitcibasi to refer to the non-Western societies that make up the majority of the world's population) (Kagitcibasi 2002), is urbanizing at a rapid rate.

Adolescence in the Context of Globalization: *"Times Are a Changing"*

In the present context of globalization and social change, societies are undergoing varying degrees and forms of transformations, and adolescents cannot remain insulated from this phenomenon. Present day adolescents are known as the *Millennial Generation* or the Generation Y, to indicate that they follow the Gen X (individuals born between the early 1960s and the 1980s). Although no definite dates are specified, the term *millennial* refers to individuals born between early 1980s and early 2000s. The *millennials* share three key features: living in an ultra-connected technologically advanced digital world with disappearing time and space constraints, being born into a post-communist world, and enveloped in uncertainty from shifting geopolitical balance (Havas Worldwide 2011). Stereotypes about this generation abound, and the general perception is that of a "me generation," one that is essentially focused on self-interests.

Today, Heraclitus's famous epithet "Change is the only constant," perhaps needs to be revised as, "Rapid change is the only constant." The vigorous and even fleeting character of change is best witnessed in the development of new technology. Examples are as follows: the flurry in the production of different cell phone models, with I Phone and Samsung for instance vying with each other to produce even more advanced models promising novel apps (applications), computer brands competing with each other in claiming the slimmest and slickest design in laptops or tablets, the television introducing a new channel almost every other day, and the Internet producing innumerable bytes of news and views every minute. Caught in the middle of this explosion and embracing it every which way, sometimes willingly and at other times grudgingly, are our adolescents and their parents.

Developmentally adolescence is the period during which individuals are more open to diverse beliefs and values (Arnett 2002). The openness to new beliefs and values brings both opportunities and risks (Jensen 2011). Globalization and increasing modernity are also likely to create cultural gaps and conflicts between young people and their parents, especially with respect to views on parental authority and adolescent autonomy. This has been demonstrated in the immigrant contexts wherein adolescents acculturate better than adults have. Further, a gap in parent–adolescent beliefs predicted less family cohesion and more conflict in Asian Indian families (Jensen and Dost-Gozkan 2015). Present day adolescents are more vulnerable to globalization as they are experiencing a double-layered transition, one that is developmental, and the other through intersection with a world in transition

(Arnett 2006). As stated in the World Youth Report (2003), "Globalization is ultimately as complex as young people's lives are multidimensional. The combination of the two inevitably creates an explosive and heady mix. Young people's transitions are to varying degrees becoming increasingly open-ended, but that open-endedness is introducing an enormous assortment of complications that are making young people's lives more difficult than ever" (p. 305).

According to Mortimer and Larson (2002), a significant developmental consequence of globalization is the lengthening of adolescent transition, especially in urban middle and upper social class contexts. Across societies, adolescents spend a greater number of years in formal education, to not only get a basic graduate degree but also postgraduate degrees or value added specializations in order to prepare for desired jobs that will bring adequate economic returns. Entry into full-time work, age at marriage, and child bearing are also delayed. These changes have led to the creation of "emerging adulthood" defined as a period of exploration and experimentation with relationships and worldviews, but also instability (Arnett 2000). "In sum, (therefore) the dawn of the twenty-first century may be considered both the best of times and the worst of times for youth, a time of ominous trends as well as new opportunities" (Mortimer and Larson 2002, p. 14).

"Growing up" in the present times is thus a unique experience as the world that young individuals inhabit today is vastly different from the previous generations. The key points of departure are globalization, technological advances and economic development (Nugent 2006), and above all the vigorous pace of change. Adolescents' daily life increasingly comprises multiple worlds (e.g., cultural, digital, generational) with distinct codes, assumptions, goals, and meanings, which multiplies the complexities and challenges that they encounter (Larson et al. 2012).

Three trends of social change affect adolescents in particular. First is the globalization of economy, advancement of communication technology as evidenced by the growing expansion of the Internet, and territorial mobility within and between countries that is sweeping all societies of the world. Consequently, preparation for future jobs is considerably uncertain and the school to work transition is rendered more difficult. Growing individualization and pluralization of life paths and the corollary flexibility in social scripts regarding developmental goals is the second manifestation. As a result, there is lack of clear guidelines for future roles and life decisions. The third trend is the demographic changes such as decline in fertility rates and patterns of immigration or emigration (Pinquart and Silbereisen 2005). Globalization is also impacting gender equality, in turn affecting available opportunities. First, since the global economy is based on information, technology, and services, families across the world including India are increasingly beginning to believe that it is in their best economic interest to educate girls so that they may benefit from the global economy. Second, there is growing international pressure on the countries of the world to address gender discrimination and enhance gender equality (Jensen and Arnett 2012). The latter is influencing government policies and programs of education, and new prospects are progressively more available to adolescent girls.

Globalization entails both economic and cultural change (Scholte 2002). Global consumerism and global media are most associated with young people, and although they may create their own versions based on their local circumstances, they are equally influenced by it. For instance, in a recent study on attitudes toward romantic relationships in Baroda, India, young boys and girls reported being influenced by American TV shows (Athavale et al. 2016). Global brands (read Western) are attractive and consumer markets target young people in selling global brands in clothes, music, and movies. Global influences may thus outweigh local influences. The term "global youth culture," a transdisciplinary category, is frequently used to describe and make sense of the hybrid culture and identity that is becoming characteristic of youth all over the world. New media technologies in particular are creating a context in which local and global influences interact and are reflected in young people's lifestyles (Kahn and Kellner 2006).

Globalization is bringing about changes across the board in all life domains. Jensen (2011) discusses three aspects that are most relevant to the cultural identity of adolescents—language, diet, and media, and the global changes therein. In the present times, the popularity of English is at its peak the world over, including India. Given the colonial history, English has always been valued in India, often acting as a divide between the progressive and *"desi"* (traditional, local). Speaking in English signifies modernity, and young individuals are especially conscious of this. The tremendous need for English is observed in the proliferation of English speaking classes as also parents' keenness to enroll their children in English medium schools. The fallout is a loss in one's own language and the parallel adoption of a hybrid language that is amply evident in the Indian context. Food is another major domain. McDonaldization is being experienced the world over, to a greater or lesser extent. At the same time, there is a bidirectional movement of cuisine, for example, the growing popularity of Indian curry or *samosas* in many parts of the world. Adolescents thus have the opportunity to learn about all kinds of cuisine, which may have positive or harmful effects on their health. The media explosion is yet another powerful domain that is thriving under global impact. The pervasiveness of communication technology in India is impressive. Internet accessibility is growing, and cell phone use spans urban, rural, and even some tribal areas. Social networking sites such as Facebook and WhatsApp are immensely popular with adolescents (and in fact across all age groups in India), and the question, *"Hey, are you on WhatsApp??"* or the comment, *"WhatsApp me"* are commonly heard in young people's conversations.

Adolescents are thus routinely acquainted with global cultures, which are likely to impact their everyday lives. As Jensen (2011) states, developing a cultural identity in the present times "…involves navigating both local and global cultures" (p. 65).

Arnett (2002) has discussed the possible psychological consequences of globalization on young individuals in terms of the development of a bicultural or hybrid identity, identity confusion, and self-selected cultures. Globalization has implications on cultural identity, which involves adopting beliefs and practices of a cultural community. The diluting cultural boundaries, increasing contact (real or virtual) with other cultures, and exchange and spread of ideas across cultures render the process of acquiring cultural identity a complex one, with many pathways to choose from. The situation may result in the formation of a bicultural identity, which means that in addition to one's culture-specific local identity, individuals develop a global identity and are able to relate to information, events, and practices that occur at the global level. Further, the beliefs and practices of local cultures are themselves changing, thereby creating a multicultural world and the likelihood of a hybrid identity. Instances of a bicultural identity are evident in the Indian society wherein on the one hand Indian youth are at the forefront of the country's technological revolution, and on the other hand, they continue to prefer arranged marriages. Identity confusion may arise from difficulty in adapting to the rapid changes in one's own culture, which may seem inadequate, and simultaneously the relative alienation that one may experience in relation to the global culture, thereby creating acculturative stress leading to identity confusion (Arnett 2002; Jensen and Arnett 2012). Research with Indian adolescents has not only confirmed the development of a bicultural identity in girls and boys, but has also demonstrated its relationship with well-being (Rao et al. 2013).

As much as young people are vulnerable to global change, they are just as adaptable and hence in the best position to take advantage of the myriad opportunities that the global world is presenting. For instance, young individuals are best informed and skilled in using new information and communication technology. Globalization has brought about considerable positive change in adolescents' living conditions, especially in the urban economically well-off middle class populations. Today's global world is providing adolescents ample opportunity to know multiple cultures, either personally or through communication technology such as the Internet or TV (Jensen and Arnett 2012).

In the growing competitive world, access to resources is important and determines options and constraints, for example, in relation to factors such as gender and family socioeconomic status (Mortimer and Larson 2002). Across the world, and especially in developing societies, there are young people who do not have the economic resources to experience the many advantages of the globalizing world, yet their cultural identity and local traditions are threatened. Social class is an important mediator of young people's experience with globalization. Globalization reinforces divides, for example, in education and wealth as the availability of resources varies greatly, especially in developing countries such as India. The relationship between young people and the globalizing world is thus ambiguous (World Youth Report 2003, 2005).

Changes are also observed in adolescents' experiences of interpersonal interactions in the community and family, including the parent–adolescent relationship. Parents are making greater economic investments in adolescents, especially for education as it is perceived as an essential aspect of socialization.

There is a growing tendency to have smaller families so that the best can be offered to children. Parents are getting more involved in their adolescents' everyday lives and are increasingly acquainted with their activities. In terms of disciplining, there is a trend toward decreasing parental authority and control, and increase in responsiveness to the needs of the adolescent, with more democratic and open communication. At the same time, generational discrepancy in parent–adolescent perspectives is evident, and brings with it misunderstandings and interpersonal conflict (Larson et al. 2002).

In general, social change has multiple, complex influences on institutions and individuals. This is especially true of the Indian society with its variegated, multilayered social structure. A single depiction of the Indian adolescent is difficult to derive, instead what emerges are "kaleidoscopic images" that represent different regions and socioeconomic contexts (Verma and Saraswathi 2002, p. 105). The next section discusses how adolescence has been interpreted in the traditional Indian-Hindu model of development and in the contemporary context.

Adolescence in the Indian Cultural Milieu

This section depicts how adolescence was construed in traditional India, followed by a description of adolescence in contemporary Indian context.

Adolescence in the Indian-Hindu Model of Development

In the Hindu model of human development, a child begins to be regarded as a person only when he or she is able to study and understand the scriptures. Hence, early adolescence is considered as the first stage in the developmental life cycle. Although there are specific stages and rituals to signify the period of childhood, according to the Hindu worldview, a young child is not considered a person before one is able to study and understand the scriptures. This process is initiated during *Brahmacharya* with the onset of a period of learning, when a child enters school and continues until he or she has finished all schooling. "*Brahmacharya*" is considered important for apprenticeship and acquiring knowledge of the tasks of adult life (Kakar 1981). The stage also included the practice of celibacy connoting chastity which is necessary for the purpose of learning from a *guru* (teacher), and during later stages of life for the purposes of attaining spiritual liberation (*moksha*). For example, in traditional India, boys (in rare cases, girls) in the "*brahmacharya*" stage were sent to a "*gurukul*" (home of the teacher) to acquire knowledge of "*shastras* and *vedas*" (Hindu religious scriptures) and also to groom themselves in other required tasks such as warfare. In contemporary India, this may be compared to the present day education system that readies the adolescent to achieve career goals successfully in order to gain adult identity. The term *Kishorawastha* is used to refer to the pubescent child and *Yuvawastha* refers to youth. The goal of *Kishorawastha* is to acquire knowledge, build character, and to learn to shoulder responsibilities. This period of life is considered significant for moral development and a time to set and pursue one's personal goals (Chakkarath 2005).

In consonance with the Hindu developmental model of "individual-in-social-world" discussed in the previous chapter (Saraswathi et al. 2011), the developmental task of the Indian adolescent is not to separate but to strengthen emotional bonds (Larson et al. 2003), and develop a relational, familial self (Roland 1988). As discussed in Chap. 1, the Indian self evolves in a complex context, changing its form across the life span. The relational dimension is valued until the stage of householder or *Grahasthya Ashrama,* whereas the spiritual self is emphasized in later life. The dominant developmental framework is one of inter-dependencies, within which autonomy is conceptualized and performed. In the present times, the dynamic and consistent interactions between culture and context are influencing the traditional outlook.

Adolescence in Contemporary Indian Society

In the Indian society, the terms "young people" or "youth" refer to adolescents and young adults. In recent years, youth as a phase of life has received considerable attention in India because of three main reasons. First, according to the 2011 census youth 13–35 years form 65% of the Indian population; second, the view that youth are most vulnerable to the HIV-AIDS pandemic, and third the recognition that youth are a valuable human resource and potential contributors to the development of the nation (Census of India 2011; Kapadia and Bhangaokar 2013). The significance of this developmental period is well recognized and accepted, not only by academicians but also, or especially, by policy-makers, particularly because of the instrumental value of this segment in contributing to national development (Saraswathi and Oke 2013). The present government is making every effort to take the youth in its fold to contribute to their own development and in turn that of the country. The age group of 15–29 years comprises 27.5% of the total youth population (National Youth Policy 2014). Adolescence is characterized by immense diversity because of wide-ranging disparities in social and economic class, caste, education level, gender, and geographical location—rural, urban, or tribal. Such diversity renders any attempts to generalize about Indian adolescence a difficult task.

Adolescence as a distinct stage of development involving preparation for adulthood characterized by a world segregated apart from adults is largely a cultural construction of technological and industrial societies in the twentieth century (Arnett 2002). In contrast to this, many non-Western societies such as India are characterized by child-adult continuity, in turn leading to the absence of adolescence as a distinct phase or stage, the latter mainly because of greater similarity in life course and continuity in expectations from childhood to adulthood.

Saraswathi's (1999) discussion on the question of the existence of adolescence as a distinct stage in the Indian society highlights relevant aspects. She contends that notwithstanding some observable markers of the social transition to adulthood, the existence of a distinct stage of adolescence similar to Western societies is a recent development, essentially observable in upper social classes. In the same vein, Kaur et al. (2001) have observed that "...childhood for majority of the Indian children is truncated and adolescence is seldom experienced" (p. 206).

According to Saraswathi (1999), child-adult continuity in the Indian society occurs differentially depending upon social class and gender, with greater continuity evident in lower social classes and among girls. From a young age, girls are socialized to be "good" mothers and "good" wives, and assigned tasks of sibling care. In the midst of this continuity, however, there is a short phase of transition before marriage, when the girl is specially trained to assume greater responsibility for household tasks with a view to prepare her to meet well the requirements of the conjugal family. Verma (2000) has also highlighted the continuity in transition for boys in families engaged in traditional occupations. In case of boys, although they enjoy the privilege of being a male child in a patriarchal society with its advantages such as more freedom, more leisure time and little involvement in household tasks, they bear the burden of beginning to earn at an early age to support the family, which causes not only a diminished possibility of adolescence, but also curtails childhood.

In middle and upper social classes in urban India, child-adult continuity is diluted and the distinctness of the adolescent phase becomes evident. The facilitating factors include parental encouragement for education and career, increased opportunity for interactions with peers, increased mobility, and access to consumer goods (Saraswathi 1999). Although the dominant developmental framework is one of interdependencies, the dynamic and consistent interactions between culture and context are influencing traditional outlooks, including notions of autonomy and authority.

The gender factor continues to play a role with greater emphasis on traditional gender role training and performance for girls. Although both boys and girls are encouraged for education, there is greater emphasis on career building for boys (Saraswathi 1999). In general, across social classes more freedom and authority are accorded to boys than girls. In matters of romantic relationships, boys are provided more flexibility, whereas for girls the boundaries are firmly etched. Both boys and girls in urban middle class families have more leisure time, however, girls are more occupied with home-based interests and hobbies and boys are observed to engage in outdoor activities, which in turn provides more opportunities for autonomy (Verma and Sharma 2006). In nuclear families where mothers were educated, girls' experience in the family was more favorable. In general, social change is bringing about greater democratization in urban middle class families in India (Larson et al. 2003).

Social class is a relevant factor to consider in the conceptualization and interpretation of adolescence in the Indian society. The complexities and opportunities of global influences are best observed in urban upper middle class populations in India, a segment that is growing at a rapid rate. An overview of the urban Indian middle class has been presented in Chap. 1. The following section profiles the middle class in Baroda, Gujarat, defining the specific context in which the adolescents' lives are situated.

The Urban Middle Class in Baroda, Gujarat

The adolescents in this book represent the urban upper middle class context in Baroda, Gujarat. One of the fastest growing states, Gujarat is a microcosm of India in terms of rapid economic growth, increasing consumerism and aspirations for upward mobility. Considered a part of the "golden corridor" of Gujarat, Vadodara or Baroda is the third largest city in Gujarat and mirrors the state in its economic and industrial growth, resulting in growing prosperity of the middle class. The city has a population of 1,670,806 (Census of India 2011).

Known as the *sanskari nagari*—cultured city, Baroda is viewed as the cultural capital of Gujarat and as an educational hub, with many activities centered on The Maharaja Sayajirao University of Baroda, which was set up in 1947 by the erstwhile ruler of Baroda Shri Sayajirao Gaekwad. Historically the city has been home to renowned scholars and artists, which has resulted in a rich cultural and educational legacy. In the early 1960s, Baroda experienced a fillip in industrial growth, which has strengthened over the years and continues to draw entrepreneurs from all over India. The recent years have also seen growing numbers of multinationals and expatriates in the city. Overall, the economic, educational, and cultural opportunities and experiences that the city offers continue to attract people from all over the world, thereby sustaining its cosmopolitan character. Visitors and newcomers to Baroda view the average Barodian as being open-minded and hospitable. Although Gujarati is the official language, Hindi, Marathi, and English are also widely used. Hinduism is the majority religion in Baroda city with 85.39% followers. Baroda has high average literacy of 90.36% (Census of India 2011). Education is valued and most middle class individuals are likely to have a graduate degree. As a rule, an overwhelming majority of young people from upper middle class families study in reputed English medium schools. Later these students prefer to be enrolled into The Maharaja Sayajirao University of Baroda, although there are other recently established private universities that are also gaining popularity. Baroda enjoys a reputation of being a safe city. This image is validated by the recent report of the National Crime Records Bureau (NCRB) Crime in India 2015 which has designated Baroda as the third safest city for women in India (National Crime Records Bureau 2016).

The city's links with Western countries, mostly the USA and the UK, are vibrant, with every third family in Baroda having relatives in either of these or even other Western countries. Non-resident Indians (NRIs) or Non-resident Gujaratis (NRGs) are an integral segment of the city's population, and much economic and social activity around the winter season, known as the "NRI season" in popular parlance, is centered on visiting NRI relatives and friends. Along with globalization and the significance attached to education, this is perhaps another factor that inspires and drives many young individuals to go abroad for higher education, with families encouraging and supporting this aspiration.

Most upper middle class families in Baroda live in what is known as "societies" or "colonies" that comprise a set of houses or apartment buildings within a designated geographical territory. A typical middle class household is well furnished with all amenities including a refrigerator, television, music player, and an air-cooler, and more recently, even an air-conditioner to deal with intense summer months. It is increasingly common for young people to have their own room, sometimes shared with a sibling. Ownership of at least two vehicles, a two-wheeler and a car (sometimes even two cars), is common. Family outings to restaurants and movies are regular, especially on weekends and holidays. Van Wessel (2011) explains how modernity is understood in Baroda middle class. In discussing social and cultural change, people indicate a divide of "people of old thinking" and "people of new thinking" (p. 104). People of old thinking are projected as those who follow tradition without thinking, and English terms such as "orthodox," or "narrow minded" are used to describe them. For young Barodians modern outlook signifies gender and caste ideals that depart from "outdated" tradition. It represents flexibility, practicability, and living life in tune with the changing times. The adolescents and families portrayed in this book represent such middle class families.

References

Athavale, U., Kapadia, S., & Gala, J. (2016). *Views of young adults on social norms related to romantic relationships*. Unpublished master's dissertation. The Maharaja Sayajirao University of Baroda.

Albert, I., Trommsdorff, G., & Mishra, R. (2004). Parenting and adolescent attachment in India and Germany. In G. Zheng, K. Leung, & J. G. Adair (Eds.), *Perspectives and progress in contemporary cross-cultural psychology: Selected papers from the seventeenth international congress of the international association for cross-cultural psychology* (pp. 97–108). Retrieved from http://ebooks.iaccp.org/xian/PDFs/3_4Albert.pdf.

Anandalakshmy, S., & Bajaj, M. (1981). Childhood in the weavers' community in Varanasi: Socialization for adult roles (pp. 31–38). In D. Sinha (Ed.), *Socialization of the Indian child*. New Delhi: Concept.

Arnett, J. J. (1999). Adolescent storm and stress, reconsidered. *The American Psychologist, 54*(5), 317–326. doi:10.1037/0003-066X.54.5.317.

Arnett, J. J. (2000). Emerging adulthood: A theory of development from the late teens through the twenties. *American Psychologist, 55*(5), 469.

Arnett, J. J. (2002). The psychology of globalization. *American Psychologist, 57*(10), 774–783. doi:10.1037//0003-066X.57.10.774.

Arnett, J. J. (2006). Emerging adulthood: Understanding the new way of coming of age. In J. J. Arnett & J. L. Tanner (Eds.), *Emerging adults in America: Coming of age in the 21st century* (pp. 1–19). Washington, DC: American Psychological Association.

Bekker, M. H., & Van Assen, M. A. (2006). A short form of the autonomy scale: Properties of the autonomy-connectedness scale (ACS-30). *Journal of Personality Assessment, 86*(1), 51–60. doi:10.1207/s15327752jpa8601_07.

Booth, M. (2002). Arab adolescents facing the future: Enduring ideals and pressures to change. In B. B. Brown, R. W. Larson, & T. S. Saraswathi (Eds.), *The world's youth: Adolescence in eight regions of the globe* (pp. 207–242). Cambridge: Cambridge University Press.

Brown, B. B., & Larson, R. W. (2002). The kaleidoscope of adolescence. Experiences of the world's youth at the beginning of the 21st century. In B. B. Brown, R. W. Larson, and T. S. Saraswathi (Eds.), *The world's youth: Adolescence in eight regions of the globe* (pp. 1–20). Cambridge: Cambridge University Press.

Brown, B. B., Larson, R. W., & Saraswathi, T. S. (2002). *The world's youth: Adolescence in eight regions of the globe.* Cambridge: Cambridge University Press.

Census of India. (2011). *Government of India, Ministry of Home Affairs.* Retrieved from http://www.census2011.co.in/census/city/338-vadodara.html.

Chakkarath, P. (2005). What can Western psychology learn from indigenous psychologies? Lessons from Hindu psychology. In W. Friedlmeier, P. Chakkarath, & B. Schwarz (Eds.), *Culture and human development: The importance of cross-cultural research to the social sciences* (pp. 31–51). New York: Psychology Press.

Chao, R. K. (1994). Beyond parental control and authoritarian parenting style: Understanding Chinese parenting through the cultural notion of training. *Child Development, 65*(4), 1111–1119. doi:10.2307/1131308.

Chao, R. K. (2000). The parenting of immigrant Chinese and European American mothers: Relations between parenting styles, socialization goals, and parental practices. *Journal of Applied Developmental Psychology, 21*(2), 233–248.

Chen, X., & Chen, H. (2010). Children's socio-emotional functioning and adjustment in the changing Chinese society. In R. K. Silbereisen & X. Chen (Eds.), *Social change and human development: Concept and results* (pp. 209–226). New Delhi: Sage.

Collins, W. A., & Steinberg, L. (2006). Adolescent development in interpersonal context. In W. Damon & N. Eisenberg (Eds.), *Handbook of child psychology, Vol. 4: Socioemotional processes* (pp. 1003–1067). New York: Wiley.

Crockett, L. J. (1997). Cultural, historical, and subcultural contexts of adolescence: Implications for health and development. *Faculty Publications, Department of Psychology.* Paper 244. Retrieved from http://digitalcommons.unl.edu/psychfacpub/244.

Dube, L. (1998). *Women and kinship: Comparative perspective on gender in South and South-East Asia.* New Delhi: Vistaar Publications.

Fuligni, A. J. (1998). Authority, autonomy, and parent–adolescent conflict and cohesion: A study of adolescents from Mexican, Chinese, Filipino, and European backgrounds. *Developmental Psychology, 34*(4), 782.

Fuligni, A. J., & Zhang, W. (2004). Attitudes toward family obligation among adolescents in contemporary urban and rural China. *Child Development, 75*(1), 180–192.

Gardiner, H. W., Mutter, J. D., & Kosmitzki, C. (1998). *Lives across cultures: Cross-cultural human development.* New York: Allyn & Bacon.

Georgas, J., Poortinga, Y. H., Berry, J. W., van de Vijver, F. J. R., & Kagitcibasi, C. (2006). Family portraits from 30 countries: An overview. In J. Georgas, J. W. Berry, J. R. van de Vijver, C., Kagitcibasi, & Y. H. Poortinga (Eds.), *Families across cultures: A 30-nation psychological study* (pp. 90–99). New York: Cambridge University Press.

Goossens, L. (2006). The many faces of adolescent autonomy: Parent-adolescent conflict, behavioral decision-making, and emotional distancing. In S. Jackson & L. Goossens (Eds.), *Handbook of adolescent development* (pp. 135–153). New York: Psychology Press.

Greenfield, P. M., Keller, H., Fuligni, A., & Maynard, A. (2003). Cultural pathways through universal development. *Annual Review of Psychology, 54*(1), 461–490.

Grotevant, H. D., & Cooper, C. R. (1986). Individuation in family relationships. *Human Development, 29*(2), 82–100.

Harkness, S., & Super, C. M. (2002). Culture and parenting. In M. H. Bornstein (Ed.), *Handbook of parenting, Vol. 2: Biology and ecology of parenting* (2 ed., pp. 253–280). Mahwah, NJ: Lawrence Erlbaum Associates.

Havas Worldwide. (2011). Millennials: The challenger generation Vol. 11. *Prosumer Reports Series*. Retrieved from havasworldwide.com/prosumer-report.

Jensen, L. A. (2011). Navigating local and global worlds: Opportunities and risks for adolescent cultural identity development. *Psychological Studies, 56*(1), 62–70. doi: http://doi.org/10.1007/s12646-011-0069-y.

Jensen, L. A., & Arnett, J. J. (2012). Going global: New pathways for adolescents and emerging adults in a changing world. *Journal of Social Issues, 68*(3), 473–492. doi:10.1111/j.1540-4560.2012.01759.x.

Jensen, L. A., & Dost-Gözkan, A. (2015). Adolescent-parent relations in Asian Indian and Salvadoran immigrant families: A cultural-developmental analysis of autonomy, authority, conflict, and cohesion. *Journal of Research on Adolescence, 25*(2), 340–351. doi:10.1111/jora.12116.

Jensen, L. A., Arnett, J. J., & McKenzie, J. (2011). Globalization and cultural identity. *Handbook of identity theory and research* (pp. 285–301). New York: Springer.

Kagitcibasi, C. (1996). *Family and human development across cultures: A view from the other side*. Hillsdale, NJ: Lawrence Erlbaum.

Kagitcibasi, C. (2002). A model of family change in cultural context. *Online Readings in Psychology and Culture, 6*(3), 1.

Kagitcibasi, C. (2013). Adolescent autonomy-relatedness and the family in cultural context: What is optimal? *Journal of Research on Adolescence, 23*(2), 223–235.

Kagitcibasi, C., & Yalin, C. (2015). Family in adolescence: Relatedness and autonomy across cultures. In L. A. Jensen (Ed.), *The Oxford handbook of human development and culture: An interdisciplinary perspective* (pp. 410–424). New York: Oxford University Press.

Kahn, R., & Kellner, D. (2006). *Global youth culture*. Retrieved from https://pages.gseis.ucla.edu/faculty/kellner/essays/globyouthcult.pdf.

Kakar, S. (1981). (2nd ed). *The inner world: A psychoanalytic study of childhood in India*. New Delhi: Oxford University Press.

Kapadia, S., & Bhangaokar, R. (2013). *Imageries of youth as a life stage in India*. In G. Misra (Vol. Ed.), XIII (3), *Psychology and psychoanalysis* (pp. 219–254). In D. P. Chattopadhyaya (Gen. Ed.), *History of science, philosophy and culture in Indian civilization*. New Delhi: Center for Studies in Civilization.

Kapadia, S., & Miller, J. (2005). Parent-adolescent relationships in the context of interpersonal disagreements: View from a collectivist culture. *Psychology and Developing Societies, 17*(1), 33–50.

Kärtner, J., Keller, H., Lamm, B., Abels, M., Yovsi, R. D., & Chaudhary, N. (2007). Manifestations of autonomy and relatedness in mothers' accounts of their ethnotheories regarding child care across five cultural communities. *Journal of Cross-Cultural Psychology, 38*(5), 613–628.

Kaur, B., Menon, S., & Konantambigi, R. (2001). Child and adolescent development research. In J. Pandey (Ed.), *Psychology in India revisited—Developments in the discipline* (Vol. 1, pp. 163–227). New Delhi: Sage.

Kuhar, M., & Reiter, H. (2013). Toward a concept of parental authority in adolescence. *CEPS Journal: Center for Educational Policy Studies Journal, 3*(2), 135–155.

Larson, R. W., Jensen, L., Kang, H., Griffith, A., & Rompala, V. (2012). Peer groups as a crucible of positive value development in a global world. In G. Trommsdorff & X. Chen (Eds.), *Values, religion, and culture in adolescent development* (pp. 164–187). New York, NY: Cambridge University Press.

Larson, R. W., & Tran, S. P. (2014). Invited commentary: Positive youth development and human complexity. *Journal of Youth and Adolescence, 43*(6), 1012–1017. doi: http://doi.org/10.1007/s10964-014-0124-9.

Larson, R., Verma, S., & Dworkin, J. (2001). Adolescents' family relationships in India: The daily lives of Indian middle class teenagers. In J. J. Arnett (Ed.), *Readings on adolescence and emerging adulthood* (pp. 133–141). Abington, MA: Prentice Hall.

Larson, R. W., Wilson, S., Brown, B. B., Furstenberg, F. F., Jr., & Verma, S. (2002). Changes in adolescents' interpersonal experiences: Are they being prepared for adult relationships in the twenty-first century. *Journal of Research Adolescence, 12*(1), 31–68.

Larson, R., Verma, S., & Dworkin, J. (2003). Adolescence without family disengagement: The daily family lives of Indian middle class teenagers. In T. S. Saraswathi (Ed.), *Cross-cultural perspectives in human development theory, research and application* (pp. 258–286). New Delhi: Sage.

Lerner, R. M., & Steinberg, L. (2004). The scientific study of adolescent development: Past, present and future. In R. M. Lerner & L. Steinberg, (Eds.). *Handbook of adolescent psychology* (2nd ed., pp 1–12). Hoboken, NJ: John Wiley.

Lerner, R. M. (2006). Developmental science, developmental systems, and contemporary theories of human development. In In R. M. Lerner (Ed.), *Theoretical models of human development, Vol. 1: Handbook of child psychology* (6th ed., pp. 1–17). Hoboken, NJ: Wiley.

Marbell, K. N. (2014). *Encouraging autonomy in a collectivist culture: Examining parental autonomy support in Ghana and the moderating effect of children's self-construal.* Retrieved from http://gradworks.proquest.com/3642806.pdf.

Maria, M. S. (2002). Youth in Southeast Asia: Living within the continuity of tradition and the turbulence of change. In B. B. Brown, R. W. Larson, & T. S. Saraswathi (Eds.), *The world's youth: Adolescence in eight regions of the globe* (pp. 171–206). Cambridge: Cambridge University Press.

Markus, H. R., & Lin, L. R. (1999). Conflictways: Cultural diversity in the meanings and practices of conflict. In D. Prentice & D. Miller (Eds.), *Cultural divides: Understanding and overcoming group conflict* (pp. 302–333). New York: Russell Sage Foundation.

McElhaney, K. B. & Allen, J. P. (in press). Sociocultural perspectives on adolescent autonomy. In P. Kerig, M. Schulz, & S. T. Hauser (Eds.), *Adolescence and beyond.* Oxford: Oxford University Press.

Mead, M. (1928). *Coming of age in Samoa.* New York: William Morrow and Company.

Miller, J. G. (2003). Culture and agency: Implications for psychological theories of motivation and social development. *Nebraska Symposium on Motivation, 49,* 59–99.

Mortimer, J. T., & Larson, R. W. (2002). *The changing adolescent experience: Societal trends and the transition to adulthood* (pp. 1–17). New York: Cambridge University Press. http://doi.org/10.1017/CBO9780511613913.

Muss, R. E., & Porton, H. D. (1990). *Adolescent behavior and society: A book of readings.* Fairfield, PA: McGraw-Hill.

National Crime Records Bureau (NCRB). (2016). *Crime in India 2015 statistics.* New Delhi: Ministry of Home Affairs, Government of India.

National Youth Policy (2014). New Delhi: Ministry of Youth Affairs and Sports, Government of India.

Nsamenang, A. B. (2002). Adolescence in sub-Saharan Africa: An image constructed from Africa's triple inheritance. In B. B. Brown, R. W. Larson, & T. S. Saraswathi (Eds.), *The world's youth: Adolescence in eight regions of the globe* (pp. 61–104). Cambridge: Cambridge University Press.

Nsamenang, A. B. (2011). The culturalization of developmental trajectories. In L. A. Jensen (Ed.), *Bridging cultural and developmental approaches to psychology: New syntheses in theory, research, and policy.* Oxford: Oxford University Press. doi:10.1093/acprof:oso/9780195383430.003.0011.

Nugent, R. (2006). *Youth in a global world.* Retrieved from www.prb.org/pdf06/YouthInAGlobalWorld.pdf.

Phinney, J. S., Kim-Jo, T., Osorio, S., & Vilhjalmsdottir, P. (2005). Autonomy and relatedness in adolescent-parent disagreements ethnic and developmental factors. *Journal of Adolescent Research, 20*(1), 8–39. doi:10.1177/0743558404271237.

Phinney, J. S., Ong, A., & Madden, T. (2000). Cultural values and intergenerational value discrepancies in immigrant and non-immigrant families. *Child Development, 71*(2), 528–539.

Pinquart, M., & Silbereisen, R. (2005). Understanding social change in conducting research on adolescence. *Journal of Research on Adolescence, 15*(4), 395–406. doi:10.1111/j.1532-7795.2005.00104.x.

Rao, M. A., Berry, R., Gonsalves, A., Hastak, Y., Shah, M., & Roeser, R. W. (2013). Globalization and the identity remix among urban adolescents in India. *Journal of Research on Adolescence, 23*(1), 9–24. doi:10.1111/jora.12002.

Roland, A. (1988). *In search of self in India and Japan: Toward a cross-cultural psychology.* Princeton, NJ: Princeton University Press.

Roth, J. L., & Brooks-Gunn, J. (2003). What exactly is a youth development program? Answers from research and practice. *Applied Developmental Science, 7*(2), 94–111.

Saraswathi, T. S., & Dutta, R. (1988). *Invisible boundaries. Grooming for adult roles.* New Delhi: Northern Book Centre.

Saraswathi, T. S. (1999). Adult-child continuity in India: Is adolescence a myth or an emerging reality? In T.S. Saraswathi (Ed.), *Culture, socialization and human development: theory, research, and application in India* (pp. 213–232). New Delhi: Sage.

Saraswathi, T. S., Mistry, J., & Dutta, R. (2011). Reconceptualizing lifespan development through a Hindu perspective. In L. A. Jensen (2011). *Bridging cultural and developmental approaches to psychology: New syntheses in theory, research, and policy* (pp. 276–299). USA: Oxford University Press.

Saraswathi, T. S., & Oke, M. (2013). Ecology of adolescence in India. *Psychological Studies, 58* (4), 353–364.

Schlegel, A. (2011). *Human development and cultural transmission. Anthropologischer Anzeiger, 68*(4), 457–470. doi:10.1127/0003-5548/2011/0155.

Schlegel, A., & Barry, H., III. (1991). *Adolescence: An anthropological inquiry.* New York: Free Press.

Schlegel, A., & Barry, H., III. (2015). Leaving childhood: The nature and meaning of adolescents transition rituals. In L. A. Jensen, (Ed.). *The Oxford handbook of human development and culture: An interdisciplinary perspective* (pp. 327–340). New York: Oxford University Press.

Schlegel, A., & Hewlett, B. L. (2011). Contributions of anthropology to the study of adolescence. *Journal of Research on Adolescence, 21*(1), 281–289. doi:10.1111/j.1532-7795.2010.00729.x.

Scholte, J. A. (2002). *What is globalization? The definitional issue—Again* (CSGR Working Paper No. 109/02). United Kingdom: Centre for the Study of Globalization and Regionalization, University of Warwick.

Sinha, D. (1986). *Psychology in a third world country. The Indian experiences.* New Delhi: Sage.

Smetana, J. G. (1988). Adolescents' and parents' conceptions of parental authority. *Child Development, 59*(2), 321–335. doi:10.2307/1130313.

Soenens, B., Vansteenkiste, M., Lens, W., Luyckx, K., Goossens, L., Beyers, W., et al. (2007). Conceptualizing parental autonomy support: Adolescent perceptions of promotion of independence versus promotion of volitional functioning. *Developmental Psychology, 43*(3), 633–646. doi:10.1037/0012-1649.43.3.633.

Steinberg, L., & Silverberg, S. (1986). The vicissitudes of autonomy in early adolescence. *Child Development, 57,* 841–851.

Steinberg, L., & Morris, A. S. (2001). Adolescent development. *Journal of Cognitive Education and Psychology, 2*(1), 55–87.

Stevenson, H. W., & Zusho, A. (2002). Adolescence in China and Japan: Adapting to a changing environment. In B. B. Brown, R. W. Larson, & T. S. Saraswathi (Eds.), *The world's youth: Adolescence in eight regions of the globe* (pp. 141–170). Cambridge: Cambridge University Press.

Trommsdorff, G., &Kornadt, H. J. (2003). Parent-child relations in cross-cultural perspective. In L. Kuczynski (Ed.), *Handbook of dynamics in parent-child relations* (pp. 271–306). Sage. http://dx.doi.org/10.4135/9781452229645.n14.

Valsiner, J. (2000). *Culture and human development: An introduction.* London: Sage.

Verma, S. (2000). The Indian social reality of passage to adulthood. *ISSBD Newsletter, 2*(37), 6–9.

Verma, S., & Sharma, D. (2006). Cultural dynamics of family relations among Indian adolescents in varied contexts. In K. H. Rubin & O. B. Chung (Eds.), *Parental beliefs, parenting, and child development in cross-cultural perspective* (pp. 185–205). New York: Psychology Press.

Verma, S., & Saraswathi, T. S. (2002). Adolescence in India: Street urchins or Silicon Valley millionaires? In B. B. Brown, R. W. Larson, & T. S. Saraswathi (Eds.), *The world's youth: Adolescence in eight regions of the globe* (pp. 105–140). Cambridge: Cambridge University Press.

Welti, C. (2002). Adolescents in Latin America: Facing the future with skepticism. In B. B. Brown, R. W. Larson, & T. S. Saraswathi (Eds.), *The world's youth: Adolescence in eight regions of the globe* (pp. 276–306). Cambridge: Cambridge University Press.

Van Wessel, M. (2011). Cultural contractions and intergenerational relations: the construction of selfhood among middle class youth in Baroda. In H. Donner (Ed.), *Being middle class in India: A way of life* (pp. 100–116). New York: Routledge.

World Youth Report 2003. (2004). United Nations, No. E.03.IV.7 Retrieved November 11, 2016 from http://www.un.org/esa/socdev/unyin/documents/worldyouthreport.pdf.

World Youth Report. (2005). *Young people today, and in 2015*. Retrieved from http://www.youthpolicy.org/library/documents/world-youth-report-2005-young-people-today-and-in-2015/.

Yau, J., & Smetana, J. G. (1996). Adolescent-parent conflict among Chinese adolescents in Hong Kong. *Child Development, 67*(3), 1262–1275.

Yau, J., & Smetana, J. (2003). Adolescent-parent conflict in Hong Kong and Shenzhen: A comparison of youth in two cultural contexts. *International Journal of Behavioral Development, 27*(3), 201–211.

Yeh, K. H., Liu, Y. L., Huang, H. S., & Yang, Y. J. (2007). Individuating and relating autonomy in culturally Chinese adolescents. In J. Liu, C. Ward, A. Bernardo, M. Karasawa, & R. Fischer (Eds.), *Casting the individual in societal and cultural contexts* (pp. 123–146). Korea: Kyoyook-Kwahak-Sa Publishing.

Yeh, K. H., Bedford, O., & Yang, Y. J. (2009). A cross-cultural comparison of the coexistence and domain superiority of individuating and relating autonomy. *International Journal of Psychology, 44*(3), 213–221.

Zimmer-Gembeck, M. J., & Collins, W. A. (2003). Autonomy development during adolescence. In G. R. Adams & M. Berzonsky (Eds.), *Blackwell handbook of adolescence* (pp. 175–204). Oxford: Blackwell Publishers.

Zimmer-Gembeck, M. J., Madsen, S. D., & Hanisch, M. (2011). Connecting the intrapersonal to the interpersonal: Autonomy, voice, parents, and romantic relationships in emerging adulthood. *European Journal of Developmental Psychology, 8*(5), 509–525. doi:10.1080/17405629.2011.567061.

Chapter 3
Adolescence, the Stage; Adolescent, the Person

Abstract Adolescence is a sociocultural construction shaped by the complex interaction between cultural worldview and contextual influences at the macro level and the family context at the micro level. How is adolescence, the stage, and adolescent, the person, constructed in the urban Indian middle class context? This chapter addresses these two aspects. The first section illustrates adolescents' and parents' descriptions of the stage of adolescence and highlights the salient features and socialization goals. Gender as a mediating factor is underlined. The next section depicts adolescent, the person, in terms of attributes, dreams, wishes, insecurities, and anxieties, to reveal the multidimensional self-construal of the adolescent, embodying the individual, relational, and encompassing selves, with glimpses of the related-autonomous self.

Keywords Adolescence stage · Self · Gender · Indian · Middle class

Adolescence, the Stage

Developmental Significance, Transition, and Vulnerability

Initial description of adolescence was characterized by a semblance of tentativeness on part of both adolescents and parents. In response to the question how would you describe the present period of your life, Amit, 18 years mused, "*Hmm… I would say I am in the phase where I consider myself a young boy – feel like I have just entered youth (juvani ma just aavyo chu evu lage che)*." The term "adolescence" or "adolescent" is not part of the vocabulary; instead, the term "teenager" occurred more commonly along with terms such as "*yuva*," "young generation," and "21st century people." Parents mostly used indigenous terms such as "*madhya avastha*," "*kumara avastha*," "*kishore avastha*," and '*yuvana avastha*', to describe adolescence. Adolescence was also described chronologically, for example, "*I am 16 years old*," "*It is the age of 15, now from childhood he enters the age of youngster*," and "*he is in his early 16s*."

© Springer (India) Pvt. Ltd. 2017
S. Kapadia, *Adolescence in Urban India*,
DOI 10.1007/978-81-322-3733-4_3

There is also a tendency to describe adolescence in terms of key goals and social expectations. Parents recognize the developmental significance of this period. According to them, adolescence marks the point in life during which one's personality and future goals take shape. In the words of a father, *"This is the starting point of his life. Main shaping of life starts from here; this is the first step of his life."* Suggesting an orientation toward deliberate socialization, a parent responded, *"It is a stage important for achieving knowledge from family, society and school."* At the same time, a few parents and adolescents described this phase as *"a period of happiness and cheerfulness."* A boy shared, *"I am in the stage for dream planning*; *"Opportunities are waiting for me,"* and another said, *"I am in the phase of reaching my goal and achieving my aim of life."* The notions of disturbance and disruption that have long defined a typical adolescent in Western societies were not readily observed in parents' or even adolescents' primary descriptions of this phase.

Both adolescents and parents interpreted adolescence as a transition period, for example, *"He is in the age of childhood and maturity,"* or *"Neither kid nor grown up mentally."* Eighteen-year-old Keyur shared, *"I think I am kind of teenage and not adult yet. I think I am in a phase of transition where I still do not consider myself mature enough to take big decisions of life and career."* The transitional feature was associated with this being a period of *parivartan* or change, and thereby critical and vulnerable, especially for socioemotional development and education. According to a mother, *"Lots of stuff is going on in their mind. They want freedom. They don't like their parents interfering in their decisions. They like to take their own decisions. They are trying to be more independent. They like to stay alone at times. They want space in this age.".*

Parents interpret this phase as one in which the individual lacks social and emotional maturity to uphold a balanced outlook that would enable one to discern "right" from "wrong." They are acutely aware of adolescents' growing interest and inclination toward romantic interests. The tension related to this aspect comes forth in mothers' apprehensive observations. *"Girls, I think they are looking for a kind of relationship. I think my daughter is happy with her family and she wants constant love and affection from the family. At the same time, they are looking out for a relationship outside the family too. It could be having a boyfriend or having somebody, even girlfriends. But, my daughter is much happier with the family because we discuss everything at home. She is much open about herself. But most girls don't have any interest in family at this age and they are looking for a relationship outside."* With regard to her adolescent boy, another mother expressed, *"I don't know how they behave at this age. They are also looking out for a relationship outside family. I think it is a hormonal thing. They want physical relationship or an emotional relationship. They don't want to listen to their parents. Parents are always telling them that your career is more important… but you know there is a hormone or a physical desire that they have at this age, so boys also want a relationship outside and they feel happier."*

Another domain that renders vulnerability to this phase is scholastic achievement. Concern about adolescents' performance in studies juxtaposed with the likelihood of distractions that would interfere with this valued goal emerges as an impending anxiety in the minds of parents. Girls mature earlier than boys do, and this is clearly reflected in their thoughtful elaboration of the predicaments that they experience.

Box 1

Jesal, 16 years laments, *"In this age, we will do what we think. Like one of my friends is very fond of music, but his parents try to convince him that music does not have any scope in life. Still he wants to go for music, because it's his dream. Thus a major concern in this age is that we want to do what we like, and here we don't bond with parents. Like sometimes we get angry. Today itself I had an argument with my mother, as she didn't allow me to go to my friend's place in the morning. She asked why do you need to go in morning, instead study. It is the 12th grade now. Why can I not go to my friend's place? My friends are not bad ones, they are studious and I know them; my going was related to studies only. Therefore, the major concern in this age is that there is no good bonding with parents and more arguments happen. Second, there is more attraction in this age; we easily and badly fall for anyone, we never know when we are off the track. We cannot do what we think and like to do as we are still below 18 years so we don't get that right. We are treated like small school children; we have no right to take any decisions related to money and all. If there is anything we want to do, like I am fond of dancing, and if I want to do it, I have to think 15 times about what parents will think. They would think that I have chosen science stream and now want to dance also. So it pinches us somewhere that why is it always like this?"*

Scholastic Achievement: A Valued Goal, a Compelling Expectation

'Scholastic work' occupies a very significant space in the Indian middle class construction of adolescence. Education is a much-valued goal for the Indian middle class and is viewed as the means to upward mobility. A central and consistent aspect in both adolescents' and parents' narrations is the expectation of getting a good education and entering into a lucrative job or career. Parents inculcate this value in children from early on with much discussion focused on the need to study well and get "good marks," as these serve as the gateways to secure the desired career stream. This phenomenon assumes powerful proportions closer to the board examinations. "Getting a good grade" and choice of career stream, especially for adolescents who are on the brink of or in standards 10 and 12, are frequently voiced. In the words of Anuj, 17 years, *"The present stage is that of studies, 24 × 7 it is studies, studies, studies. We cannot do other new activities."* Kunal, 16 years offers a rather detailed description, *"Career is a concern. Because it is ultimately the time where you have to decide what you want to do with your life. You are not going to be promoted to the next grade like in school. Parents are also concerned about what would be good for their kids. What to do next is of concern, especially how this will impact a person's future. Seeing career as a long term output is something that makes you worried. During this phase, attractions happen, mostly with all of us. So we need to make sure that attraction and dating do not distract our life goals and dreams."*

Adolescents' frustration with the focus on academic performance is evident in the following lament, *"Also they have made such a system—the semester system has made it so boring and hectic. Even if we study for the whole day, we don't get desired percentage. And with such percentage you know well, what happens in admission. Run from one college to the other for the whole day for admission, and you're not sure to get admission"*, sighs Ronak, 16 years. The concern with academic performance is representative of the Indian middle class context of high school education in which the 10th and 12th grades are extremely critical in determining an adolescent's further education and career path. Given the instrumental value of education for enhancement of one's social and economic status, the entire family is heavily invested in this domain. In the present milieu, increased opportunities for education and career have intensified competition, and consequently greater pressure for academic achievement and entry into the preferred career.

Parents as Mentors and Family Concerns

Parents drew attention to their role in shaping the adolescent's development. One father said, *"This is a very important age and this is a very slippery age, and decisive age also. So how we deal with it is crucial."* Adolescents too highlighted the need for support and guidance from parents through descriptions such as, *"This is a crucial period in which we need support—one guide, which is parents."*

Adolescents' description of this stage as one for, *"understanding and fulfilling parents' dreams,"* reveals the integration of parents and family into their worldview. In the midst of the focus on self, adolescents manifest a parallel concern with how one's actions may impact the family. Tapan, 18 years, expresses, *"Though family is important for me, I like to spend more time with friends. We are of same age and can easily share everything with each other. But to decide when to be with family and when to be with friends, and that too without hurting anyone is a major concern."* A similar sentiment is evident in the comment of 17-year-old Radha who expresses, *"People get into relationships more in this stage and they are less interested in studies so they should focus more on studies and spend less time in relationships. If my family gets into any trouble because of my actions then I get tensed easily."*

Gender Mediating Adolescence

Gender concerns are evident in parent and adolescent depictions of the stage. Parents voice apprehensions regarding girls' sexual vulnerability. As one mother justified, "*I trust my daughter, but how can I trust the people who are going to be at the party?*" Girls, perhaps because of faster maturation, make more references to romantic friendships than boys do and complain about the regulations and restrictions that parents impose on their mobility. Sixteen-year-old Dharti expresses, "*Safety is of course one thing but besides that how to convince parents that what others are saying is not much important if they are ok with it. For example, if I go somewhere and don't come home by the time they have asked me to come, then they will say that you are a girl and you should not be out all the time because people will think that you are a spoilt daughter. Why are my parents worrying about others more than my happiness? If it is a boy and he stays outside home until 12.00 am, I don't think he would get a call from parents. But if it is 10.00 pm and I am out, I will get 15 calls asking me to come home soon.*" Gender-based expectations irk the adolescent girls and also create a ground for disagreement and argument. Seventeen-year-old Pooja's wish for the future is perhaps a reflection of this. She wishes, "*I would like to become a boy because boys are always allowed to do anything they want and the other thing is that boys are bolder and less sensitive, and I always wanted to be so because in this world I am such a person that I can easily be manipulated as compared to a boy so…*" In the same vein, Renita, 17 years shares, "*I do not wish to get married because after marriage, especially girls, can't live their lives independently. They have to take care of husband, kids, elders and they can't do what they want.*"

Gender also mediates career choices with parents urging the adolescent to opt for careers that will be "suitable" in the sense of not compromising on the gender roles. Along with the instrumental value of augmenting economic status, education also accords a social status that is useful in selection of a suitable marriage partner. Eighteen-year-old Jaimil says, "*Being a boy, my special concern is to get into a perfect stream for a good career. Girls also need that but as a boy it is more important because if I don't get a good career, I won't get a good girl, simple!*" Being educated is an important criterion that both girls and boys in urban middle class families seek in a prospective partner. Girls in particular wish for the removal of gender-based restrictions. As Sonal, 16 years, expresses, "*First I want to clear all obstacles which can stop me from reaching my goal of career. Life will be easy thereafter. Second, I want to make this world free of fear for safety reasons. I would do something with the magic stick, which can make society sensible, a girl braver and a boy more afraid of their negative actions. Then we can go out for all night fun… we can do it even now but don't do because of parent's concerns regarding girl's safety and all.*"

The focus on selecting a career that is financially stable and has wider social approval also interferes with one's actual interest. According to 17-year-old Tushar, "*Being an artist, if I think of making my career in this, then I would need to convince myself and others that this is not a fixed job. You may earn a lot during some months and nothing in other months. So life would not be like that of other boys who get a salary every month; so to accept this kind of life style is also a concern. I am still in a dilemma whether I want to make a career in this or do it as a hobby.*" Similar concerns in choice of career are also voiced by girls. "*Actually I am very fond of football but people think that it is only for boys. Even making a career in sports is considered as only for boys. I am not interested in making that as my career but even if I want it as a hobby, I can't have it because at this time, yes studies are important; but after school if I want to go for one or two hours and play then I can't do it. My parents are ok with it, but this is what people think. Also there are some slots which are only restricted for boys*" (Kunjal, 17 years). In addition, another girl shared, "*I like bike riding, but people think it is for boys...*" Apprehensions of abiding by and yet feeling constrained by societal gender stereotypic expectations thus feature notably in girls' and boys' worries about choice of career.

Correspondingly, gender is highlighted in parents' description of an ideal adolescent girl and boy. Whereas certain ideals such as obedience, respect for parents, and social responsibility are highlighted for both, there is greater emphasis on a familial orientation for a girl along with stereotypically feminine attributes such as caring, tender, sensitive, and devoted, as these are believed to contribute to the successful enactment of the roles of wife and mother. An ideal girl is expected to maintain tradition and culture and follow overt manifestations of the same by wearing a sari, applying a *bindi*, entering an arranged marriage, and observing religious fasts. Traditionally female spheres are thus emphasized equally alongside encouragement for educational and career achievement. Evidently, gender essentialism, the belief that men and women are innately and fundamentally different in interests and skills (Charles forthcoming cited in England 2010), encourages traditional choices and remains untouched by upward mobility in education and career. The cultural scripts related to gender thus mediate and likely constrain girls' long-term career choices and personal growth.

Adolescence is thus understood as a phase of transition and vulnerability during which children need to be socialized for responsibility. The vulnerability is associated with scholastic achievement and growing romantic interests and the perceived risks it potentially entails. The changing landscape of the urban middle class context is offering several opportunities for interactions among girls and boys, and the macro contextual influences render romantic encounters and relationships more attractive and acceptable. Not surprisingly, therefore, concerns about romantic interests assume greater significance in the urban middle class construction of adolescence. Romantic interests are viewed as interference that is likely to divert the adolescents from pursuance of the vital goal of education. Parents perceive themselves as actively involved in their role as mentors who guide the adolescents through any challenges that the phase may present. Education and career choice are highlighted, and academic stress hovers over this period. Gender looms large, particularly in the form of restrictions on choice of career to fit within the conventional gender-based framework and freedom in mobility for girls.

The socialization goals of adolescence resonate with the traditional goals prescribed in the *Brahmacharya Ashrama*—knowledge acquisition, character building, and learning to shoulder responsibilities. Contrary to Western ideas, in the *Ashrama Dharma* model, sexuality is sanctioned during the next stage of *Grahasthya Ashrama* (Chakkarath 2013). Apparently, this continues to be the favored social framework even today.

Adolescent, the Person: Attributes, Dreams, and Wishes

Adolescent, the Person: A Blend of Multiple Selves

The adolescent self reveals the multidimensional nature of the Indian self, with both individual and relational self-conceptions reflected. The descriptors of self fit broadly in the framework of within-self, self-relating-to-other, and other-relating-to-self dimensions across the domains of emotions and feelings, roles, identities, and dispositions (Mascolo et al. 2004). The gendered nature of self-conceptions is evident across the different dimensions.

Individual within-self conceptions revolve around physical characteristics and dispositions, along with activities, habits, and interests. These descriptors comprise both positive and negative characteristics or dispositions, and habits and activities in which adolescents may typically engage. Well-liked positive characteristics include descriptors such as, "emotional, funny, jovial, smart, innovative and creative, sensitive, sincere," whereas the not liked ones are "laziness, being too emotional and overreacting, arrogance, negativity, egoism, and having a lot of attitude". Within-self identity descriptors also include activities in which adolescents are involved (e.g., playing pranks and playing games), their habits (e.g., punctuality and sleeping for long hours), and their interests and hobbies (e.g., listening to music, love for driving, dancing, and playing cricket).

A within-self characteristic that parents appreciate is the openness that their adolescent has with them as well as the independence that they demonstrate. According to a mother, "*I think she is open to me, she tells me everything that goes on in her life. I like this kind of innocence. She is also getting more independent and less dependent on us. I like her maturity; she has definitely grown up. She can think on her own, take her own decisions.*" On the other hand, lack of perseverance, short temper, over sensitivity such that it impacts mood, and lack of focus and concentration on studies are some characteristics that they do not like in their adolescents. Gender-specific attributes emphasized in within-self physical characteristics include descriptors such as weak, slim, gentle, and fussy about looks for girls, and well-built, courageous, and frequenting the gym for boys. Physical attributes focusing on appearance are especially highlighted for girls. In the words of a mother, "*This is the time when girls try to look beautiful and smart and wish to dress according to current fashion.*" Similarly, emotional characteristics such as sensitive, jealous, caring and shy, and easily tacked with love are commonly used for girls, whereas not very emotional, innocent, and strong willpower are used for boys.

Within-self descriptions also refer to academic and career success (e.g., typical careers such as engineer, doctor, civil services, and business, as well as atypical careers such as football player, singer, or a career that will make one famous), and changes in lifestyle. The latter incorporate a range of material wishes and fantasies such as earning lots of money, having a luxurious lifestyle, becoming rich and owning big cars and a bungalow, going on a Disneyland tour, going on a world tour (*"alone, not with mummy or daddy"*), and getting an autograph from a Hollywood superstar from action movies. The middle class aspiration for an enhanced materialistic lifestyle is thus clearly indicated.

In consonance with the goal of education, interest, sincerity, and commitment related to education and career emerge as valued attributes. Yet again gendered expectations in this domain are evident. Responses of parents and adolescents in this area referred to the need for *"equal opportunities for girls"* and need for *"white-collar jobs for boys."* Reference is also made to a highly competitive employment scenario for boys. Studious, ambitious, and concerned about career are other typical characterizations, voiced more by parents than adolescents.

Insecurities, worries, and anxieties. The challenges presented by the flux in the macro context introduce insecurities and apprehensions in adolescents. Factors such as the increasing competition in education and multiplicity of new emerging careers exacerbate anxiety for one's future. Kunal, 16 years, reflects, *"Hmmm one anxiety that I have is definitely related to education, because the world is becoming so competitive and as everyone wants to have a good career, I am worried that whether I will also be able to compete with others and make my own career which will provide me my own identity. So, there's tension that if we do not get admission in a particular field in college, what will happen. It is said that life is a race; we have to keep running to get success in our aim. There is a fear whether that aim will be successful or not."*

Further, the imminent transition from school to college creates apprehension, mainly related to the uncertainties that the new context would bring and the fear of losing school friends. Varun, 17 years, says, *"It may not be so important, but still when I think of it, it bring tears. It's now 12th standard and after parents if anyone is closest, are friends. Sometimes we feel insecure, that what will we do without our friends. They are very supportive in this age."* Matters related to romantic interests and relationships add to worries. *"I have seen my friends running behind their girlfriends everywhere. I just started dating someone and I am worried that she does not make me her bodyguard all the time as I want to have my personal life as well,"* quips Sapan, 17 years. Adolescent girls especially voice gender-based constraints. *"One insecurity is that we are girls, and it's not safe in night. We have to complete projects and for that we have to stay late at friend's place, but parents don't allow because of this reason—that you are girls, anything can happen. They are also right; it is insecure to go out, boys can harass, and these things make you weak mentally,"* justifies Arpita.

Where some insecurities and apprehensions occur by virtue of the developmental stage, others clearly stem from the macro contextual changes. Together these impact the adolescent's experience of this transitional developmental period. Chapter 5 further discusses the range of issues that cause insecurities, worries, and anxieties in both, adolescents and parents.

The relational self-construal is manifested in conceptions that include the dimensions of self-relating-to-other and other-relating-to-self descriptions. The relational aspects focus upon family, peers, and the larger society. There is a greater leaning toward self-relating-to-other rather than other-relating-to-self attributes. Self-relating-to-other attributes that are considered positive comprise prosocial characteristics such as being caring, understanding, helpful, trustworthy, faithful, sincere, and sociable. On the other hand, self-relating-to-other attributes that are not welcome are bullying and making fun of peers, bad mouthing, and disrespect toward teacher. Girls tend to refer to opposite sex interactions (self-relating-to-other and other-relating-to-self) as behavior that is not welcome. Anuja, 16 years shares, *"I don't like when girls or boys talk with one another just because they want to become popular in school. Being friends with boy/girl is fine but to meet secretly and moving here and there in spite of knowing that you are losing study time is something I don't like"*. In a similar vein Jesal, 17 years, opines, *"In this age, one gets distracted very easily, like attraction of boys and girls. If I talk about my friends, they are addicted—I mean few of them smoke and drink. In this generation, if we want to move ahead in life, it stops us from doing so. These are the things I don't like. Some people have right dreams in life, they are moving ahead in life, but then there is love and affairs, which is very common in this age. And as a result, one is left behind. Nowadays, there are so many technologies and people are on Facebook or WhatsApp, I am not there on WhatsApp, thank God! (Laughs)."* The extent to which these opinions are valid or guided by social desirability is an arguable matter. Nevertheless, it points to girls' greater preoccupation with romantic interests.

Parents place greater emphasis on self-relating-to-other attributes such as loving to everybody, respecting of elders, and caring for others. Gender differences are "naturalized" and highlighted. One parent comments, *"Girls are very sensitive. They know their responsibilities and importance of life. They know that this is the time when I have to perform well in my life and make parents proud. Girls are very adjusting."* On the other hand, *"Boys have a 'Chalta hai' and 'Dekha jayega' attitude* (colloquial expressions that convey a careless, laissez-faire attitude). *They don't take responsibility or initiative. For example, if I am sick and he has to go to his friend's place, he will not change his plan for my health. He would just say I have to go, so please Mamma you take care. Or, he will be busy with his mobile. Whereas if it is a girl, she will make sure that she stays around me so that if I need any help, she can do so. For education also, boys are not goal oriented most of the time. They just conform to the minimum merit or 'cut off' for admission, and don't try to score more than this cut off."*

Other-relating-to-self attributes are expressed mainly in relation to parents, for example, *"My mother cares about me," "She is always there to support me," "My parents are there to guide me."* Few adolescents shared negative attributes, for example, *"My father is very strict with me,"* or *"He is partial toward my sister."*

Overall, the self-relating-to-other and other-relating-to-self orientations comprise descriptions of girls and boys in relation to their family and parents, peers and society at large. Parents mention more parent- and family-related descriptors, whereas adolescents mention more peer-related descriptors to describe a "typical" adolescent. In describing an ideal adolescent, parents emphasize relational characteristics involving parent and family such as understanding and solving problems of the family and abiding by family discipline. Simultaneously, undesirable characteristics such as disobeying parents and having conflicts with parents (e.g., girls do not help mothers in household chores and boys demand more facilities from parents) have also emerged. Parents of girls more than boys describe an ideal girl largely within the "self-in-relation" framework and expect a familial orientation.

Ideal Girl and Ideal Boy: Salient Themes

Obey and respect parents and others: *An ideal girl and ideal boy should first of all face the society, stand up in the society, respect and obey, be disciplined, give respect to others, understand what others are saying, show manners in behavior toward others and do one's own work by oneself.*

All parents like children who obey and respect them. Those children who ideally instill the values (samskaras) given to them are liked by parents. If they deviate from it, parents don't like it. An ideal girl or boy is one who behaves properly, who does things as we say, obeys us; nothing is more ideal than this.

Cultivate a balanced outlook: *An ideal girl has to know what is good and what is bad. She should know the difference. She should not get carried away by emotions. This is the phase where their hormones are at the highest point; they can get carried away very easily. She should not get influenced and make bad decisions. You know I am not saying that you should not have relationships, or that it is bad, but they should know what is good for them. She should be smart, intelligent and well mannered. If all these qualities are present, then she is an ideal girl. She should help mom and dad in whatever way possible. She should be efficient in household chores; if she can do that it is good, and if she can cook, that will be great!*

Be responsible, goal oriented, and abstain from bad habits: *An ideal boy should help mom and dad around, be smart and he should know what is good for him and how his future should plan out. If he knows what he wants to achieve in his life that will be great. In this age boys tend not to listen to parents. A boy should be responsible and sincere in behavior and actions. He should respect elders, not get into any bad habits. This is a very important thing for boys because they can get carried away easily. They feel it is something great to smoke cigarettes, take drugs and all that, but it's not good and they don't realize that.*

Adolescent as a person: *"One who has 'good' work habits and values"*. "Parents expect their teenagers to develop good work habits and good values. Common responses included descriptors such as becoming a 'wise person,' an active individual,' 'rational,' 'practical,' 'should do work with responsibility,' 'works as per her requirement in time,' 'do own daily routine work herself,' 'stable under stress condition,' 'do work according to importance of time,' and 'acting according to the requirement of the present situation.' Both parents and adolescents referred to the acquisition of good values such as 'be honest in all walks of life,' 'always do the right thing,' 'observe self-discipline,' 'discriminate between right and wrong,' 'must have a good character *(charitravan),*' and 'lead a good and peaceful life'. Parents also voiced that they expected their adolescent to become independent. Eighteen-year-old Karan shares, *"In all arguments that we have, mom would surely ask what I shall do when she will not be there to feed me. Mummy na rotla pachi shu (what will you do after I will not be there to cook for/feed you?)."* It *is her indirect way of saying that I should become independent."* According to adolescents, parents expect them to focus on studies, keep good company, choose wise friends, and be aware of one's limits. Tanu, 17 years, complains, *"If we are out with boys, then they want us to be more careful. If we are out with girls then we are allowed until 11 p.m., but with boys we are allowed until 9.30 or 10.00 p.m."*

A few parents and adolescents shared that they expected adolescents to contribute to the country, help the poor, and become a good citizen. The concern for the "other" reflects the inherent connectedness articulated in the Hindu-Indian dictum *Vasudhaiva Kutumbakam*—viewing the world as one large family. In this vein, parents and adolescents also refer to the responsibilities and contributions that adolescents make toward the society, for example, helping the underprivileged. Some of the responses in this domain are, *"they are aware of their duty toward the nation,"* and *"they take interest in national and international events."* Referring to the contribution of girls to society, a parent commented, *"Girls play an important role in social revolution of the country."* Qualities such as being patriotic and being a good citizen are also included in the description of an ideal adolescent.

The **encompassing self-construal** is observed in adolescents' articulation of their dreams, wishes, and ideas of success. In general, parents and family feature prominently in adolescents' thoughts and worries. Parents' influence on one's individual wishes is apparent in articulations such as, *"My dream is what my parents dream about me. They want me to become a doctor so it is now my dream as well…;"* *"I wish to make my parents proud of me;"* *"I want to be a successful person, I want to support my family, fulfill their desires;"* *"They should not regret the efforts and money that they have spent on their son."* There is ample demonstration of adolescents' awareness and sensitivity toward the efforts that parents have put in for them. Gauri, 17 years, expresses, *"…I want to earn so much in life for me and my parents. My father is striving very hard for my studies and for donations and admissions. They are always standing behind me, persuading me to study. They ask me where do you want to go for further study? Go ahead, we are behind you, whatever money it takes. I want to earn much so that I can give satisfaction to my family and live a luxurious life. I wish to do everything that can*

give contentment to my parents. They should have everything they wish to have.
I wish I get all the facilities for them."

Wielding a Magic Wand, Cherished Memories, Notions of Success, and Future Projections

If adolescents could wield a magic wand they would make themselves free from school and examinations and the stress associated with it, choose a career based on one's preference and liking (e.g., musician), remove gender-based restrictions, and ensure parents' and siblings' contentment and happiness.

In response to a question asking the adolescent to share any three wishes that one may have, 16-year-old Sonal discloses, *"First I want to clear all obstacles which can stop me from reaching my goal of career. Life will be easy thereafter. Second is to do all things which can give contentment to my parents. They should have everything they wish to have. I wish I get all the facilities for them."* Whereas 18-year-old Arpita expresses, *"I want a change in my lifestyle; I would love to be in a foreign country. I always wanted to … I wish my brother was with us, wherever we are, not so far. I wish he could find a job here and live with us so it becomes a happy family and we don't need to worry about this."*

> **Wishing on a Magic Wand…**
> *We have a new wish every day in life. Like we wake up in the morning wishing that today this should happen. When I was a child, I wished to become a fairy once in my life (Laughs). Now the thing I wholeheartedly wish for is to successfully become a doctor, that's my first wish. What my mom–dad dreamed about for me, I want to fulfill that. My second wish would be to belong to an upper class family. At some point in life, we are tagged as middle class family, I don't want that. Today if we go somewhere, if we want to buy something, we have to think before doing—what would be the price, how costly it would be, how much will we spend and save. So if I want to do something in life for me and my parents, it would be to have a life like that of one who is 'born with a golden spoon', where food is also served in golden dishes. I wish to earn so much in life, that I am able to treat my parents the same way that they have treated me. They have never denied me anything, whether they are able to afford it or not. So, after I start earning, my wish is to do all the things that my parents want. My father is fond of traveling, so I wish that after he retires or after I start earning, I will take him for a world tour, both my mom and dad. Till then, my brother would have got married (laughs), so he won't come leaving his wife behind. My third wish is to be with someone in life, who will treat me like a princess. Today when I see my parents, I feel very happy. They don't live together, as such, as my Mom is here because of our studies and my Dad is in Rajkot, but still they have that*

bonding. So I want the same thing, I would also like to get someone who treats me like that and is meant only for me. He should never try to become my husband, but remain a friend forever.
Komal, 16 years

In sharing a most cherished memory, adolescents predominantly referred to events related to academic achievement (e.g., securing good marks in Xth or XIIth standards) and occasions involving the family such as a surprise birthday party, a surprise holiday trip, or a surprise gift. Pooja, 17 years, says, "*Most cherished moment for me is when I got to know that I have scored maximum marks in the class in 10th std. and stood 1st! Actually I was happy thinking that my parents would be happy at last because for 5–6 years from almost 4th standard I have never got the 1st rank.*" Alluding to the freedom from academic pressures, Surabhi, 16 years, wistfully expresses, "*My childhood memories are dearest to me. I used to play a lot and there was no pressure and stress that what I have to do next for my life. It was simple fun life. Though I am still enjoying my life, yet those moments were very nice and beautiful.*" Ruminating over non-academic events, Saloni nostalgically shares, "*My most favorite memory is my first trip without family. I went with a group of friends from school and we had so much fun. I did not know that I could handle so many things on my own till I actually did during that trip.*"

For adolescents the definitions of success range from achieving the goals that one sets for oneself, especially career goals, material acquisitions such as money, reputation, and being a good person. Pratik, 18 years, philosophizes, "*According to me a person is successful if the person is going to die next minute and at that time he thinks that everything I did in life is right, I am a good person, good in everything, be good to everyone, everyone likes you, everyone likes being with you. If you make such a nice life that inspires someone else to be like you, that's success.*" Along similar lines, 17-year-old Kunjal states, "*Success is satisfaction, simple! Whatever we are earning, how we want to earn, we should feel satisfaction. Today my papa has money and everything, but still he is struggling. No one is stable here, anybody in middle class is running around here and there; you have money but there is no satisfaction and peace in anyone's life.*"

Expression of the encompassing self runs in tandem with ideas for individual self-enhancement. Success for adolescents is linked to one's own as well as parents' satisfaction and happiness. "*When you do something and if you as well as your parents are satisfied, it is success. But if either (parents or me) is not happy and satisfied, then even if you have achieved what you have wished, you will not be successful because that happiness will not be there*" (Anuja, 16 years). The anxiety of fulfilling parents' dreams for one's career and in relation to other aspects is clearly articulated. For example, Namrata, 17 years, shares, "*First, I sometimes feel that I am weak in studies and cannot cope up so I have a fear that I may lose mine or my parent's dream. Second, sometimes I make mistakes and then later I realize that so I feel that my parents should not feel bad or get hurt because of me.* Parents' health and their apprehension for the adolescent are also worrying factors. *"First concern is health of my parents. I am the only child of my parents and I am dependent on my parents. So if anything happens to them, my life would be affected adversely. One of the concerns is also safety and security. If I go somewhere out of Baroda, then parents would be worried about me and I would be worried about them. They will be alone here and if anything happens, who will help. So, to find a good career in Gujarat is also one of the* worries. *I want to do things that will give contentment to my parents; I wish to get all the facilities for them"* (Anita, 16 years). In a similar vein, Kruti shares, *"I don't want to go away from my parents. So marriage and further studies out of state would be big concerns. I am much attached to my masi (aunt—mother's sister) as well and I don't want them to go anywhere. They are planning to shift little far from my place, though it is in the same city, I am really worried that what I will do if I won't meet them daily. She is my second mom. Losing people or friends with whom you are close is one more concern."*

Adolescents' projections into the future are positive and indicative of education and career accomplishments as well as enhanced lifestyle. Parents continue to feature in these projections. For instance, Mukta, 18 years, says, *"I will be a successful woman, I would have fulfilled my aim. Papa may retire and I will be standing on my own feet and taking care of him."* The lure of foreign shores and their potential to offer a comfortable lifestyle is reflected in adolescents' future projections. Seventeen-year-old Pooja reveals, *"After 5 years I will definitely be studying abroad, as I know that the field I will be choosing is not valued in India. So I am going out like USA or other place. The success I want is not possible staying here in India. For earning, I will go US or any other country and earn very much. After 10 years I will be a perfect individual standing on my own feet, earning very high, having good husband and good house, be at peace in short."*

More girls than boys referred to love and marriage in sharing about their future. Ranak, 16 years, ruminates, *"After five years I would have completed my MBBS and would be doing a job in a good hospital. And, I will be with the boy whom I love. After ten years, I will not be studying. It's my dream to live in a wood house. I will have such a house, and the boy whom I love will be with me in the house. So I will be living a successful and happy life."*

The cultural construction of adolescent, the person, represents multiple self-conceptions including the individual self, evinced in within-self descriptions, the relational self, comprising self-relating-to-other and other-relating-to-self characteristics, with parents favoring the former; and the encompassing self is evident in the integration of parents in adolescents' wishes and dreams. For example, the wish for a "good" lifestyle with all material facilities is intertwined with the desire to reciprocate to parents by presenting them with a better lifestyle. The worry about fulfilling parents' expectations is pervasive. Adolescents' thoughtfulness and reference to parents flow across the different domains.

Notwithstanding the primacy of the relational and encompassing dimensions of self, instances of the individual or autonomous self are also observed. Adolescents demonstrate clear articulation of their personal wishes, dreams, and anxieties related to self as well as parents and family. This is suggestive of both individuating and relating autonomy, which contributes to creating the related-autonomous self-construal (Yeh et al. 2007). This aspect is discussed further in Chap. 4 in the context of conceptions of parents, issues of interpersonal disagreements, and parent–adolescent relationship, and also in Chap. 6.

Figure 3.1 illustrates the salient features of adolescence, the stage, and adolescent, the person.

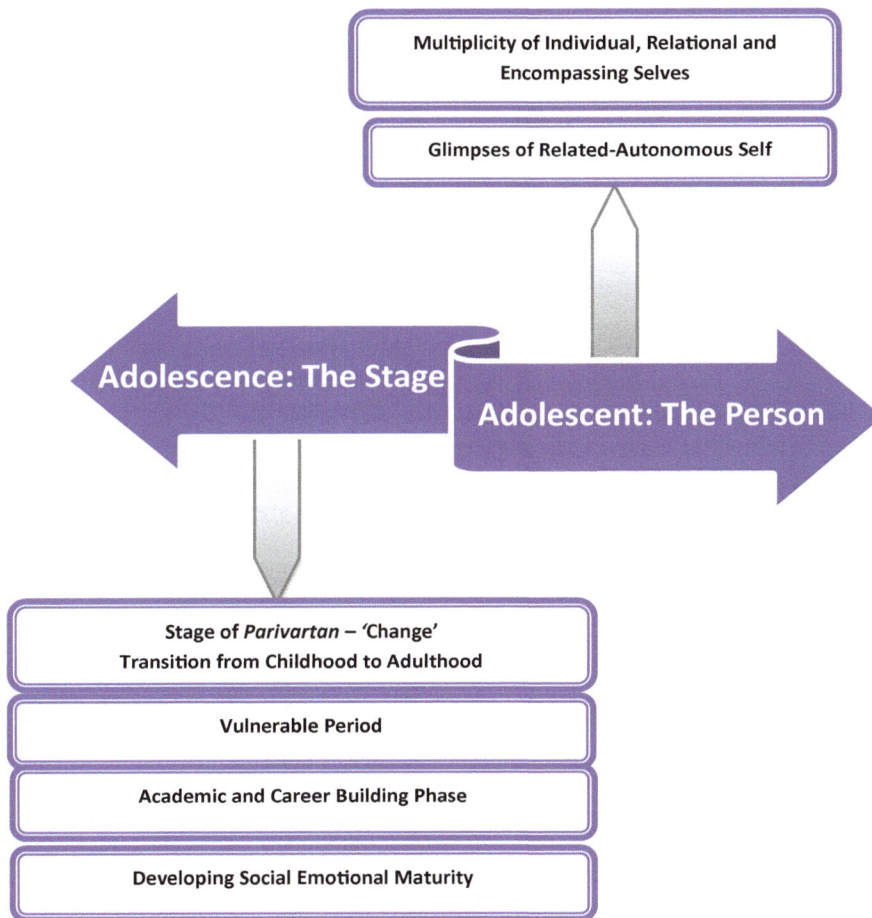

Fig. 3.1 Adolescence, the stage, and adolescent, the person

References

Chakkarath, P. (2013). Indian thoughts on human psychological development. In G. Misra (Vol. Ed.), XIII (3), *Psychology and psychoanalysis* (pp. 167–190). In D. P. Chattopadhyaya (Gen. Ed.), *History of science, philosophy and culture in Indian civilization*. New Delhi: Center for Studies in Civilization.

England, P. (2010). The gender revolution: Uneven and stalled. *Gender and Society, 24*(2), 149–166. doi:10.1177/0891243210361475.

Mascolo, M. F., Misra, G., & Rapisardi, C. (2004). Individual and relational conceptions of self in India and the United States. *New Directions for Child and Adolescent Development, 104*, 9–26.

Yeh, K. H., Liu, Y. L., Huang, H. S., & Yang, Y. J. (2007). Individuating and relating autonomy in culturally Chinese adolescents. In J. Liu, C. Ward, A. Bernardo, M. Karasawa, & R. Fischer (Eds.), *Casting the individual in societal and cultural contexts* (pp. 123–146). Korea: Kyoyook-Kwahak-Sa Publishing.

Chapter 4
Parent–Adolescent Relationship: A Circle of Care, Respect, and Faith

Abstract Much writing, both scientific as well as popular, has highlighted the rather trying time that parents endure in dealing with their adolescent children. The burgeoning contextual changes are only expected to exacerbate this phenomenon. Concerns along these lines are expressed in contemporary Indian society, especially with regard to dissipating traditional cultural values and the challenge of reconciling traditional beliefs and practices with new realities. This chapter probes into the phenomena of parenting and parent–adolescent relationship from the perspectives of both adolescents and parents. The following questions are addressed: What kind of parenting is preferred in the present milieu of flux of social change? How is the changing context affecting the traditional hierarchical authority structure of parent–adolescent relationship? What are the defining features of the parent–adolescent relationship? The chapter begins with an overview of parents' and adolescents' descriptions of parenting adolescents. It then presents the nature of parental authority as revealed in the different conceptions of parents described by adolescents and parents. Subsequently, the guiding elements of the parent–adolescent relationship are discussed as evinced in the interpretation and resolution of interpersonal disagreements.

Keywords Adolescence · Parenting · Parent–Adolescent relationship · Interpersonal disagreements

Parenting Adolescents: A Multilayered Phenomenon

Cultural worldview and goals shape parenting beliefs and practices, and these are mediated by contextual contingencies. The world over, including India, families are trying to adapt to the global changes which are refracted through distinct cultural systems (Larson 2002). Parenting is a lifelong responsibility comprising vicissitudes at every developmental stage of the child and the parent.

Across societies, parent–child relationship represents a hierarchical structure, with authority as the primary constituent. In cultures such as India, the hierarchical

© Springer (India) Pvt. Ltd. 2017
S. Kapadia, *Adolescence in Urban India*,
DOI 10.1007/978-81-322-3733-4_4

83

authority orientation is even more firmly entrenched in families and is infused with a moral subtext. In the present times, global factors are compelling parents to introduce adaptations in parenting ideas and practices to facilitate their own as well as children's adjustment and development. This is revealed in the multifaceted conceptions and expectations expressed by both adolescents and parents in response to two questions:

Parent: "How would you describe yourself as a parent of an adolescent?" "What are your expectations from your adolescent child?"
Adolescent: "How would you describe your parents?" "What are your expectations from your parents?"

Opening responses to these questions reveal a largely positive perception of parenting, albeit with reference to the changes that parents need to introduce into the parenting process.

Parents

How would you describe yourself as a parent of a teenager?

> *Parents of children at this age should behave like their friends. We should solve the questions that come in their life. We should counsel them for their studies, life style and career. We should talk with them about their future, sit and talk with them, we should eat together.*

> *As a parent it is necessary to be flexible and try to understand the adolescent. Times have changed and mostly adolescents are living in their own circles—school, college, friends... they tend to compare us with friends' parents, so we need to change ourselves accordingly. We have to keep patience. Our parents used to tell us things directly like you cannot do this or you have to do this...But now we have to make adolescents understand in a nice way. So see, earlier also we had to understand as children and now also we only have to understand, even as parents.*

Adolescents

How would you describe your parent?

> *My mom and dad are there whenever I need them. My mother always cares about me; she always thinks about me first before herself, she always tries to sacrifice for me, for my welfare. She understands me and I can share everything with her. Many problems are such that we cannot share with our friends. When I got my periods for the first time I didn't know who to share with so I directly went to my mother and she explained everything to me and guided me. She helps me do my homework, and also in co-curricular activities. When in school I had participated in a 800 meters race. She accompanied me every evening and recorded the time when I practiced running. When I am confused she helps me to sort things out. She gives me the answer that is right for me (Devi, 16 years).*

Dad is very supportive. If I do anything, wrong at any time, he will sit with me and explain this is right, this is wrong and that this is what you have to do. He never scolds me but always tries to explain to me because he knows that at this age you might tend to do this wrong. He sits with me and he is absolutely frank and tells me what is wrong. This is satisfying because parents have also gone through our age and they know what is right and what is wrong. They know what kind of feelings we have right now… they can understand us much better (Renita, 16 years).

My mom is really sweet and caring. But sometimes she is too interfering… and that bothers me. I know she is saying things for my good, but it is too much sometimes… and I also know my good… (Rahul, 18 years).

Both parents and adolescents describe parenting in terms of multiple conceptions and expectations from each other that comprise a combination of traditional and "new" images. Appendix E gives the percentage distribution of the themes of expectations of adolescents and parents from each other, drawn from the survey data. Further description of these themes was derived from the qualitative interviews with parents and adolescents. The conceptions and expectations are suggestive of the types of parental authority exercised in the present context. One is conceptualized as nurturant, anchoring authority and the other as an adaptable and relational form of authority. The former represents the traditional orientation, whereas the latter reflects a contemporary orientation.

Nurturant, Anchoring Authority

Hierarchical authority is integral to the Indian societal framework. The nature of authority exercised by parents draws from the Hindu notion of *dharma*. The child in the subordinate position is expected to show obedience and respect to parental authority and the parent in turn is responsible to guide and protect the child. Parents thus act as anchors for the child. This phenomenon reflects the concept of "anchoring function" put forth by Omer et al. (2013). It is proposed as an integrative concept used to bridge Diana Baumrind's notion of authoritative parenting with Mary Ainsworth's concept of parent–child attachment bond. It integrates parental authority and the concepts of safe haven and secure base. The concepts of safe haven and secure base indicate the refuge and encouraging function of parents, whereas the anchoring function refers to the protective function of the parental role, which needs to be well anchored. The anchoring function becomes particularly relevant during developmental periods in which the child's explorations expand and exposure to risks increases (Omer et al. 2013). Adolescence is perceived as just such a vulnerable period.

Conceptions of parents and expectations from parents shared by adolescents and parents suggest the traditional nurturant and anchoring authority that parents enact, which corresponds well with the interdependent relational cultural outlook.

Parent as guardian, guide and support. Parents and adolescents both expressed that the parent cares for the adolescent's safety, corrects, guides, and advises when wrong, helps and supports, teaches and explains in case of personal problems and problems with friends, and helps to deal with any other difficult situation. Parents shared that it is their duty as parents to *"show the child the right way if he or she was going wrong."* A mother expresses, *"Whatever problems come they should share even if they have done wrong… I will be able to guide them better… I feel my kids should tell me everything and treat me as a friend. We should solve the questions that come in their life. We should counsel them for their studies, life style and career. We should talk with them about their future, sit and talk with them in general, and we should eat together."*

Adolescents highlight the support and help that parents offer, and their input in showing the "right" path. Anuj, 17 years expresses, *"If I am doing something wrong she (mother) will definitely stop me… she is also encouraging like if she finds out something about scholarships then she will get me to do it… she will help me fill a form and help me write an essay… actually I am into debates and quizzes and she has a hand in it… she is an inspiring force for me."* In the same vein, Reena, 16 years, describes, *"My dad is always ready to solve my problem for me. He's very good at that. So every time I have a problem, he gives me a step-by-step guidance for the solution. He pampers me, really cares for me… he is very concerned for me. Whenever I want to buy something he lets me and tells me how to care for it."*

Parents also shared the need to be proactive and involved in adolescents' everyday activities, especially academics. A father explains, *"You have to be, you know, very active because there are lots of things going on; there are lots of opportunities so being a parent you have to be aware of all that is going on around you or the kids. And you should be aware of all the possibilities for your son in future or for his present education. Even now, we cannot take for granted that since he is going to school everything will be taken care of by the teacher and that our job is just to pay the fees and all that stuff. No, it's not like that. Now parents have to make extra effort for researching what's going on around them, giving the best kind of knowledge to children. So even parents have to make more efforts, searching and researching…"* The increasing responsibility that parents are required to shoulder is evident as also their conscious efforts in this direction.

A Father's Conception of an Ideal Parent
An ideal parent I feel should have no expectations. They should not force upon the children that this is what you have to do in life. Children have to be given independence. They should be given freedom. We cannot force our wishes, our whims and fancies on the child. An ideal parent should know what the child wants and give them the freedom, but I am not saying that we should give too much freedom and just leave them like that. It is just that we should realize what the child wants and not force our expectations on them. That is what I feel. An ideal parent should show love and affection, have trust on children, and not keep on questioning why he/she is doing something. That

doesn't mean you can completely trust them also, but you have to know how to balance and give them credit for what they do.

Parent as disciplinarian. The image of parent as a disciplinarian mainly refers to the parent regulating the adolescent's behavior and activities (e.g., not allowing the adolescent to go for late night parties). Adolescents express having differences of opinion with their parents as according to them their parents' ideas are "outdated" and "biased." Girls tend to describe fathers in more positive terms whereas boys feel that their fathers are short tempered, rigid, and strict. This may be perhaps because the fathers impose more regulations on boys or the boys tend to "break rules" more than girls. One father expresses special concern related to disciplining. He clarifies, *"As a parent I do expect good behavior from my children…that is, maintaining time in coming home on time, timely waking up, timely studies, obedience, outing with friends sometimes, but punctuality is important, and also openness…if you are going out with friends you must tell us and tell us when you will return…I prefer my children come home at night, that is, they don't stay out during the night."*

Father, a "distant" figure. The traditional image of father as a distant figure in the adolescent's life is reflected in a few responses such as, *"He gives less time at home," "He is not as close as mother," "He does not trust me,"* and *"Hard person to judge."* Jigar, 17 years, shares, *"My father is also friendly, but still father has a different respect. I can share everything with him but I don't. It's like there is some respect which father has to be given, so things that I share with my mother I can't share with my father. But he understands me…"* Adolescents made many references to father's anger and bad temper.*"Like…sometimes when I am not studying he is so angry that sometimes he can beat me…like at that time I don't like it because now I am grown up and when he does all those things I don't like it. And he feels that whatever he tells is only good, he does not listen to me…whether I am right or wrong he does not listen to me…he does what he knows, nothing else"* (Kunjal, 16 years).

Girls express a two-dimensional relationship with fathers, one wherein they feel close to the father and specially cared for and another wherein they feel distanced from the father. Radha, 17 years, said, *"I am quite free with my father. Things for which my mom says no, I go to him and he never says no, he allows me. He is more possessive and protective about me than my brother."* On the other hand, Ashita, 17 years, regretfully shares, *"My father doesn't understand me as well because that's girl stuff and all that. I love him but I am scared of him. He gets angry; I am scared of his anger. He controls himself but he gets angry. Like if I do something wrong I feel scared ki (that)… papa will scold me."* Adolescents also complain about the long absence of father from home, mainly on account of his job.

Parent as provider. The traditional parental responsibility of providing for children, which is inherently tied to parental authority in the Indian context, is well ingrained. The role of parent as provider is taken for granted in urban middle class families in India and is voiced in adolescents' and parents' expectations from parents, and adolescents' satisfactions in the relationship. In addition to providing for the adolescents' needs, parents also wish to give those facilities that the parent may have missed as a child.

In keeping with the contemporary contextual exigencies of the urban middle class, adolescents expect parents to make provision for some entertainment every 10–15 days, for example, take them on vacations, buy video games, and eat out. There is the expectation that parents procure necessary items for the adolescents' needs (e.g., a vehicle—mostly a two-wheeler, study books, cell phones, computers) as well as facilities such as tuitions, good schooling, cable TV, and Internet access. In the words of a mother of a girl, *"My daughter expects a lot from me. She wants love, affection. She wants financial assistant, give her money whenever she wants. She wants expensive clothes, so if we can provide these she is very happy. She wants support in everything. I think she has a much longer way to go before she realizes that someday she has to do everything on her own. Right now we are providing everything."* In the Indian context, this responsibility of parents continues well into children's adulthood and begins to cease, although not completely, only when the boy begins to earn and when the girl gets married.

Love and blessings. "*Love*", "*inspire adolescents to keep up their morale*," and "*spend time with them*" are primary expectations voiced by both parents and adolescents. These also emerge as more satisfying elements of the relationship. Adolescents expect their parents to bless them in fulfilling their ambitions, provide them love, show interest in their life, be their well-wishers, and keep them happy. In the Indian culture, parents are attributed a godlike status—*matrudevo bhavah, pitrudevo bhavah (*mother and father are equivalent to God*)*. Blessings (*ashirwad*) from elders, especially parents, are highly valued, and it is common for young people to take parents' blessings before beginning any significant activity, for example, appearing for an examination or a job interview or taking a trip.

Academic and career achievement. Parents' anchoring authority is markedly evident in their input in adolescents' scholastic work, a significant developmental task of adolescence in middle class families. Parents are actively and vigilantly involved in ensuring that adolescents focus on their studies. Parental involvement and authority in this domain range from advice in selecting a career stream and setting career goals to providing all support in the path toward the same, for example, arranging for tuition classes and everyday monitoring and supervision in studies. Whereas adolescents expect their parents' help in setting and achieving academic and career goals, this often becomes a matter of dissatisfaction and conflict, as adolescents perceive that parents nag them constantly on this aspect.

In general, academic- and career-related expectations of parents from their daughters and sons include pursuing a specific career (e.g., doctor, aeronautical engineer, or pharmacist), being highly educated, studying a lot in order to earn well, and building a bright future. Adolescent girls and their parents emphasized that parents expected their daughters to study and make a career. This is a reflection of young urban Indian women's increasing aspirations. Further, in the present times, education is an essential attribute that gives an advantage to the girl in the marriage market. In the world of the "aspirational" middle class, boys are observed to prefer an educated wife as it enhances their social status and also because of her potential to earn and contribute to the family income, thereby enabling the couple to augment their life style.

The increasingly competitive scenario of academics and employment raises serious concerns for the adolescent's future, and much parenting during this stage revolves around encouraging and enabling children to pass through this critical phase as effectively as possible. Successful accomplishment of this goal brings a strong feeling of achievement to parents as they feel content that they have fulfilled one of their major responsibilities of "putting the child on the right track" or "making the child self-reliant" *(amare ane page ubho karvano che-we have to ensure that he stands on his feet)*; whereas adolescents feel that they have made a mark for themselves in some way. The downside of expectations related to academics is the immense pressure on adolescents, both in school as well as at home, to perform well, which produces considerable stress often resulting in dire consequences such as adolescent depression and even suicide in some instances.

Role-related duty toward parents and family. A core element of parental authority is the focus on role-related responsibility, which has emerged as an underlying theme in the expectations of adolescents and parents and is evoked in discussions during interpersonal disagreements. The anchoring function is represented not only in terms of the parents' responsibility toward the adolescent, but also in the notion of the adolescent's duty toward parents. In line with the Indian concept of *dharma*, fulfillment of the adolescent's duty as a daughter or son emerges as a leading expectation. Gender differences are evident in that the daughter more than the son is expected to fulfill the role of a good daughter. Echoing adolescent self-conceptions (described in Chap. 3), more girls and their parents expect girls to be a "good daughter," defined as one who has good *samskaras*, is cultured and family oriented, and has good education. The daughter is also expected to be affectionate, loving, and peaceful in her relationships with others.

Support and help is another significant expectation endorsed by both parents and adolescents, especially extending care to parents in old age and in time of need. For example, a mother of a girl said, "*I don't expect anything from her but she should at least have time for us when we become old. For now, we are staying together, we are always with each other so I don't expect anything, but in future if she goes abroad for further study, she should at least remain connected with us.*" Adolescents too shared that they want to "give back" to parents and fulfill their wishes and needs. In this regard,18-year-old Ankur says, "*Sometimes we are discussing movies or with parents' friends from the USA who share their experiences saying how children don't care for their parents after a certain age. So many a times my parents say, in a lighter vein, that we expect that you won't put us in an old age home when we will be old.*"

Parents and adolescents also shared their notions of responsibilities toward each other, the crux of which was mutual expectation of active involvement of parents in the adolescents' lives and the corresponding acceptance of it by the adolescents. Illustrative quotes are given below.

Mother of Kavita (18 years)

Interviewer: *What do you think are some of your responsibilities toward her?*
Respondent: *My responsibility is right from her birth to her marriage. I feel that I am responsible for bringing her up, and give whatever she wants to satisfy her...I should be a dutiful mother...she should be given meals on time...I want to be home whenever she comes from school or from play or whatever...I want to be with her and ensure that her needs are fulfilled.*

Kunal (16 years)

Interviewer: *What do you think are your parents' responsibilities toward you?*
Respondent: *I think they have a lot of responsibilities, because until I turn 18 they are fully responsible for all my decisions... they have to help me because they are the ones who are experienced. They are the ones who know life. They are the ones who help me out in each and every situation. They do have a lot of responsibilities, from waking me up in the morning to giving me all the materialistic things I want such as, paying school fees, getting me to a good tuition class... I cannot do anything without them.*

Ruchita (17 years)

Interviewer: *What do you think are your parents' responsibilities for you?*
Respondent: *Be there when I want to ask them anything... hear me out... like when I am having a bad time... they should be there. I should always be able to talk to them... they should be there to console me... anytime I want something... makes me feel good.*

Adaptable Authority

The adaptable form of authority signifies parental flexibility and consideration of the adolescent's perspective. This form is emerging in response to changes that are filtering from the macro context. Conceptions and expectations suggestive of this form are described below.

Parent as friend. Both parents and adolescents perceive their parent as a "friend." "Close and frank relationship," "friendly," "broad minded about heterosexual relationships, parties and clothes," "open communication," "understanding and adjusting" are some descriptors that are used. Aparna, 16 years, says about her mother, *"My mom is so free... like other girls can't speak freely to their mother, but I tell her everything, things that I don't even tell my best friends. She's really a friend, my best friend."* Similarly, Ankur, 18 years, shares, *"My mom is very open with me. There are no secrets between us. We have a frank relationship. If I am feeling anything—sad or happy or there is something wrong she can make out immediately without my telling her."*

A daughter's special relationship with the father is observed in the response of 17-year-old Roma, *"Actually between my brother and me he is more fond of me. We have a father and daughter bond. He is protective about me. My father is as helpful as my mother. They are equally good. He is helpful and kind to me. My mother does scold me at times, but my father never scolds me. He is too lenient and open with me and I never hide anything from him. I do not have the fear that he will disclose what I share with him to others, I mean any other family members…"*

Adolescents have also referred to their parents' leaning toward a liberal attitude signifying the notion of a friend. *"My mom is very liberal. She never puts any restrictions on me. She'll let me go for a movie at any odd hour of the day. She'll even provide me transport for that as far as possible. She's not possessive about me. Any phone call from boys, no questions, it's ok. She never comments on my clothes, my friends, their boyfriends and she's open to me having a boyfriend. My father, he's also same (like mother); in fact he's more liberal. He encourages me to have a boyfriend and he's very you know like 'why don't you have one?'. He'll also allow me anywhere at any time of the day, provided I'm in good company and he stresses on my having a good academic performance"* (Ruchita, 17 years). Keyur, 18 years, comments, *"My father is a very cool, calm person. He won't interfere in my matters. I think he is the best person who understands me…he knows what teenagers are up to…he won't nag me 'do this and don't do that'…he is more of a friend to me than a father."*

On their part, parents too endorsed this characteristic as manifested in the following excerpts.

An Ideal Parent: Parents' Perceptions

An ideal parent should be like a friend with children at this age. By being a friend and talking with them like a friend, the adolescents will be also free to share things with the parents. Otherwise they will not share what they are doing or feeling. Many children don't share what they are doing outside the home, but if you behave like a friend they will share" (Mother).

Parents should have an open sharing attitude, they should not be authoritarian. This is a very important phase for a child and the children should not get distracted. If we have a sharing and friendly nature, they would feel comfortable in sharing things with us and that way we can help them in taking life decisions during this stage. If you keep after them or if you keep on watching over them, they start hiding things and that is most dangerous. Learning to create a friendly space between you and your kids is most important. We should not doubt them. The child should feel that parents are here to help, not to scold and demoralize the child (Father).

"Understanding" parent. Adolescents and parents emphasize the characteristic of being understanding. Parents, especially, feel that this attitude is necessary in view of the vulnerability of this phase of life. Deliberate attempts to maintain a balanced approach in socialization are evident with an eye on the sensitive mind-set

of the adolescent. A father shares, *"The parents should be very understanding. They should know the psychology of a child. They should understand what their child is going through at this age and time. Because see, as I told you, they are going through a very delicate age. At this point of time, even if we scold them or we tell them something then they would not be able to digest that. They would feel ki (that) no this is wrong. They will think ki (that) what dad is saying or what my mom is saying is totally wrong. So they won't be able to take that easily. And they could react in a different manner. And this may create a different impact than what the parents might be expecting—a very negative impact. That's why I would suggest that parents of kids this age should be very understanding; they should understand the psychology—what your son or daughter is going through. We have to see things from their perspective…. Then and only then we can solve their problems also."*

Open-minded parent: "A little less restriction, a little more freedom." Parenting is a bidirectional phenomenon and parental authority is transacted in a relational context. How adolescents perceive and accept parental authority is relevant in determining the nature of authority that is applied. Adolescents complain about parental restrictions and express a clear wish for relaxation in the same, expecting their parents to *"…provide freedom to take decisions in life and let me live the way I want to."* Parental regulation and disciplining such as being strict, over protective, nagging, and over directive (especially the mother) as well as some personality characteristics such as being short tempered, conservative, and rigid emerge as a predominant source of dissatisfaction among adolescents. Misunderstandings due to generation gap, mostly with the mother, are also voiced. Namrata, 17 years, explains, *"She doesn't allow me to go somewhere. She's a bit conservative you know. I'm not as open with her as I am with my sister. I don't share everything with my mother. She might understand, but there are gaps like you know this generation gap that forms between us. That is a problem."*

Gender differences are evident in that more girls shared about the over protectiveness of the mother as a source of dissatisfaction. *"Ya … sometimes … she behaves like a kid. For instance…she acts a little immature. A little stubborn and … I mean I can't really explain that. And sometimes she acts a little too motherly. Like … if a guy likes me, then she is like 'I don't want him to call up too often and all'. She's just overprotective and too concerned sometimes"* (Avni, 16 years). Ruchita, 17 years, comments about her mother, *"Ya … like whenever we sit and discuss anything she looks at it from her perspective only and she weighs everything in comparison to her time, when she was young. Now I am in a totally different world. It is not the same. It was very different in her time. So then she is not able to fit herself into my shoes or see things from my viewpoint."* In such situations, the perceived double standards of parents also cause dissatisfaction. For example, Neena, 17 years, cribs, *"Ya actually they say something else but in reality it is something else. Like they say that 'ya, you should go out with friends and enjoy', but when such a situation does occur they refuse."* Such instances also point to the discrepancy between belief and behavior. Much as parents believe in giving "freedom" to adolescents, in actual situations, they experience the "cold feet syndrome" (Saraswathi and Pai 1997, p. 91) and may hesitate in sanctioning certain activities. Often parents themselves are tentative in articulating behavior and activity boundaries, especially for girls, and more so in matters involving potentially romantic interests. Issues involving parental regulation are a major source of anxiety and interpersonal disagreements.

Restrictions on speaking one's mind also bother adolescents. *"When I sometimes speak my mind... she thinks I am being rude. So sometimes, I just feel the need to say things you know when I am upset or something, so I just speak my mind. I don't mean to be rude and that is sometimes... when I have to go somewhere or something, like I have to ask her quite a few times before I go somewhere"* (Ishita, 17 years). Such incidences indicate the rules of authority that operate in hierarchical relationships wherein the one who is lower in the social hierarchy (e.g., child, student) is not supposed to talk back or talk over the person who is higher up in the hierarchical order (e.g., parent, teacher).

The traditional hierarchical authority between parent and child wherein authority was more parent-centered is being relaxed, giving way to a child-centered outlook to better accommodate to the changes and challenges of the present context. Adopting a friendly attitude which would make the adolescents comfortable to share openly with parents regarding their activities, tensions, and troubles is considered as the more effective way to parent adolescents. Much like a friend, the parent is expected and expects to make an effort to understand the perspective of the adolescent. Parents' motivation for being friendly with their adolescent centers upon the need to remain actively involved in the adolescent's life and preclude any distancing in the relationship. In general, a combination of "strict and liberal" attitude is highlighted, at the same time stressing the need not to compel or nag the adolescent, lest he or she may rebel. Instead, parents prefer to use subtle tactics to monitor the adolescent, for example, offering to drop the child when she or he may be going somewhere in order to get to know the place where she is going.

What Kinds of Challenges Do Parents Experience in the Process of Parenting Adolescents? What Parenting Practices Are Most Effective to Meet These Challenges?

In discussing the challenges of raising adolescents, parents tend to look back on their adolescence and draw comparisons in parent–child interactions then and now. A mother shares, *"In earlier times, when father's friends would come home, I would have to stand up and go inside. There was no question of going out anywhere, just go and come from college. We did not have many clothes or footwear. We had to get the results expected by parents. These days anger does not work with children. Unko samjhana padta hai (We have to explain to them). Earlier we used to respect our elders so much."* Parents realize that they need to change their ways and become more flexible and understanding with their adolescents. Lack of seriousness about studies and resistance to parents' views or directions are pet peeves of parents.

Adolescents' assertion and argumentation in certain domains also presents a challenge to parents. Parents are frustrated when the adolescent makes choices that according to them are not appropriate for him or her. A mother elaborates, "*My elder son took a 2 year drop from studies. Now he wants to take admission in Fashion Communication. We are saying no for it, but he wants to go in that field only. One has to think why I am taking this course, not just because your friends are doing it. When we ask him how will it be useful, then he searches the net (Internet) and gets back to us with all the job prospects in this field. But you don't know all this I say, and he says, I will get to know it once I study it. I am suggesting that he goes for Hotel Management which will be helpful in future also, as he is planning to stay abroad. He does not realize that we know better what kind of career would be better for him, so we should guide him.*"

How to deal with the adolescent's tendency to keep information away from parents is also a challenging task, especially in matters concerning friends. "*When he goes out with friends, he often lies to us. No doubt, all his friends are good, but as a parent we have the right to ask with whom he is going, where did he go, what did they talk, but he never tells us the truth. Even when I will go home from here then he will say that I was at home only but actually, I reach home by 2.30 pm and he knows it so he will come back by 2.00 pm so we should feel that oh he was at home only. So he will not share on his own. I have to ask and then he will say where he was or with whom. My concern is just that someone should not come and tell us that your son was roaming with this one or that one or somewhere; that we don't want to listen to and that is why we ask. So many times I make him understand that 'sole shaan, vise vaan' when you reach 16, you get knowledge and when you reach 20, you get your skin tone, body etc… so I told him that this is the stage and you have to make the most of it and study well.*"

Parents also put the accent on making time for adolescents and initiating "peaceful conversations" that would enable knowing the "inner feelings" of the adolescent. Parents acknowledge that the present milieu is challenging for the adolescent and in turn for the parents as well. In such a context, their support and efforts to reach out to the adolescent are central. A mother describes, "*My parents brought me up differently where they didn't have these challenges. Now I have different challenges, which are increasing day by day, so I don't know exactly what practices I should follow, what are the set rules we need as a parent. We are also trying to get smarter as parents, and we are also trying to see what is going on in their lives and what are the challenges that they are facing, and trying to give them support for the tensions they go through. This is what happens when they are chatting on Facebook. They feel it is okay, but what happens is when you are addicted to it, you can get carried away with it… so you know we have to keep on telling them that it is not required at this age. You have other things to worry about. We as parents are also learning how to bring them up. It is really difficult at times.*"

Gender differences are brought to light with parents acknowledging that it may be necessary to use different strategies for girls and boys. According to them, girls need a friendly approach, whereas boys need stricter handling. A mother articulated, "*For boys, I think your treatment should be little bit strict whereas for girls, you have to be very friendly. If you are too friendly with boys, they will start taking you for granted and will not listen to you seriously. As I already told you about the 'Chalta hai... ho jayega... Mummy dekh lenge... papa set kar denge' ('it will happen, we'll see... mummy, papa will sort it out') kind of attitudes boys have. So to make them responsible, you have to be strict and friendly both, but more strict. For girls, they are very sensible and can understand others' views as well. So I think you have to be friendly enough so that they can easily share what is happening with them. The major challenge is to learn to behave in these different ways with your kids, yet not make them conscious about this partial treatment."*

Balancing Strict and Liberal Approaches
She is 16 years old. I think that we should not compel the child. We have to support the child and at the same time help her to choose right things. We cannot force her to obey and say that do this and don't do this. At the same time, I do not mean that we should give her full freedom without any supervision. For example, if she is going somewhere, we just need to ask that with whom you are going and by what time you will be coming back. If she is going alone and if you are unsure, let her know that, you will be comfortable if she would allow you to drop her. That way, you can see the place as well and also she can be free in the sense that even if it is late, someone will come from home to pick her up. But during her party or gathering, we should not constantly ask her what is happening, what you are doing etc. because such questions will irritate them. Instead, we should make them responsible that if they are in some problem, they should tell us or if they are late, they should report to us before we ask them many questions. To learn when to be a friend and when to be a parent is really the most effective practice I feel. Trusting your children and letting them know that you trust them is also important. For instance, I go home from office and if she is watching TV, I won't get upset with her. I will just check with her whether she has studied or not in a causal way. She herself will give a reason. As a parent, I have to trust whatever she tells; many times one has to go along with children.

(Mother of Ankita, 16 years).

Figure 4.1 depicts the conceptions and expectations of parents and parenting adolescents in the urban middle class context.

The perspectives of parents and adolescents reveal considerable harmony. Both endorse the traditional ideology of respect, duty, and care, albeit infused with certain changes. The conceptions and expectations depict an interesting mélange of "traditional" and "contemporary" elements. Traditional elements suggestive of nurturant authority include expectations of discipline, guidance and support from parents, and respect and obedience from children, whereas "contemporary" parenting embraces a more democratic stance with a form of authority that is adaptable and relational. It emphasizes aspects such as friendliness, space for sharing and

Fig. 4.1 Parenting conceptions and expectations

discussing matters in an open and friendly ambience, and taking proactive interest in the adolescents' academic and other activities. Thus, although the traditional cultural roles and responsibilities of the parents persist, the way in which these are enacted is changing from a strictly hierarchical, authority-oriented style to a more flexible and child-centered mode, laced by a strong desire to continue to remain an active part of the adolescent's life. The approach also signifies support for adolescent autonomy as evinced by adolescents' tendency to be more open with parents and expressing many of their views explicitly, especially during episodes of interpersonal disagreements. How interpersonal disagreements are dealt and resolved reveals the defining elements of the parent–adolescent relationship.

Duty, Respect, Faith, and Care: Guiding Elements of the Parent–Adolescent Relationship

In the urban middle class Indian context, the parent–adolescent relationship and the exercising of parental authority evolve in a circle of duty, respect, faith, and care. This is demonstrated in the ways in which disagreements are resolved and the salient themes of adolescents' reasoning during such episodes.

Interpersonal Disagreements: Pervasively Present

Adolescent–parent disagreements are not alien to the non-Western world. Disagreements occur mainly on mundane everyday issues such as chores, academics, regulation of behavior and activities, and finance (McElhaney and Allen in press; Schlegel and Barry 1991). A similar pattern is observed in the Indian urban

Table 4.1 Themes and definitions of interpersonal disagreements

Themes	Definitions
Chores	Doing chores such as cleaning the room, helping in cooking and washing dishes
Academics	Concerns regarding choice of subject, method of studying, preparation for and performance in examination
Regulation of interpersonal activities	Regulation of one's choice of friends, decisions regarding when to see friends, participation in social/familial/religious activities
Regulation of behavior and activities	Concerns regarding choice or timing of activities such as watching TV, talking on the phone and watching movies; taking decisions regarding buying or driving of vehicle
Finance	Concerns regarding spending habits, pocket money and being responsible with money
Physical appearance	Concerns regarding acceptable standards of appearance and grooming

middle class context. Table 4.1 provides the themes and definitions of parent–adolescent disagreements.

Appendix E provides the percentage of occurrence of different disagreements. Adolescents have more disagreements with their mother than with their father. The mother is the primary caregiver who monitors adolescents' everyday activities. She is generally present in the home for longer periods, which is likely to result in greater interactions with children and hence scope for differences in opinion. Parental regulation of the adolescent's behavior and activity emerges as a common area of disagreement between adolescents and their parents. Some behaviors and activities that parents frequently regulate are amount of time spent on computer games, watching television, texting or talking on the phone with friends, spending time with friends like going out for a movie or a party, and spending the night at a friend's place. Another frequent area of disagreement concerns the matter of study. Time devoted to studies, choice of subjects, and method of studying are some of the main issues causing difference of opinion in this domain. Finance-related disagreements, for example, spending money on clothes and extravagant use of money are also common. Girls more than boys have disagreements related to physical appearance (e.g., sporting a particular hairstyle) and household chores.

Adolescents perceived most disagreements as being minor because according to them these did not last long but only a few minutes or a few days ("*…it came and went*"; "*It didn't go on for a long time and it was not wherein we had cold war*"); the incident did not involve much argument, parents did not compel or force them but "*just gave their opinion;*" it did not evoke long-lasting anger; adolescent's wish was fulfilled resulting in a "*happy ending;*" after the event occurred the adolescent realized one's own mistake and recognized that the parent was right; or that such issues also happened with their peers. A disagreement was interpreted as major when it continued for a long time, involved studies or money, if the activity was much cherished by the adolescent, if the issue involved much discussion and occurred frequently, or if it involved a matter that had significant impact on the adolescent's life (e.g., choice of major subject or continuing a hobby that was much desired).

Everyday Disagreements: Themes, Resolution and Reasoning

Hypothetical and actual interpersonal disagreements between adolescents and parents are described in terms of the resolution process and the reasoning used in the course of the disagreement.

Hypothetical Situations: Mixed Group Weekend Picnic, Career Choice, and Marriage Partner Selection

Mixed group weekend picnic. "Samir/Reena has an invitation to go out for a weekend picnic with a group of boys and girls. However, the parents are not giving permission to go, as they are not in favor of heterosexual friendships."

Both adolescents and parents favored negotiation and mutual accommodation to deal with this disagreement. The adolescents believed that they would be able to convince their parents that the adolescent would be safe. Hence, they were keen to offer detailed information to their parents regarding the picnic, that is, the venue, who will be going together, and the time when they will return home. In the words of Arpita, 18 years: "*I shall discuss with my parents, tell them why I want to go for the picnic… persuade them… I will also ask them what are their reasons, is there something specific stopping them… I will try and see what they feel. Still I will try my level best to convince them, tell them that all my friends are going. I can tell my friends' parents to talk with them. I will be adamant that I want to go. I will discuss with them openly, but then if they feel bad I will not go. I know they are concerned about my safety… they feel insecure.*" Parents on their part felt that they should explain the pros and cons of the situation to their adolescent (for example, possibility of falling in "bad" company). Both parties felt that talking about the issue with each other would help resolve it, and in fact strengthen their relationship. Concern about relational harmony is also evoked. "*It's a small matter, going to picnic is not a big thing-your life does not depend on it. Unnecessarily parents will be hassled. They'll be worried. It's not right for such a small matter. I must listen to my parents. It's better than creating a fuss in our relation…creating a barrier between me and my parents, the relation will be strained,*" Ankit, 17 years.

Gender-based concerns were articulated by parents and even some girls. Mothers seemed to be more cautious about allowing the girl to go for the picnic, whereas for boys they appeared to be more relaxed. A typical response for a boy was, "*I always allow him to go for such outings. But I tell him that he should have a check on himself, have control over himself.*" For a girl, however, there were more considerations involved. For example, a mother said, "*I would want to see how the group at the party is going to be, how the boys and girls are. Only then I would give permission.*" In the same vein, an adolescent girl said, "*If it were a boy he would not be asked many questions about who will be there for the party; there would be fewer problems for him to get permission to attend.*" The vulnerability of girls was evoked with the belief that a girl would not be able to protect herself if anything untoward were to happen. For boys, mothers used the strategy to explain guidelines for proper conduct, whereas for the girls the stance was one of "inquiry," to procure as much information as possible about the scenario. A father expressed, "*When faced with a difficult situation boys can still come out of it...girls are weak and might get carried away; her security and safety is most important for me...I will not allow her to go.*" In addition, a mother worried, "*I cannot afford to spoil the reputation of my daughter...who will marry her? People will say she goes out with boys for outstation picnics.*" Fathers shared some interesting views. One said, "*Since childhood my son has studied in a co-educational set-up...so girls and boys are friends...one has to look positively at relations...they can learn a lot from each other so why can they not go out together? I would send my daughter as well.*" Yet, another father said, "*Today girls are cleverer than boys. I have given my son proper samskaras, but if I feel the girls are not good I will not let him go lest he gets into trouble.*"

Parents expressed concern about the safety and affordability of sending the adolescent for the trip. "*One must look into the situation, where is the picnic, how they are going...anything can happen. If I am not convinced, my child will not go.*" A few adolescents interpreted going on a picnic as a "*small matter*" and hence not worth trying to convince their parents. "*Going out with friends is a very simple matter...my life does not depend on it. It is not like marriage or career where my life could be made or ruined...so let parents decide.*"

There were minor instances of self-assertion in which adolescents voiced that one may not tell parents everything all the time as, "*What they do not know will not hurt them,*" and hence it may be okay to tell an occasional lie.

Career choice. "Vikram/Pooja wants to pursue a career of his/her own choice. However, the parents have thought of another career which they think will be the best for him/her."

Negotiation and mutual accommodation emerged as the predominant approaches, with adolescents preferring the former. Two patterns were demonstrated. One in which parents tended to leave the choice on the adolescent, as they perceived their adolescent to be mature and sensible to take the appropriate decision. A father of a boy proudly said, "*Today's generation is well-informed and technologically advanced. I will in fact respect my son's decision and encourage him. He has to study and he knows his potential...why should I decide for him? The duty of a parent is to make them aware of their capacities and tell them about prospects and guide them all through...they are sensible and can decide.*" In the other pattern, however, a few parents felt that the adolescent was immature and shortsighted, and hence it was necessary to prevail upon him or her through appropriate negotiation. Girls demonstrated greater inclination to negotiate and convince parents of their choice. "*A person needs freedom in matters of career. It is a personal decision to think for yourself... to plan for your future,*" shares Kruti, 17 years. This also reveals girls' increasing aspirations for education and career. The downside of compelling an adolescent to decide for a certain choice was also revealed in a mother's reasoning, "*Forcing children for their career can take them into depression or mentally strain them...with serious consequences like suicide.*" A few adolescents relied on parental advice based on their wisdom which they believed would lead one toward an appropriate choice. As Karan observed, "*Parents are a better judge... I am aware of only the current trends. Parents see long-term benefits and have past knowledge...they know better where success lies.*"

Marriage partner selection. "Arun and Nisha want to get married to each other. But their parents are opposed to this marriage because they both belong to different castes. The parents feel that their children should get married within their own caste and to someone that their parents choose for them."

Mutual accommodation was the predominant strategy used. Marriage is a significant collective event in the Indian society and although dissipating in select regions of India, caste remains a strong criterion defining in-group and out-group with clear rules regarding who can and cannot marry. Even if education and economic status are becoming more important in present-day Indian society, given a choice, marriage within one's caste is preferred, especially if it is an arranged marriage where parents are actively involved in seeking a partner.

A typical response on part of adolescents and parents was that, "*The children will have to convince parents that there is nothing wrong in selecting their life partner because it is their life and they want an inter caste marriage; there is nothing wrong with it.*" Some adolescents also said that they would bring the prospective partner home to meet the parents so that they may be convinced of the appropriateness of their choice. Gender differences were most evident in this scenario with parents showing greater inclination to inquire more about the partner in case of a girl. A typical response was, "*We would like to see the boy, talk with him, and judge how he is. If education wise they match and he has a good career, only then we will give our permission.*" Another parent commented, "*The parent will evaluate the relationship based on various criteria like future prospects of the relationship, family background, career growth, qualification and the like. In case they find all this is okay then the children can go ahead, otherwise they should compromise (and not get married).*" For boys, however, parents felt it more important to "explain" to their sons about the adjustments that the boy and the family would need to make if the girl were from another caste.

Real Life Disagreements

Actual disagreements represent situations that adolescents commonly experience in the domains of academics and regulation of interpersonal activities and behavior. Illustrated below are disagreement dialogues related to choice of major subject, use of cell phone, and girl–boy friendship.

Amit, 17 years
Major Disagreement: Topic, Resolution, Reasoning
Theme: Choice of Major Subject

Can you think of a specific disagreement or difference of opinion that you have had recently with your parents?

Regarding studies is the main thing now. We have options between Math, Computers and Geography.

So actually I didn't want to take Math, but my parents forced me. They told me that in future you need to be proper in Math because in you will need Math in each and every stream. If we do MBA then Math will be there or if we do anything else Math will be there. So they forced me to take Math.

Who was more involved, your mother or father?

My mother; because as a teacher she asked her old students about what I should select. First of all I was interested in Computers, but my mother said you take Math.

So what actually happened?

When I got the form to fill the subject options that day my mother asked one of her previous students and one of her colleagues who has done commerce. He said let him take Math because Math is important. Even if he opts for any other stream Math will be included, for example, if I take MBA Finance then Math will be there. Computers we can do afterwards also, means after completing 12th. We can go for classes anywhere but for Math no one has separate classes. Actually I wanted to take Computers but she forced me to take Math.

What were your views/reactions?

I reacted okay I will take Math. I told that I will cope with it, but Math is not my cup of tea. Even though I practice regularly, I can't remember. When the question paper comes, I get tensed and even though I know the answer I write wrong things and that's why I lose marks in the exam. So, my mother said that even if you lose marks you have to take Math. I said okay but my decision was to take Computers.

What were the views/reactions of your parent?

She also said okay I know your decision is to take Computers but seeing that in the near future Math is going to be a major subject for you when you go to college or do MBA, it is better to take Math as it will be helpful. Computer will help you but only if you opt for Computer stream.

How was the difference of opinion/disagreement resolved? What was the outcome?

After 1 or 2 days after thinking a lot I said okay I will take Math. But after taking Math I will not be able to score that well. I will not score 90 in each and every exam so she said okay don't score 80 or 90, but get above 70. The average for me in Math is 70 only because above that I can't do it; every child has his own capacity. She said okay don't go below that or much above, but if you get above then that will be good. So I ended up taking Math. I ended up accommodating to my mother. The reason was that I thought okay I should listen to parents also, and go with their decision so that they will also be happy and I will also be happy.

At the same time, my parent also ended up accommodating to me. I was ready to take up Math although I was not very familiar with Math. She thought okay he has taken Math he has to do a lot of hard work and my father also said, I will teach him Math. That way I said okay it will be fine because my father has a good method of teaching so I was happy. She wanted I take Math and I took it. She was also happy. She felt that since I have taken Math so she should now help me so that I can do well.

Were you satisfied with the way the disagreement/issue was resolved? Why or why not? How did you feel?

I wasn't actually satisfied because the decision was made by my mother. So I was not okay with the decision. From my mother's viewpoint the decision was right, but from my side I wanted Computer subject. I am not interested in Math and we don't study for subjects in which we are not interested. But then I felt okay, the decision taken was right; it was in my mother's favor. The decision taken was helping me but it was against my wish.

Do you think your mother/father was satisfied with the way it was resolved? Why or why not? How did she/he feel?

Yes, she was satisfied because the decision was in her favor, and I also became a part of that decision. And she felt she had explained to me how things will work out so she felt I have understood and will work now. She felt good that the decision made by her was right.

Do you feel that there is a responsibility or obligation to accommodate in some way to what your parents wanted you to do in this situation or do you consider it your own business?

In this situation it was obviously my own business. First I have to study these subjects, not my parents so studying was done by me and what I had thought was that Computers will be easy for me and studying will be easy for me; Maths I generally don't prefer.

Do you feel that your parents have a responsibility or obligation to accommodate in some way to what you wanted to do in this situation? Explain.

Yes they also should equally think that the studying part has to be done by the child and not by them, so he has to choose what subjects he has to study. If he chooses the subjects that he likes only then can he study properly. If he doesn't like that subject he will generally not study that subject or he will not feel attached to that subject. She could also have understood me.

Do you consider it a minor or a major disagreement?

It was a major issue. This was important as it will influence my life afterwards. If I have chosen Maths in which I am disinterested, I will tend not to study. If I would have taken Computer subject I would naturally study that subject with great interest and put in a lot of hard work. Also, if I would have taken computers it would have helped in college.

Nidhi, 16 years
Minor Disagreement: Description, Resolution, Reasoning
Theme: Lending Cell Phone to Mother

Can you think of a specific disagreement or difference of opinion that you have had recently with your parents?

In fact just yesterday, I had my cell and my mom was going out of station and as she is a housewife she doesn't require a cell as landlines are there. So she wanted my cell for 3 days and I said no I can't give it to you. I said, anyways you don't need it as such you are going to grandpa's house, and you have a landline so I can give you a call anytime. Anyways Dad will join you in a day or two and he has a cell. So she said but why can I not have your cell; so I said you can always have it, you can use it anytime it is always at home. Whenever you are going somewhere locally I can give it to you, but I can't give it for 3 days, I am sorry. She was like what is so special, I mean what is wrong in it that you can't give me. I said nothing wrong but I am not willing to give it to you. Everything was fine I went to tuitions that day and everything. But she was angry with me and when she went to the station, Dad went to drop her and Dad just called up and said mom wants to talk to you. So I said okay fine. I said sorry and I was like I am sorry I didn't give you my cell and please understand from my view, I am really sorry. She said it's okay but the way you refused to give it to me was not right. I said sorry and she excused me.

What were your views/reactions?

My reaction was horrible. I know I made a mistake, I said no. I was like please Mom I can't give, I don't want any arguments on this.

Why did you react in this way?

I don't know…seriously I regretted that why didn't I give her the phone. It was just an intuition that I felt I can't give her the cell, not for 3 days.

What were the views/reactions of your parent?

She was extremely angry and she rang up Dad immediately and she was like what is your girl up to, she is not giving me the cell, and it is all because of you, you don't scold her, and she has become so dominating and pampered. After 10 min it cooled down.

Why did he/she react in this way?

She felt I am not giving her importance, she is my Mom and I am not giving her importance. I can't lend her my cell for 3 days. Just a little thing and she made a chaos.

How was the difference of opinion/disagreement resolved? What was the outcome?

I was after my mom saying that I am sorry, I am sorry. She finally gave in… you know Moms they are sweethearts; they finally agree with you, they are really nice. She was also like it's alright but don't do this to me again. I was literally sorry from my heart and I felt I had done something wrong.

So in a way I ended up accommodating or giving in to my parent's concerns because I felt that I was wrong, absolutely wrong and I did a very wrong thing by telling her that so that's the reason. And my parent also ended up accommodating because I had just said a few sorry's and she said it's okay. She was very good about that. She didn't contradict much, and it was like it's okay so I feel she is much better than me.

Were you satisfied with the way the disagreement/issue was resolved? Why or why not? How did you feel?

First see I was not at all satisfied, but slowly I realized she was right and I was wrong. Yes, I was satisfied because you do wrong and your parents forgive you, what else do you want. I felt bad with the way I reacted because they are the ones who are giving us all these things, these facilities and we are the ones who are telling them not to use it. They are the ones who are paying for this, education, cell phone and I said no to them – the ones who are supplying. That was absolutely wrong.

Do you think your mother/father was satisfied with the way it was resolved? Why or why not? How did she/he feel?

She was satisfied because somehow she was also convinced that I am not wrong. At this age teens do get hyper about some little things and she understood that. And she never wanted to get into conflicts and all because you know it's bad to get into conflicts and it's better to resolve things in a better way, so there was understanding from both ends. She was feeling at that moment that I am portraying her wrong and as if she does not have any right over me. She was frowning as if she would kill me. After the resolution I did talk to her yesterday, she was in her usual mood, very good, very pleasing, very caring.

Do you feel that there is a responsibility or obligation to accommodate in some way to what your parents wanted you to do in this situation or do you consider it your own business?

I think it is none of my business right at this age as they are my parents. I consider they know better for me what is good and what is not. Sometimes they can be fussy but it's not always the case. So I may not agree at that moment but later on I do realize. It was nothing personal that I should have kept the cell or anything would have come out had I given it to her. I could have given her without any problem.

Do you feel that your parents have a responsibility or obligation to accommodate in some way to what you wanted you to do in this situation? Explain

At that moment I had told her I can't give you my cell, it's my personal cell and that was wrong... it's not personal, she is my mom and she can use it whenever she needs it and she has been using it and I have never objected on that part, but yesterday I did. Yeah, may be somewhere somehow I did wrong. I mean parents are a bit tensed about their children and worry that they might choose a wrong path, so maybe something may have come to her mind and she revolted against me. The way she reacted should have been less intense, I feel she over reacted. I mean keeping herself in my place she should have realized what kind of a person I am... I would not go on any wrong track. And generally she is satisfied with me. When anyone says your daughter might have done this she always disagrees with them... she says, oh she can't, I know her better. When she is so confident about me then where was that confidence now?

Do you consider it a minor or a major disagreement?

The issue was minor because it came and it went. Some part of realization from my side and some part of understanding from her side. So I was satisfied that I realized I did wrong. And the conflict ended in just one day.

Abhay, 17 years
Major Disagreement: Description, Resolution, Reasoning
Topic: Texting/SMS

Can you think of a specific disagreement or difference of opinion that you have had recently with your parents?

This was not an instantaneous disagreement; it was about sending SMS. It went on for days. I would SMS in breaks or at night. When at night you are really bored and when you have to be awake late in the night to study then it is like a company and we can communicate if even he/she is 3 kms away. My mom wasn't very happy about my messaging. I was like I am studying and it helps me stay awake. This went on till my sim card expired. And they said no recharge. It happened last week. No recharge was two weeks ago and for 1 week I lavishly spent whatever money I had. Now, no sending SMS.

What were your views/reactions?

I had this sim card and I would SMS and then that also went away, and in between there was a period when I had no mobile... then the recent one came in. She (mother) saw me messaging and I saw the whole thing coming and it was not a shock, I was ready for it and was bracing for it, and was knowing it will stop one day. It was a surprise as it wasn't in my mind that she would just walk away and say no more.

What were the views/reactions of your parent?

We have four phones at home right now—a Vodafone phone, a BSNL, an Airtel post-paid and an Airtel prepaid. The sum of all this was an enormous amount. So, my dad said drop one phone. My dad had a post-paid as he goes to the office and he needs it. He has a job at a pipeline and he has to work in places where there is no network but only cell phones work. We have two landlines and numbers that we have given to people; so the only connection that can be cancelled is my prepaid. So, that was the first reason and the second reason was maybe the result of my SMS sending spree.

How was the difference of opinion/disagreement resolved? What was the outcome?

I just put my head down and said that's about it. Although it wasn't something big but it was important, it was fun, it was full time entertainment and a great way to stay in touch with your friends and other people out of India and in India. It's quick, it's cheap. Yes it was a disappointment that it was gone. The disagreement was more like it was something passive. It was a passive resistance me giving up the phone and she trying to stop me from messaging. It was a disagreement stretched for a long period of time with an abrupt end.

I ended up accommodating to my parents. I just put my head down and said you want it so I do it! There was only little arguing and stuff because it would lead to a fight and that was just after my first term result and it wasn't the best time to revolt. Things are not going my way. They want it and let them have.

My parents also ended up accommodating a little because they let me SMS through their post-paid a little. Once in a while I pick up the phone and SMS.

Were you satisfied with the way the disagreement/issue was resolved? Why or why not? How did you feel?

Not at all, they would have limited messaging hours, they could have compromised. But it was abrupt stop. I felt really bad. Next day my friend came and said "why didn't you reply last night?" I was like what the hell would I reply!

Do you think your mother/father was satisfied with the way it was resolved? Why or why not? How did she/he feel?

Yes because I don't sms anymore; according to her I am only studying. In fact I am only studying. According to her I didn't really pay much attention when I was sending SMS, according to her it may be good for me to just stop this. She was feeling good.

Do you feel that there is a responsibility or obligation to accommodate in some way to what your parents wanted you to do in this situation or do you consider it your own business?

In this case I certainly feel it was my responsibility to accommodate, as it is a very important year for me. It's something that not only I want, but my parents, my friends want and this is something I have been prepared for last 11 years by my parents. Every time they must have helped me in something they might have thought this might be useful for me in next few years. Then of course they want to see me doing well and that's why I think this year being such an important year it's my responsibility to accommodate to their way.

Do you feel that your parents have a responsibility or obligation to accommodate in some way to what you wanted to do in this situation? Explain.

Yeah, she could have had a pact or compromised that you can sms from 9 to 10 or that sort or 9 to 11 or I give you at 11 pm and then till you sleep you can have it.

Do you consider it a minor or a major disagreement?

Major. I sort of really enjoyed messaging, it was a great way to stay in touch and stay awake. It's a lot less cumbersome than taking a phone and dialing up. One thing leads to the other and leads to the other in a phone call, whereas in SMS, "do you have a test tomorrow or not?" full stop. It's cheap, what else do you want? I pay 30 bucks for a month and everything is free.

Seema, 17 years
Minor Disagreement: Description, Resolution, Reasoning
Theme: Girl–Boy Friendship

Can you think of a specific disagreement or difference of opinion that you have had recently with your parents?

Recently my friend (a boy) used to call me. My parents were very concerned that why is he calling so much and all. My mom and I then had a fight on this, did not fight exactly but she was dissatisfied that why is he calling and all. So they don't have that much faith in me. At a certain time I argued. This happened recently and my mom thought he is my boyfriend or something. He calls me every evening. He called me at 5:00 p.m. once and we talked for 1 hour and my mom was angry. She got suspicious and I said he is just a friend. She asked whether he is my boyfriend or what. She then listened to me, whatever I say she trusts me. It's not that she doesn't, she was not against me.

What were your views/reactions?

First of all I tried to explain to her that there is nothing like that, and seriously nothing of the sort was there. Later on she was like okay she listened to me but if there will be too many calls then she will be like that na (no). My sister also had a boyfriend recently and she came to know about this; they are more careful and conservative so they didn't want me to be in any relationship.

What were the views/reactions of your parent?

She was feeling a little insecure and she told Dad that I talk on the phone a lot in the evening. Later on my father and I had a talk in the night. So he said you should avoid being in a relationship. She thought that I was doing something wrong. I was going around with somebody and she didn't like it.

How was the difference of opinion/disagreement resolved? What was the outcome?

So I just told her there is nothing like that. I told him (my friend) also not to call so much, so now he doesn't. I ended up accommodating to my parent's concerns. Mainly they were concerned about me that I should not get into a relationship. Later on I still talked for a long time sometimes. In a way I did accommodate a little.

My parents also ended up accommodating to me a little. I thought they will not react in such a way but they did. I thought they will not think about such things and they will listen to me. I thought they will not lose trust in me. But somewhat they did not come up to my expectations. They didn't talk about this, they don't have problems with me and now it's okay, they don't mind if we talk. He calls but they don't have a problem. They are concerned about me; they now know that there is nothing like that. They don't have a problem if I talk but they have a problem when I talk a lot.

Were you satisfied with the way the disagreement/issue was resolved? Why or why not? How did you feel?

Yes because now they are not putting any restrictions, they are allowing me to talk and act in a manner I want to and they don't have a problem. It was not a serious issue. I felt good. Because many parents put so many restrictions on their child, for example, they will not allow any calls, or they won't allow to go to parties. But my parents are very broad-minded.

Do you think your mother/father was satisfied with the way it was resolved? Why or why not? How did she/he feel?

Yes, she didn't have a lot of problem, but she did mind me talking to that boy; mainly she was afraid that we will have a relationship. I have decreased the span of talking now. She is feeling good, she doesn't complain now as much as she used to earlier.

Do you feel that there is a responsibility or obligation to accommodate in some way to what your parents wanted you to do in this situation or do you consider it your own business?

It is not my own business. I think my mom will be concerned as I am her daughter, she will be concerned with what is right for me. She was not satisfied with what I was doing. She respected my views also when I said we are just friends. Yes, it was my responsibility to accommodate as I am her daughter and I always respect her views. She is my mother after all. She is always telling me this… and she is more experienced.

Do you feel that your parents have a responsibility or obligation to accommodate in some way to what you wanted you to do in this situation? Explain

No, because she is concerned about me and it is my mother's responsibility to guide me. Yeah, in a way yes because now I am growing up, even I can decide what is right and wrong. So even she should adjust to my views sometimes.

Do you consider it a minor or a major disagreement?

Minor, because it happens in everyone's house.

Accommodation and Reasoning Used During Disagreements

As illustrated in the dialogues, the resolution process involves varying degrees of accommodation by adolescents and parents. Across disagreements, adolescents accommodated more than parents. Appendix E presents the descriptive statistical results related to the degree of accommodation by adolescent and parent during situations of disagreement, and the considerations regarded as important for the same. The salient themes for adolescent and parent accommodation are discussed in the following section.

Adolescent Accommodation to Parents

Role-related duty and obligation to accommodate. Respect and acceptance of parental role-related authority and a duty to monitor and advise the adolescent, and in turn, the adolescent's social-moral duty to accommodate to the parent are significant considerations. Across disagreements, especially the ones related to studies and regulation of behavior and activities, adolescents believed that it was their responsibility as children to accommodate to parents. Namrata, 18 years, expresses in relation to a disagreement regarding buying a two-wheeler, *"Being my parents they have full right to tell and guide what I am supposed to do. Actually its 70% their business, but 30% mine as well."* Similarly, 17-year-old Simran observes, *"Yeah, I feel it's my responsibility to accommodate because she is my mother, we have such a bonding between us, she loves me and I love her. Also, I am their kid and they are my parents, so there will always be an obligation on my part to adjust to them."* In some cases adolescents felt that accommodating to parents is a way to reciprocate what their parents have done for them. More girls feel that they have a responsibility to accommodate to parents, suggesting greater cooperativeness and empathy on their part.

Faith in parents' experience and concern for child's welfare Adolescents are inclined to accommodate to parents as they have faith in parents' experience and their intention of doing what is in the best interest of the child. Pranay, 16 years, shares, *"She always cares about me; she always thinks about me first before herself, she always tries to sacrifice for me, for my welfare. She loves me very much… she also scolds me for not studying or something like that but she loves me and she will always stand by me for whatever I want.*" Adolescents firmly believe that parents are "more experienced" and "more learned" than the adolescent, and hence they know better. Amit reasons, "*First I was angry that due to generation gap my parents are not allowing me to go to the party, but when I thought calmly I found that they were right. Next day my friends were tired and were not attentive in the class, I felt that my parents were thinking for my good. In a way, it was good not to go to the party. I was quite attentive in the class and I could answer almost all the questions and this way I felt not going to the party helped me in the class by paying more attention and answering in the class.*" There is also the feeling that parents need not accommodate to them, as it is their (parents') prerogative to decide what is in the best interest of the child and regulate adolescents' behavior accordingly. Girls tend to be more forthcoming in recognizing their own fault in a situation. Renita, 17 years, notes, "*No, my mom should not accommodate, as I was wrong but she cannot be, she is older than me so she will do whatever is right.*" And Ishita, 17 years, comments, "*I don't think it is my mother's responsibility to accommodate because she is elder to me and she knows what is good for me and what is not; and if it's not good for me why should she accommodate to me?*"

Sensitivity and concern for parents. The concern about one's behavior or actions causing hurt and unhappiness to the parents is deeply ingrained in adolescents. Hence, even though they may not be convinced about parents' opinion, they may act in accordance with it. In the words of Keyur, 18 years, "*Because I thought okay I should also listen to them, stay with their decision only so that they will also be happy and I will also be happy. So I said okay, the decision that you are taking is also right and I will go with that decision only.*" Adolescents' interpersonal sensitivity in their relationship with parents is thus evident, which in turn enhances their capacity to take the parents' perspective.

Adolescents' accommodation to parents is thus purposeful, based on deliberate reflection; there is little evidence of it being a consequence of parental control or coercion, except perhaps in matters such as coming back home at a certain time or devoting adequate time for studies. In fact, adolescents expect and accept parents to impose such rules, and although they may complain about it, they reflect a sensitive understanding of why it may be necessary for the parent to act in a certain manner. The common thread running through the reasoning process is the adolescents' perception that it is their moral duty and responsibility to accommodate to the parent.

Parent Accommodation to Adolescent and Adolescent Self-assertion

The active participation of adolescents in influencing parental authority and glimpses of autonomy is revealed in the parallel perception that parents should also accommodate to the adolescent. Karan, 18 years, reasons, "*See, dad has got certain principles that he follows at each step in life. Well at my age we can't be restricted to the principles and rules that come from parents. When we deviate from these rules we begin to form our own principles, frame our own rules, which cannot be done by our dads. Then the way we look at a situation becomes very different. We have a more liberal outlook whereas my Dad has a stricter outlook so that's where the gap comes in."*

Insistence on parental accommodation is justified if the wish or demand in question is occasionally expressed or if it is rather intense. Sixteen-year-old Meghna describes, *"About a week ago it was my best friend's birthday and I really wanted to go to her party. My Dad said it was too far away. The place was too far away and my Dad had a very important meeting, and he couldn't drop me and there was no other way I could reach there. He did not allow me to go with either of my friends neither did he let me go alone. A birthday comes once in a year, that too of a very good friend, so for me it was a major issue."*

Parents' accommodation is also desired in matters that the adolescent considers as one's own business. These include choice of career stream, choices related to personal grooming (dressing or hair style), or engaging in an activity in which the adolescent is not interested but compelled by the parent (such as attending singing classes or learning to skate), or the other way around, that is, the adolescent may be interested but the parent feels otherwise. Boys are more inclined to think that parents should accommodate because according to them they (adolescents) were "right" in a given situation.

Instances of self-oriented reasoning and assertion are evident in adolescents' support of the stance that the issue in question is one's own business. The following quotes illustrate this sentiment.

Simran, 17 years: *You see, my mom has such a nature—I mean all moms have this nature of guiding us, pushing us toward the right direction, showing us what is wrong and what is right. So a point comes when you feel you can manage by yourself and you don't need that constant pushing and guiding, you can decide certain things for yourself. So many times I feel I am also correct and she is also correct but neither of us can explain what we mean or think to each other and so there is a communication gap.*

Vivek, 17 years: *A person needs freedom in matters of career. It is a personal decision to think for yourself… to plan for your future. Even I know what is good for me; I am not a child anymore.*

Manish, 16 years: *Even they should accommodate, because it's after all my life and like trying to be a person the way others want you to become does not make a successful life. Of course, it's their duty to guide… I mean like 70% as I say it's their duty. But then they should accommodate also. They should take my point of view into consideration and then it's up to them to accommodate or not.*

Gopika, 17 years: *I feel that parents and me, both should look into the matter as I have to go for the school trip; so they should listen to me once at least. If they think it is right then only they should let me go and if they think it makes sense. But not listening to me and just deciding that you don't have to go means don't have to go! She (mother) didn't even see the school circular; she just said "no" means "no." At least, first they should listen to me and then they should decide what they should do. They should help me out with that. It's my life and I should get the chance to enjoy. They have had their school life and they did what they wanted and now they are stopping me from doing that and I don't feel it is right.*

Nidhi, 16 years: *My parents then did allow me to go for garba* (dancing during Navratri– a popular festival in Gujarat) *for the last 7 days. See, you cannot force any person completely to do anything in one's life. Like after all, it's a person's life. Like if you have to drive someone else's car and hold someone else's steering wheel then the only thing that happens is an accident!*

Patterns of Resolution Across Interpersonal Disagreements

Across the disagreement scenarios, hypothetical and real, both parents and adolescents primarily use the process of mutual accommodation to deal with disagreements. Gender plays a significant role in certain scenarios such as mixed group weekend picnic, marriage partner selection, and friendship with a boy. Parents' active input is more evident in such instances perhaps as these concern romantic and intimate relationships with significant short- and long-term implications. The concern is with regard to protection of sexuality and the social reputation of the girl and thereby the family. Marriage is a family affair in the Indian cultural context, and hence approval of parents is vital. However, both parents and adolescents favor the adolescent's perspective more in relation to personally consequential issues such as career choice and marriage, yet again indicating the increasing space to exercise adolescent choice. Adolescent self-assertion is particularly evident in career decisions. Although there is openness to seek parents' advice if necessary, imposition of parents' views meets with much dissatisfaction.

The primary tendency in all disagreement scenarios is to engage in negotiation and discussion toward resolving the issue. Adolescents express respect for parents, and firmly believe that parents have their best interest in mind and that one needs to listen to them by virtue of their age, experience, knowledge, and wisdom. The deference that they show to parents stems largely from their sensitive outlook rather than power assertion by parents. In fact, assertion of authority without offering any explanation elicits resentment. Parents on their part may "put their foot down" as far as some situations are concerned, yet they are also inclined to take into consideration the adolescent's perspective. This demonstrates the growing tendency of parents in the urban middle class to adopt flexible approaches to child rearing and "change with the times." "*My children should remain happy, and that is where my happiness lies,*" is the parents' *mantra* along with the concern that the adolescents may not accept the parents' views readily or unquestioningly so it is better to accommodate rather than to create unpleasantness and perhaps strain the relationship.

Adolescents express more satisfaction in instances when parents offer reasonable explanation leading to adolescents' understanding of their perspective, in turn facilitating mutual accommodation. This outlook yet again indicates a rejection of unilateral authority, emphasizing the desire for a more pliable attitude. Adolescents also express satisfaction when they feel that parents have understood their perspective and cooperated with them. Ronak, 16 years, says, "*I am satisfied with the outcome because although they felt otherwise, I explained to them that going to school (during the period of exam preparation) is just a waste of time; rather I sit at home and complete the course; and my parents understood my problem and accordingly they thought that what I was saying is right.*"

A shift in outlook toward hierarchical authority from unquestioned compliance to a more democratic approach, with an expectation of understanding from the parent is also evident from the dissatisfaction that adolescents express with the way an issue is resolved. Dissatisfaction was evident when parents compelled adolescents to follow their (parents') decision and adolescents had to concede unwillingly, even though out of respect for parents. Renita, 17 years, explains, "*I felt bad that she (mother) never tried to understand me. If I wanted to go for a movie, she should have allowed me to go. She just said I cannot go!*" What dissatisfies the adolescents most is the feeling that their parents did not understand their perspective and compelled them to follow what they (parents) thought was right. In the same vein, 18-year-old Karan remarks, "*Because they didn't agree to my viewpoints partially also, not even 1% they agreed to my viewpoint, and I had to agree to their view point 100%; so I think that was unfair on their behalf that they didn't agree to my viewpoint.*"

Overall, adolescents experience greater satisfaction with the resolution when they understand the parent's perspective and when there is mutual accommodation between adolescents and parents. Some adolescents acknowledge that they realize that parents always think about the adolescent's welfare and benefit, and this is what satisfies them, irrespective of whether their wish is fulfilled or not in that particular instance. In this vein, some adolescents feel dissatisfied when they follow their own wish disregarding parent's opinion. They express guilt about disobeying, upsetting, or behaving rudely with parents (e.g., showing defiance toward parent's opinion either overtly or covertly, like not having lunch or dinner with family). Tejas, 17 years, gives an example, "*After mother scolded me to switch off the TV, I just gave her that look and continued to watch. I should have told her that I know when I have to go inside, but I did not. I was feeling bad that I did not explain to my Mom but gave her the cold look.*" Regret and guilt were especially evident when the adolescents realized their mistake. Rarely are adolescents satisfied when they go ahead with their own wish, despite parents disagreeing with the same, even if they may think they are right in that situation. Such a situation evokes guilt regarding hurting and upsetting parents by not obeying them. Anuj, 17 years, in relation to an issue regarding a girl that he was seeing expresses, "*I was not satisfied because my views were not considered and I was also feeling bad because I lied to her that now I am not going out with the girl.*" The most acceptable approach is one where each party attempts to dialogue and share one's own point of view, with an intention to understand and accommodate to the other.

The interpretations that adolescents attach to the issue of disagreement and the reasoning that they offer reveal the core elements that guide the parent–adolescent

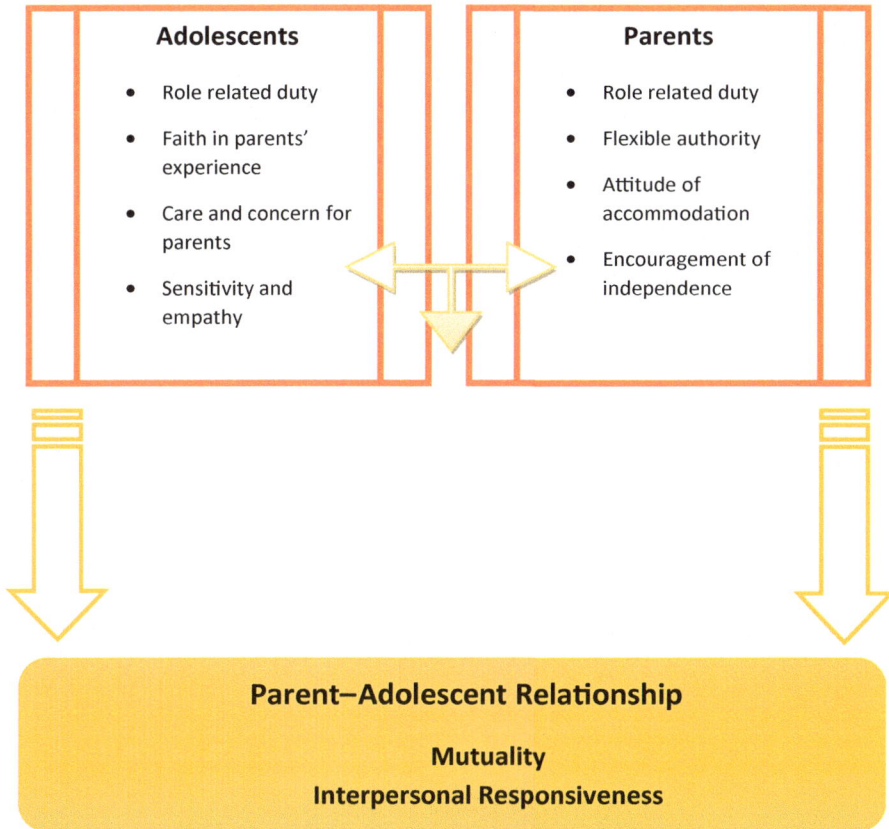

Fig. 4.2 Parent–adolescent relationship: Defining elements

relationship. Figure 4.2 presents the defining elements of the parent–adolescent relationship in the urban middle class context.

Overall, the parent–adolescent relationship depicts mutuality, with both parties trying their best to understand the other's perspective and integrating flexibility in the resolution process. The resolution process and reasoning across episodes of disagreement reveal the adolescents' capacity for empathy, an aspect that has received little research attention. The core values of mutual care and concern, and adolescents' respect for parents and faith in their experience and attention to the adolescent's well-being emerge as the core factors that shape the relationship. Equally, the changing dynamics of the relationship are also evinced. With reference to authority, the pattern is seen to be changing in the present times with parenting and socialization processes revealing a shift away from a unilateral outlook characterized by unarguable submission to a perspective that suggests the diluting of the traditional hierarchical authority-oriented relationship between parent and child. Adolescents expect that parents should not only fulfill their traditional role of a guardian and a provider, but should also try to "understand" them, which is a relatively new expectation from an Indian parent, one that shifts away from the traditional hierarchical model and cultural norm. Further, the approach and reasoning also reflect select elements of parental support for autonomy (Marbell 2014) such as perspective taking on part of parents, listening to children's views on an issue, consultative decision making which involves taking into consideration the adolescent's wish, and an overall environment that allows for mutual exchange of views. In general, the prevailing tendency on part of both adolescents and parents is to try to understand each other and to accommodate to each other's perspectives, either fully or partially.

References

Larson, R. W. (2002). Globalization, societal change, and new technologies: What they mean for the future of adolescence. *Journal of Research on Adolescence, 12*(1), 1–30.

Marbell, K. N. (2014). *Encouraging autonomy in a collectivist culture: Examining parental autonomy support in Ghana and the moderating effect of children's self-construal.* Retrieved from http://gradworks.proquest.com/3642806.pdf.

McElhaney, K. B., & Allen, J. P. (in press). Sociocultural perspectives on adolescent autonomy. In P. Kerig, M. Schulz, & S. T. Hauser (Eds.), *Adolescence and beyond.* Oxford University Press.

Omer, H., Steinmetz, S. G., Carthy, T., & Schlippe, A. (2013). The anchoring function: Parental authority and the parent-child bond. *Family Process, 52*(2), 193–206. doi:10.1111/famp.12019.

Saraswathi, T. S., & Pai, S. (1997). Socialization in the Indian context. In D. Sinha & H. S. R. Kao (Eds.), *Asian perspectives on psychology* (pp. 74–92). New Delhi: Sage.

Schlegel, A., & Barry, H., III. (1991). *Adolescence: An anthropological inquiry.* New York: Free Press.

Chapter 5
Uncertainties, Insecurities, and Worries: The Bane of Globalization

Abstract The intricacies of present-day social change, particularly globalization, and the impact on young individuals, have been discussed in the previous chapters. Adolescents today are required to navigate not just one culture embedded in one context, but multiple cultures and multiple contexts. The frame is vibrant and appealing, yet simultaneously uncertain and fluctuating. This chapter discusses the challenges and risks of globalization as these intervene in the everyday lives of adolescents and parents. It begins with an overview of globalization as interplay of opportunities and risks. The subsequent sections discuss the major insecurities and anxieties that adolescents and parents experience across domains.

Keywords Adolescents · Globalization · Insecurities · Anxieties · Gender

Globalization: Interplay of Opportunities and Risks

The present context is offering myriad, old, and new developmental pathways, presenting thereby opportunities as well as risks. Young individuals from urban upper middle class families are at the forefront of technological and cultural changes set in motion by globalization, and at the same time vulnerable to the challenges and risks that the phenomenon unfolds. As discussed in Chap. 1, globalization elicits both positive and negative outcomes. Positive outcomes include increased exposure to new ideas, new opportunities, and quality of life, whereas negative outcomes may be in the form of breakdown of traditional values and customs, generational conflicts, and decreased predictability and control (Marsella 2012). Adolescents and parents are caught in a milieu laced by rising aspirations, ever-increasing desires for individual achievement, and growing competition. The complexities of globalization and the multiple new developments surfacing at a brisk pace are urging young individuals to engage in rethinking and revising, especially their sense of identity (Bourn 2008). Jensen and Arnett (2012) use John Berry's concept of acculturation to explain young individuals' adaptation to the globalizing world. Berry's model outlines four possible patterns of

© Springer (India) Pvt. Ltd. 2017
S. Kapadia, *Adolescence in Urban India*,
DOI 10.1007/978-81-322-3733-4_5

acculturation; (1) Assimilation: where one rejects original cultural identity and embraces a new identity, (2) Separation: where greater value is placed on one's original culture, avoiding contact with the new culture, (3) Integration: where original cultural identity is combined with the new culture, and (4) Marginalization: where there is little interest in maintaining one's own culture, at the same time rejecting the new culture. In the context of globalization, assimilation may occur in countries with rapid socioeconomic changes, and young individuals may find local cultural patterns of little use, and prefer to embrace the global culture. The concept of "culture shedding," which means unlearning that which is no longer appropriate, is applicable here. Separation is likely to occur for people whose culture is being really impacted, but they prefer the local culture and resist the global culture. Integration implies the development of a global identity and the desire to belong to the global culture, a phenomenon that is greatly facilitated by communication technology. At the same time, local identity is retained and actively manifested in everyday behavior and interactions. An example is the continuity of the cultural practice of consulting family elders for any major life decision (marriage, job change) in the Indian society. Also relevant here is the degree and nature of change in local cultures themselves, and the extent of discrepancy between the local and global cultures. Young individuals are thus caught in a multilevel and multidimensional change cycle which may lead to the development of a bicultural or even a hybrid identity that integrates local and global elements in new ways. Notwithstanding the form of acculturation, a fallout of the global changes is cultural identity confusion.

The urban upper middle class context in India is hovering on the threshold of integration as a way of acculturating to the transforming society. Research with Indian-immigrant populations across the Indian diaspora has shown that Indians have a tendency for bicultural functioning (e.g., Juthani 1992). Although integration may be best adapted to global changes, the identity confusion, the myriad choices, and the increasing competition and comparisons in all walks of life are likely to affect not only adolescents, but parents as well.

Although parental interest and involvement in adolescents' lives are observed across societies, the intensity is perhaps much stronger and obvious in Indian families. The mixed bag of opportunities as well as insecurities and anxieties emanating from the global influences renders much complexity to the scenario and creates the likelihood of anxiety and stress for both adolescents and parents. Parents appreciate the advantages of globalization in terms of better education and career opportunities, including the easier access to education abroad, improved job prospects, greater likelihood of traveling to distant places occasions, and an overall environment of possibilities. At the same time, they are equally conscious and wary of the negative fallouts. A mother's comment on her understanding of globalization is rather telling of the anxiety and insecurity that they experience. *"The things which should not come up are happening in today's world and I guess that is globalization. 'Vinash najik avi rahyo che' (destruction is nearing)."*

The major insecurities that impinge upon adolescents and parents comprise short-term everyday matters and issues with long-term implications. On the face of it, some of the everyday issues seem trivial; however, when these persist and if these carry much meaning for the adolescent or the parent, there is anxiety and stress. Vogli (2004) has put forth a framework to understand the link between globalization and stress. According to this framework, rapid change is likely to influence social and economic uncertainty such as job insecurity and related loss of resources like health insurance. Individuals engage in primary appraisals of the situation such as fear of inability to support family in case of job loss, as well as secondary appraisal, for example, assessing adaptive capacities to cope with the situation. Effects on physical and psychological health follow. The model can be applied to parents and adolescents in contemporary India to draw out the dynamics of anxieties and insecurities that they experience across domains such as scholastic achievement, issues of privacy in the face of new technology, the phenomenon of social comparisons, renewed generation gap, romantic interests, peer influences, and gender issues. These are discussed in the following sections.

Fixation on Scholastic Achievement:
Will the Adolescent Make the Cut?

Adolescents' scholastic achievement, a quintessential developmental task in urban India, features as a primary source of anxiety for the adolescent, and perhaps even more for the parents. As mentioned in Chap. 3, it is also an aspect that renders vulnerability to this developmental phase. In terms of Vogli's (2004) framework, the multiple options and opportunities of globalization are bringing about intense competition in getting admission in a particular educational field or a specific college. The intense anxiety that surrounds academic performance during the XIIth standard is rationalized on the basis of it being the only means that will lead to a lucrative job and ultimately socioeconomic advancement. Primary appraisals related to this and thereby the decisions are long drawn out and guided by an uneven combination of the adolescent's interest, ability (or inability), the percentage that one secures in the XIIth standard, which is most important, well-intentioned advice from relatives and friends, and parents' financial status. One or the other factor may be prioritized depending on the situational contingencies. The repercussions, not only on the adolescent, but also the parents and the entire family whose reputation is tied to the adolescents' performance, are immense. As discussed in Chap. 3, much apprehension occurs, and it peaks especially around the board exams. This often results in psychological health issues such as depression and even the tendency toward suicide. It is not uncommon to read newspaper accounts of adolescent suicide around the exam period or when the results are about to be announced or have already been announced.

Preparation for the board exams is like preparing to run a marathon, with parents running side by side holding the baton. The entire family, relatives, and even neighbors are heavily invested in this venture and do all they can to facilitate the prized goal of scoring maximum percentage. Studies with school students have reported the impact that academic stress has on adolescent mental health. For example, a mental health survey of 150 educational institutions in New Delhi found that 40% students feel overwhelmed by exams, whereas another study reported that 57% students were depressed, and 9% had considered suicide because of academia stress (Pasmantier 2005). In a time-use study with mid-adolescents, Verma et al. (2002) found that girls spent more time in school than boys, and generally schoolwork, especially homework, generated negative subjective states such as low affect state, below-average activation levels, lowered feeling of choice, and higher social anxiety. Lower educational achievement has emerged as one of the reasons that drives youth into depression and suicide (the others being substance abuse, violence, and poor reproductive and sexual health) (Pillai et al. cited in David 2013); in fact, suicide is the second leading cause of death in both genders (David 2013). Not only the pressure from parents and family, but also the schools and tuition classes further exacerbate the scenario. Schools and tuition classes vie with each other to publicize and "show-off" the results that their students have achieved, and in the process inflict even more pressure on the students. This is especially evident in newspaper advertisements of tuition classes soon after the board exams, with photographs of students who have secured the highest marks or are in the top five or ten in the city and state.

Parents pull out all the stops in their effort to enable the adolescent to achieve the highest percentage. The schedule of the entire family undergoes a change in the best interest of the adolescent's studies. Cutting off or reducing social engagements, TV viewing, and even taking time off from jobs are common occurrences during the board exams. The intention is to ensure that the adolescent maintains single-minded focus on studies. While such actions and inputs are appreciated, the downside is that these also increase the pressure to perform. Interwoven in these actions is the strong narrative of expectations for a certain percentage. As 18-year-old Pratik quips, "*All my parents are interested in is MARKS!*" Considering all that the parents are doing, which is often articulated by parents themselves, the adolescents feel pressured to secure a certain percentage, as pleasing their parents is the overriding concern.

Compounding adolescents' own anxieties regarding education and career is parental anxiety and pressure, sometimes even more so than what adolescents may experience. This is abundantly evident from adolescents' complaints about parental pressure and nagging related to studies. Hrithik 17 years, explains, "*In this age, major concern is our studies, it's our priority. It's a hectic schedule every day, and we cannot give 100% to it. We go to tuition and school. When we want to start studying, we cannot, though we try much. So major concern is we cannot study well. Another worry is that parents keep on pressurizing to remember. I get to hear at least once in a day that you are in 12th with science major. It feels like pressure. If I want to do anything beyond studies, this constant nagging stops me from doing so.*" Parents on their part justify this "nagging" as perceived by the adolescents, as necessary in order to keep the adolescent on the "study track," and prevent him or her from getting distracted. A mother expresses, "*Keyur is lazy, he is just not serious about his studies. These days there is a break in his tuition classes. So he says I need a break. And all day he keeps watching TV or playing cricket outside or sleeping. His argument is 'Anyways after a week I will have to study, so let me relax now'. See, my view is that he should make headway now so that it will help him later. He is also not sure what he wants to do later. His father gets upset too. He says, with this attitude, what will Keyur do in his life? Kya dekhega humko, kaise support karega? (How will he look after us, support the family?).*" In the same vein another mother shares, "*Anuj is obsessed with 'screens,' be it TV, computer, tablet, or cellphone! Ek var screen same aavi jaye etle time nu bhan na rahe. (Once he is in front of a screen, he just does not pay heed to time). I always worry about his studies getting neglected. So need to keep pushing him. He of course has his arguments. He complains, 'Aakho divas shu bhan bhan karvanu? Mare pan entertainment joiye. Hu thaki javu chu. Karu shu? Tamne mara upar vishwas nathi —trust nathi. Hun kari laish' (What is this study, study all day? I too need entertainment! I get tired. What do I do? You do not have faith in me. I shall do it— studying).*"

Running parallel to these considerations are one's own insecurities and doubts related to scoring the marks that will enable them to get admission in the desired educational stream. The stress on boys is especially high. Kunal, 16 years who has just completed his XIIth standard board exams shares, "*It is more important for me as a boy to get good marks so that I get into BCA (Bachelor's in Computer Applications) and then I can do my Master's and later perhaps go abroad and get further education, and then a good job. Being a boy, I am responsible to support the family and keep the family reputation positive, so even though education and career are important for girls, for boys it is a mandatory requirement. There is constant pressure that in the long run you have to earn for the family, and for that, being conscious about life decisions is important. Being free of fear regarding my decisions is also a concern. So, there is more pressure in that way. I got 65% marks, which is not that good. I scored more in subjects like English but less in scoring subjects such as Math; but let me see how I do in the BCA entrance exam...*"

The multiplicity of new emerging careers presents a double bind. On the one hand, the scenario offers new opportunities and choices, thereby accommodating myriad and varying individual interests, yet on the other hand, the scenario instills a sense of confusion and insecurity in the adolescents. "*About me, at present I don't know which field to go into. We don't have an idea about how our life would unfold on choosing a particular field. We don't know the scope of that field. Every year something new is added or changed in each course, so the scope also changes. If we study any course now, which has less scope and value in future, then it is useless to choose such a course. There is fear always about the future. What if I have made a wrong choice in my career?*" worries Pooja, 17 years.

Adolescents are aware of the increasing competition and fear that they may not be able to enter the career of their choice or create their own distinct identity as far as career is concerned. Ankit, 17 years shares, "*One worry is definitely related to education. Because the world is becoming so competitive and as everyone wants to have a good career, I am worried whether I will also able to compete with others and make my own career, which will provide me my own identity."* In this vein, Nikhil says, *"My first worry is to not be able to achieve my goal, which is to become a successful businessman. If I don't succeed in that then it would hurt me."* Girls too harbor similar anxieties. Ritu, 16 years asserts, *"We have to make our aim successful. So there's tension that if we do not get admission in this field, in this college, what will happen. It is said that life is a race; we have to keep running to get success in our aim. There is a fear whether that aim will be successful or not."*

Further, parents' interventions in adolescents' career choice are also a cause of frustration. While some involvement in terms of suggestions and discussion is welcome, imposition of parents' views is what annoys adolescents. Eighteen-year-old Arpita explains, *"My mother insisted that I should go for engineering. I was not for it. But she said it is better than doing XIIth standard. So I took admission. But in the second year itself I started to get so bored. I did not say anything to my mother. Now in the third year I told her that I just do not like it. Actually, I am interested in music—playing the flute. Finally, my mother understood. But see, I wasted three years and now I will get admission in music which was always my first choice. I hope I get it."* Similarly, Jasmine who has just completed her XIIth says, *I got 89% in XIIth. My parents are keen that I do MBBS but I do not want to. I would rather do scientific research. So I am applying for admission in a research institute. Just because I got good percentage in certain subjects does not mean I like these. Anyone can get good marks by studying hard for a few months. My parents feel that becoming a doctor is better—it has more scope and status. Also for girls, it is better than engineering, because girls need to manage house and family as well."* Correspondingly, Jasmine's mother shares her views. *"She has done very well in 12th standard and from childhood she feels like I want to do something different and we want to support her. Right now, we want her to take the medical field but she is rejecting it, she says that she wants to go in the research field. Where I work the people advise me that it is very difficult to get a job in a research field. Her father is very much interested in her doing MBBS; he will be very happy. She argues so we said yeah it is ok, but still inside us we feel that it is good if she does MBBS. It has more status. Also since she is a girl, we have to think more carefully. If it is a boy, he will go anywhere and study but if it is a girl, we have to take care."*

In the Indian context, even if one may be currently living in a nuclear family, there is much continuous interaction and sharing with relatives, including grandparents. The extended family expects to be informed and involved in major decisions concerning children such as career and marriage. Hence, one is required to deal with the network of extended family members, all of whom are enthusiastic in giving well-intentioned, even if unsolicited, advice. Adolescents thus need to deal with differences with parents if any, as well as with relatives. Although the social support that the extended family offers is valued, navigating the different advices tends to cause anxiety in both adolescents and parents. Parents in particular find themselves in a position where they are expected to balance the two sets of views. As Shruti's mother says, *"We have to respect our elders (mother-in-law), and listen to them as well"*. Navigating these networks is a cause of anxiety and sometimes tends to create even more strain in the parent–adolescent relationship. Akruti exasperatedly retorts, *"What will people say? This is my mother's favorite line. Sometimes she may be ok with something, but then she feels people may be critical. And then parents and relatives even compare us with their children."* Similarly, Tanu bemoans, *"Such conversations confuse us. Are we making the right decision for ourselves? And we also feel worried that if we do not succeed in our chosen field, then what will relatives say? They will taunt us and our parents too."*

According to a school counselor, parents tend to impose their choices on the adolescents and force them to select a particular stream, either because they feel it is the "right choice" for the adolescent or it is a way to fulfill their own dreams and wishes for self that they could not meet. Often, however, down the line when the child does not do well or remains uninterested, they realize that they should not have forced the child to opt for a certain stream and then want to retrace. This wastes time and in the process affects the adolescent's self-esteem. In her words, *"Often parents do not realize what the adolescent's interest or potential is. They impose their own thoughts or even their dreams. Adolescents have little personal space to identify their own dreams. We have aptitude tests in the school and we share this information with parents. But some parents do not accept this. Goals that they perceive as 'unsuccessful' are just not accepted. Then much later they may realize that this was not the right choice for their child."*

It is relevant to note that the relationship between domains that cause insecurity and anxiety is bidirectional in the sense that academic stress also affects other life domains. Further, although scholastic achievement is the major stress-inducing factor, the extreme and overzealous focus on it often eclipses other issues that adolescents may be experiencing, and which in turn may affect scholastic achievement.

The Cell Phone: *An Instrument of Privacy or a Lurking Menace?*

"Any argument that my parents and I have ends in the cell phone!" retorts 17-year-old Kruti, in an exasperated manner. She grumbles, *"If I am not eating, they will say I must be doing something on the phone; if I fall from the vehicle, they will say I must be driving with the phone in hand or may be texting while driving; so anything happens they will blame on the phone only"*. Parents' exasperation with the centrality of the cell phone in the adolescents' lives is evident in 16-year-old Ritu's revelation, *"My mom used to say that whoever has created this phone, I will kill him. Actually, my mom is a homemaker and she doesn't like mobile, computers or laptop and me and my dad are very fond of mobile and laptop and internet. When mom calls me for some work also then I say mom I am busy with laptop or internet doing some work, so she gets angry"*.

India is one of the fastest growing cell phone markets, and mobile subscribers grew from 2 million in 2000 to 939 million in 2012. The penetration of smart phones has accelerated with the numbers rising from 2.5 million handsets in 2009 to about 27 million in 2012 (IPSOS Business Consulting 2013). Youth are the largest consumers of cell phones. Today the cell phone, even more than the computer, is young people's lifeline. In urban upper middle class households in India, cell phones are pervasive, with each member of the family owning one's own. A survey across the major Indian cities Bangalore, Mumbai, Delhi, Hyderabad, and Chennai has revealed that cell phones are the primary mode of online data usage by youth. The wide-ranging options of smart phone models, attractive features, and apps with competitive pricing have facilitated this pattern (India Onward 2013). Cell phone companies are having a field day introducing new models every day, and young people get particularly enticed.

Research on cell phone use has found that there are intended and unintended uses of this technology. Cell phones are responsible for forming subcultures among youth, they are blurring the boundary between work and private life as well as between public and private space, and the cell phone user is susceptible to social control by friends and family (Aoki and Downes 2003). For young people, the cell phone has multiple uses, which include making friends, initiating romantic relationships, ongoing exchange with friends, keeping up-to-date with other people's lives, and keeping parents informed regarding one's whereabouts. Most popular are text messages and chatting through services like WhatsApp which has become India's most popular social networking site across age-groups. A study in Mumbai mapping cell phone use patterns in youth 15–30 years revealed that adolescents 15–19 years used the cell phone to communicate with friends. Local calls and texting were most popular and more girls than boys preferred talking with friends for long hours (MACRO April–May 2004). Adolescents in Baroda depict a similar pattern of use. Rijuta says, *"The cell phone is awesome! We use it for everything—staying in touch, planning what to do and where to meet, and of course for talking with friends."*

For adolescents, cell phones provide a communication route that is potentially free from the watchful parental eye. Cell phone related disagreements with parents occur on an everyday basis. Arguments with parents regarding upgrading to the latest model, and frequency and nature of cell phone usage are commonplace. The usual issues are talking for long periods of time, frequency of making or receiving calls, texting during a family activity, and timings of calls or text messages or chatting. Kruti, 17 years laments, *"My mother is against any calls or sms from 10.00 pm to 7.00 pm. It is like maintaining office timings. And if ever there is a call late in the night then her bombardment begins, 'Who is it, What does she want?' If it is a boy, then the questions are even more frantic. Why does he call in the night? If he is just a friend as you say, then what does he want at this time?' My cell phone will be taken away for some days. This is not fair. See during the day we are busy in school or tuition classes so we do not get the time to talk with friends. It is only later in the evening that we are free. Sometimes I argue that if you want then I will stop studying and attending classes in school and talk with friends on the phone. She does not understand that we are free only in the night so that is the good time to talk with friends and relax."* Along similar lines, 17-year-old Simran shares, *"Earlier I had a plan with a cap on text messages—100 messages was the maximum limit. So these would get over fast. And my Dad would start questioning—'what is it that you message about? Say hi, hi, hi to each friend'? Now how do you make them understand?"* As discussed in Chap. 4, despite such protests, adolescents are also sensitive to the parents' perspective. Nishi says, *"I know parents are protective and they have these rules out of concern for us. But they should give us some freedom, no? Their favorite line is 'tumne duniya dekhi nahi abhi tak, duniya bahut kharab hai' (You have not yet seen the world, it is a bad world out there). But then I feel agar aap dekhne nahi denge, allow nahi karenge toh duniya kaise dekhenge? (If you do not allow me to, how will I see the world?)."* Boys have disclosed similar issues and strategies of circumventing parents' interference in their digital world.

Adolescents' are fiercely protective about the privacy that the cell phone potentially provides, and they tend to assert their autonomy in this regard. *"The smsing is great! You can send and receive messages without talking so there is more privacy. In few words, you can say what you want to say. Also, there is no fear of parents hearing what you are saying. And the best part is that you don't need to be online for this. It feels good to chat with a friend and share things that you cannot share with parents."* (Ritu, 16 years). Along similar lines, Surabhi explains, *"See parents may be right in their view, but then we too need our space. It is a very bad feeling when parents check my phone. It is my phone after all, so why should they look into it? I always wonder why they do not trust me."*

Apparently, parents and adolescents play a "cat and mouse game," with the parent trying to regulate the duration and nature of cell phone use, and the adolescents on their part making any and every effort to devise different ways and means to circumvent this intrusion on their privacy. Eighteen-year-old Anupa explains, *"See my mother is very curious about my phone. Sometimes I have a password and she gets angry. She says, see I also chat with my friends and you can check my chats when you want. So then I too should be able to see your chats if I want to. But see I am not interested in her chats. So then I may remove my password and let her check and on purpose leave some chats with boys else she will get more suspicious. See my thing is even if they check our chats, what will they understand? They do not understand the emojis and short forms we use."* Kunjal has devised a clever way to circumvent parents' "poking" as she terms it. *"You know what, my mother does check my phone secretly, and she thinks I do not know, but I am aware. Purposely I do not keep a password on my cell phone as it makes parents even more suspicious. So I leave it on the table where they can have access to it* (laughs)."

Clearly, adolescents share what they want their parents to know so as to assure them that nothing untoward is going on in their lives. Similar issues arise with other social media sites such as Facebook, and especially with girls. Surabhi, 16 years shares, *"You know I have many friends on Facebook including boys of course—just friends ok, not boyfriend. So then sometimes when I post pictures of me then I get comments from boys too such as, 'Ay Surbhi mast lage che (Hey Surbhi, you look great!)' or Hey cutie pie! These comments are harmless and in friends, chalta hai (it is ok). Once my mother saw these so she got very upset. So then I unfriended Home* (laughs). *I do not want any fuss about such things. After all what is Facebook for?*

Hum Facebook pe thodi burkha pehen ke jayenge?" (*Are we going to wear a burkha on Facebook?*). Similarly, 18-year-old Mukta gleefully quipped, *"You know I did not teach my mother how to make friends on Facebook,"* even as Nikhil laughingly revealed, *"I show my parents what I want, but not what I do not want. In fact showing them chats or leaving the phone around off and on is good as it takes them off the detective track!"* Interestingly, adolescents like the small structure of the cell phone and use their smart phones for all purposes, including access to Facebook. Reema explains, *"Cell phone is better than a computer as the computer has a wider screen so parents can easily see, but the cell phone is smaller and it may be difficult to see even if they are trying to see when you are chatting."* The gender factor is also at play in the cell phone context. Girls complain that the rules are different for them and their brothers. For example, the brother is allowed to have a password or even chat for longer hours than the girls. The unfairness of this frustrates the girls and they also complain to their parents. However, the recurring response that they get is that "It is different for girls, so do not argue." Ruchi exclaims, *"We may have privacy like our own room or our own phone, but not parents' trust!"*

Parents on their part feel that it is their right and duty to monitor closely the adolescent's cell phone use patterns. One mother exasperatedly retorted, *"The cell phone is indeed a menace! It is very distracting for the adolescent, and then there are also comparisons with friends, like so and so has an IPhone, so I would like to have one too! So, it is actually a drawback in our life. It's really, really very convenient, but at the same time it is troublesome* (Phew!)." In their effort to "beat the system" so to speak, some parents do not buy an individual phone for the adolescent, but allow him or her to use their phone or they insist that no passwords may be used. Ankur's mother divulges, *"My husband has kept this condition from beginning, that no passwords. I will buy you a phone on the condition that I have full right to check it anytime and also take it away anytime. As soon as you reach home, you've to keep it aside. You are not supposed to use WhatsApp and all at night. Its okay, they use in vacation period, talk with friends, everything … we give freedom, but right now they are under our control. We have strictly told them not to misuse it. Two of the students, I know, lost their lives, while taking selfies. One should not talk on phone while driving. Mobiles are becoming a nuisance. If someone sends a 'hi', one has to reply."*

At the same time, parents also show sensitivity to the adolescent and are conscious about respecting their privacy. A mother earnestly elaborates, *"I don't check my children's phones because some things are there which are personal. Till date, I have never checked my daughter's phone. Yes, after I reach home, I do keep my cell phone aside. Because I think that we should spend time with each other. Yes, 2–3 times I have slapped my daughter because of the cell phone. My thing is when I am at home why are you on the phone all the time and what are you chatting about? I never allow them to chat at night. I don't like that at 12.00 o'clock at night you message someone to say 'good night'. I don't do it, you also don't it. After 10.00 pm, no WhatsApp with anyone, no 'likes', nothing. If your mind is always in the phone, when will we talk with each other?"*

The Gender Factor: *Resilient and Restrictive*

The earlier chapters have discussed how gender is interwoven in the construction of adolescence, the stage and adolescent, the person, as well as in family socialization. For adolescents, girls especially, this causes immense frustration and even insecurity. Parents' views reflect contradictions and ambiguities, which are manifest in their socialization practices. To a direct question regarding the need for differential treatment of girls and boys all parents unanimously respond in the negative, that is, there should not be any differential treatment. It is only in the course of the interview that mothers highlight the vulnerability of girls and the greater risk of harm to self and family. A phrase with which mothers frequently begin to share their views is, "*Aaj hum kharab time mein reh rahe hai (Today we are living in bad times)*." The statement alludes to the threat to girls' sexuality, and restrictions are linked to this primary concern.

Parents' preoccupation with safeguarding girls' sexuality is a major cause of anxiety and insecurity, which in turn is transmitted to their daughters, ad infinitum. For girls, this causes much frustration and insecurity, and interferes in their aspirations, ambitions, and ability for independent thinking. Restrictions on girls range from everyday dressing and behavior to choice of friends and selection of education stream and career, as well as long-term decisions related to marriage partner selection. Eighteen-year-old Neha cribs, "*There are so many rules for me, but not for my brother. Like keep distance from guys, stay away from friends with bad habits, no hanging out with friends after 11.00 pm...the list is endless. My brother can wander around until 2.00–3.00 am in the night. Even for meeting with friends my mom says, 'Roj roj shu malvanu? (What is the need to meet every day?)'. I feel angry and so bad about it. Is it a crime to be a girl?*"

How to dress and what clothes are most appropriate is a contentious matter between girls and parents. Ritu elaborates, "*Shopping is always with my parents. They do not allow me to go shopping with my friends. The other day we went shopping and I wanted to get a frock—it was so pretty. So then my mother said now you will go to college so you have to think of your status. Wear kurtis with tights or jeans, and with sleeves. So I argued that I can wear the frock in parties, but then even though I liked the frock so much I did not buy it (sighs).*" Similarly, Rijuta says, "*No shorts or one-piece (dress)! They would be happy for me to always wear anarkali (Indian full-length dress with full sleeves) if I allowed them. We had our school farewell party a few months back and I wore a one-piece (a dress). So my dad said why don't you wear a sari instead. Now imagine, how can I wear a sari to a party—how can I dance in a sari? And of course, no sleeveless ever! Imagine wearing a one-piece with sleeves! Eeks! I tell my parents that everyone wears such clothes.*"

Parents are even more wary about their daughters in view of several incidences of sexual harassment that have received much media attention in recent years. The phrase "*Duniya kharab hai*" (*the world is a bad place*) is repeatedly invoked and justified in reference to such instances. It also leads to closer monitoring of adolescents. A mother shares, "*I don't want her to feel that mother has said no, so supposing she wants to go somewhere alone at 7.00 or 8.00 pm, then I drop her. When she knows she's getting late, she'll drop a message otherwise I will call her tuition fellows or her teacher. She may be on the way, driving so I do not call her. If the tuition gets over at 8 o'clock and it gets 8.30 and if she has some work, she has to explain the reason for coming late. She of course gets annoyed...*" Girls on their part resent parents' protective attitude and present cogent arguments with regard to gender equality. Hetal, 18 years, complains, "*My parents always give examples of others. Did you hear what happened to that girl? She was wearing revealing clothes, no wonder guys get wrong ideas. 'Hum ko apni izzat rakhni aana chahiye' (We should know how to guard our honor). 'Hum ko kabil samajhna chahiye' (They should consider us capable). We can protect ourselves. Parents say 'buri nazar se bachna chahiye' (be safe from the evil eye). And there is constant commenting on 'dhyan se baitho' (sit properly, decently). Now tell me, is it the fault of the girl or the guy who harassed her, his mentality? Wish they would understand. See, at home I am allowed to wear shorts. But if someone comes, a relative or guest then my mother tell me to go and change. My thing is tell that person to change his mentality, why should I bother to change my clothes?*"

In a departure from the dominant narrative of girls' vulnerability, one mother wistfully revealed, "*I wish I had a daughter, then I could have fulfilled my dreams through her. See I wanted to complete my post-graduation but could not because I got married after first year of my masters program. So I could have educated my daughter well. Also, if I had a daughter she would have helped me with household chores. Sometimes I get tired as there is so much to do and boys are no help as such.*"

Adolescent boys express two types of views in relation to gender. One is an egalitarian outlook wherein both girls and boys are considered equal and hence should be given equal opportunity. Nikhil expresses, "*I think girls are more creative, they have a better dress sense, knowledge of color coordination... so they should be given more opportunity. They can be very successful if they want. And Baroda is a safe city so they are free to go anywhere they want. Of course one should be careful as it is never perfectly safe. But they should enjoy life as much as boys.*" The other view overlapping with that of parents is that girls are vulnerable and hence need to be careful. Ankit says, "*Girls should be treated equally, but then in India the atmosphere is not good, so one has to be careful. Friendships with boys are ok if the boy is good, but if he is ganda (dirty) then it would be a problem and the girl would be in trouble. Boy thodi affect hoga? (The boy will not get affected).*" Gender-based mentalities are clearly indicated and become particularly evident in matters of girl–boy friendships.

Girl-Boy Friendships: *"To Have or Not to Have"* *Is the Question*

As discussed in Chap. 3, romantic interests and friendships are seen as a vulnerable aspect of adolescence, and hence a source of anxiety. Parents' views on this subject range from a definite "No" to a tentative "yes" or "maybe" to an absolute "yes, but within limits." For adolescents on the contrary, it is a unanimous resounding "Yes!" Anuja quips, *"See there are guys who are friends and girls who are friends. What's the fuss about? After all it is no big deal."* Mansi adds, *"Sometimes in fact boys are more useful as friends. They have less jealousy and envy than girls. See we need all kinds of friends as we cannot share everything with parents, nor can they help in everything. Sometimes for some things boys are more helpful and for some things girls. For example, if I need to go somewhere far, then having a boy with me makes me feel protected."*

Most adolescents study in coeducational schools or attend tuition classes where there is a mix of girls and boys; hence, the environment offers plenty of opportunities to be acquainted with each other. Much as some parents may want, there is little that they can do to prevent this. Therefore, they take recourse in constantly reminding their adolescents to be cautious about the kind of friends they make, especially of the opposite gender, and this occurs more strongly and articulately in case of girls.

The gender factor is conspicuous with clear references to the vulnerability of girls. Arpita, 18 years retorts, *"For anything parents have this tagline, For girls... and they go on from there...."* Adolescents complain about the flurry of questions regarding guy friends, and often resort to making up stories about who a certain guy is and how she may have met him. Kunjal elaborates, *"What I do is that whenever I make a new friend, guy or girl, then very soon I try to bring them home and introduce to my parents. Then later my mother would comment on that friend, whether according to her she or he is nice or not nice—not in your class, she would say. See I have more guy friends so my mother is always commenting, why do you have so many guy friends? Where did you meet this person? How did you meet him? It is so irritating. But then I spin stories like remember I had told you he is this person's brother or the friend's brother. Jhooth bolna padta hai (have to tell lies), what to do?"* Likewise Anuja, elaborates, *"The other day was my birthday party. Now if I am going to invite guys then the party has to be at home. So I invited my friends. There were four girls and seven guys. So the questions began—how come you have more guys as friends than girls? Now come on, friends are friends. All guys are not bad and sometimes girls also can be bad. We cannot find friends only in girls. Parents have a problem if we are comfortable with boys. 'Is he only a friend?' is the first question that is posed. Obviously, I say! So then it is ok. God forbid if you say you have a boyfriend, because then it will be house arrest for sure and my phone will be taken away as well! Boys do not face this; it's more cool for them."*

Girls have a way of getting the best of their parents and seem to be mostly successful in doing so. Kirti shares, *"I have a friend who is a boy and it happens that we regularly meet so they (parents) know, but they told me that no, you should not talk to him and all. But I know how he is and in what ways he is helpful to me so then with parents I just ignore this topic. Now I don't talk to him when I am at home but when I go out I meet him so we talk face to face. When I come home I just message him that now I am at home so we will not chat; we will talk when I am out."* Boys share that they are confronted with similar questions, but perhaps not as intensely. Nikhil says, *"My parents just want to know which girls are my friends. Then they are ok. And she has told me that if ever you have a girlfriend just let me know. Parents' minds are like children's. You explain and they understand. Samjhi jaye (they understand)*" (smiles).

Parents are aware of their adolescents' romantic interests. "*He doesn't share anything with me but I have observed that he is looking at some good looking girls. He silently observes everything. Even if we are going out, he takes more time to get ready. I guess he must be feeling for girls, but he is not sharing with us. If some day he will come and tell me that mummy I like this girl or she is my girlfriend then I will ask that girl that why have you chosen him? It will feel awkward. If she is ok and good then I will accept it,*" confesses a mother. On the face of it, parents seem to be in favor of girl–boy friendships and express that these may be necessary so that the adolescents get to know of each other. They are not in favor of a romantic relationship, however, lest it distracts the adolescent from his or her studies, along with the equally strong, although less openly articulated fear that the relationship may get their adolescent into trouble. Ankit's mother says, "*Boys and girls should mix and spend time in each other's company, else there will be more curiosity. But we have to keep in mind that this stage is vulnerable physically and mentally. So sambhaline rehvu pade (One needs to be cautious). I would not allow my son to go for an overnight outing in a mixed group. These kids are young and can succumb to attractions. So it is like inviting trouble. That way I am strict.*" Kruti's mother worries, "*Kruti is a bindass (carefree) kind of girl—rather childish. I do not want that anybody takes advantage of her. It can lead to serious consequences for her. This really worries me and so I always make it a point to get to know her friends—girls and boys.*" Mothers of boys also express concern about how "*forward*" and "*smart*" today's girls are and hence boys need to be careful. Nikhil's mother elaborates, "*See my son is handsome and girls get after him. He shares this with me. There is this incidence that occurred with him and he only told me about. One day they went for a day picnic from school, and teachers were there too. There was this one girl who sat close to Nikhil and put her head on his lap, and that too in front of the teacher! Can you believe? So girls are also more 'forward' (a term typically used by Gujaratis to mean 'bold'). What if they take some step? (alluding to sexual involvement), then the boy would be held responsible. So boys need to be careful of girls, else they may create trouble for them.*" Beneath the recurring notes of caution and restrictions is the parents' anxiety for their adolescents' safety and security, and the striving to ensure that focus on studies is never compromised.

The frustrations caused by perpetual gender-based restrictions from parents manifest in protests and arguments that may be short-lived, but in the long run such messages are likely to impact girls' personality, perhaps rendering it more tentative and ambiguous.

Marriage: *"Advise, But PLEASE, Let it be My Choice"*

"*Tumko doosre ghar jaana hai (you have to go to another's house)*" is the refrain that girls constantly hear. Although marriage may still be far away for urban upper middle class adolescents, socialization for it begins very early on, especially for girls.

Adolescents and parents tend to ponder over this and have conversations related to it. Girls especially, are largely against parents deciding who their marriage partner will be. Eighteen-year-old Pallavi retorts, *"I really get worried that my parents will choose someone for me and expect me to get married to that person. If they are not allowing us to choose our clothes, then what else can one expect? Why should parents choose for us? See in any case in an arranged marriage both sets of parents meet and they share all good things about their children. Who will share bad things? For example, my mom will not say that I am the 'cool' type. So in that short time how will they know? They will say 'tere liye achha hai' (He is good for you). How can you know? Mujhe rehna hai (I have to stay with him). Also, these days' parents often do not know what their son is doing. He may be telling lies to his parents. And it is I who is to spend my life with that person, so hamara choice hona chahiye! (it should be our choice). We need to be comfortable with the person".*

Parents share that they will be flexible regarding their children's marriage partner, although with some riders. *"We have some expectations for them so it should be up to that mark also. It is not that they choose anybody and say we want to get married—that I will not allow. Even my daughter knows it. She is still too young, but still she knows this. She knows that 'mein koi bhi pasand karungi, to meri mummy wo pasand nahi karegi' (I will not approve of just anybody). I am not going to allow that. I don't believe that he should be of same caste or community, but he should have his own identity and image. Image means he should have looks, career, growth and scope for going ahead in life. See name and status are important, nahi toh koi nahi puchta (else nobody bothers),"* clarifies Radha's mother. Education is a significant criterion that parents look for in a prospective partner. Commenting on the nature of marriage partner selection, Ronak's mother explains, *"It's not that they should not have a love marriage at all. However, there should be at least one or two plus points. Like if the girl is educated, it will be useful in their future only. Even though the financial status is good, it is also important to have an educated family. Some families have rigid norms; the family background is totally different. If she is my daughter and they don't understand her, what to do with money then, her life gets affected. So main thing is education, lots many things are affected because of it. Educated people at least know they should do something, that after marriage they realize it is their duty to do something to take care of family needs, give time to family. Where there is low education, they don't understand anything."* Parents' perspectives highlight the emphasis on education in middle class families, who view it as instrumental to an enhanced lifestyle that constitutes both material comforts and social status.

Involvement of parents and family in matters of marriage is inevitable in the Indian cultural context. The notion of marriage as an event between two families is firmly entrenched across social class, and consultation with and approval of parents in partner selection is the expected norm. Assertion of individual choice may be accepted as far as it meets with parents' expectations, largely. Even though issues with regard to marriage partner selection have always existed, the globalizing context offers increasing opportunities to meet people and form relationships, thereby exacerbating such matters. Young individuals experience much anxiety and guilt in situations where parents do not approve of one's choice, and whereas some may assert one's autonomy and take recourse to extreme measures such as eloping, others sacrifice personal choice out of respect and care for parents and the reputation of the family. Either ways, the individual and the parents experience much anguish in situations of disagreement regarding a prospective partner (Kapadia, unpublished manuscript).

Social Comparisons: *Vying to Get the Best, Be the Best*

The dazzling influences of the globalizing world are creating attractions and possibilities that are difficult to disregard. The attractions range from technological gadgets and gizmos, personal accessories and clothing, variety of leisure options to opportunities for friendships and relationships, education, and career. The cultural identity confusion that young individuals experience (Jensen 2011) brings with it uncertainties and insecurities in everyday life, prompting social comparisons on all fronts, either with direct or vicarious role models who range from peers, classmates, cousins, and neighbors to movie stars, musicians and singers, television celebrities, models, or sportspersons. Social comparisons are used to cope with negative affect, for self-enhancement, to affiliate upward, or to enhance well-being (Wheeler and Miyake 1992). The world is witnessing a high-consumption culture, and India is close on the heels, especially the youth. In this scenario of a fast-growing consumerist outlook and the spiraling spending power and aspirations of the urban middle classes, material acquisitions are increasingly being linked to social standing and social comparisons. Media influx and aggressive advertising makes young individuals even more prone to engage in short-term comparisons of material items such as clothing and accessories. Empirical research in India has found that young people's purchases often happen from non-utilitarian needs that emerge from social pressure such as social comparisons and peer pressure (Thomas and Wilson 2012). Further, interpersonal influences are observed to be stronger than media and advertising (Chan 2013).

Adolescents typically like to be 'like their peers' and stay up-to-date with what is in vogue. As Nikhil's mother remarks, *"My son is fond of phones. He often takes photos, listens to music and uses WhatsApp. He wants that everybody should appreciate it, that he has a nice phone. He sees a good phone and says, 'Mummy I want that phone…' He has changed his phone four times!"* The trend of keeping up with friends also extends to leisure activities like watching movies in multiplex cinemas or hanging out in one of the coffee shops that have become popular hangout places for young people in Baroda. Further, in this context of diluting geographical boundaries, the canvas of comparisons is wider and adolescents compare with youth in other countries, whose lifestyles become known through either direct interactions or via media. Nandini, 18 years, comments, *"See, young people in the West have it so good. They can wear whatever they want. No restrictions on how to dress. When will Indian society become broad minded?"* (sighs). Such comparisons tend to give rise to a sense of inadequacy and a continuing need to attain something better. This is indicated in the adolescents' wishes, imaginations, and aspirations for future discussed in Chap. 3, for example, *"I wish I had a house on the beach, like what we see on travel channels on TV. That would be awesome!"*

"Branded is better" is a favorite *mantra* of the new age generation. Adolescents today are "brand conscious"; they have their favorite brands and are insistent on buying only branded items. Seventeen-year-old Ashwini shares with pride, *"My favorite brand is Van Heusen. I only like to buy clothes from there. My Dad too is keen on brands. See, status toh hona chahiye (you should have status). The other day I needed to buy luggage and my mother said let's go to the city to Surti Theli Bhandar (an old luggage shop in the old city with a Gujarati name), imagine! I said no way (laughs). So then, we went to the luggage stores in Alkapuri (a well-known posh area of Baroda). I decided on American Tourister which cost about Rs. 3500/."* Similarly, Akash's passion is shoes, but only Nike's! The influx of online shopping sites offers many attractive choices and even autonomy to the adolescents. Priya shares, *"I keep browsing shopping sites and place items in the wish list. Then if my birthday is coming up, I tell my parents that I want this dress and then order it online. Sometimes we also tell friends to gift us a certain item. The wish list is always long."*

In general, materialistic inclinations are at an all-time high and are abundantly revealed in short-term desire for belongings as well as long-term wishes that are largely characterized by possessions such as a luxurious villa, a fancy car like a Lamborghini or Ferrari, personal jet, and the like. Adolescents are candid in their affirmation of the significance of money; *"No money, no life!"* is their guiding motto. Extreme instances of serious fallouts of the desire for material items and enhanced lifestyle are evinced in occasional newspaper reports about an adolescent committing suicide, as the parents did not grant her wish of going out with friends for a movie!

Parents present a mix of both supportive and disapproving attitude toward adolescents' demands. Whereas some parents themselves are keen to shop for "branded goods," others are obliged to reconcile to adolescents' demands. One mother shares, *"Ankit is obsessed with brands! He is very particular to buy only branded clothes or perfumes. His jeans have to be Levi's. He is very fashion conscious. And he discards clothes that are out of fashion according to him. He complains, 'How can I wear this? It is no longer considered hip', he says."* And Pinakin's mother describes, *"The brand of cell phone is very important for him. He wanted to buy an IPhone but I said we could not buy you one now. What is the need? But he was so determined that over one year he saved money from whatever he got including for example, monetary gifts during Diwali or for his birthday or any other occasion. Then I added some and only recently, he bought an IPhone. For kids these days a smart phone is a must have."*

Parents support and indulge adolescents if according to them, their demands are "within limits"; also, they may resist in the beginning, but tend to give in over a period of time, and adolescents are aware of this. Many share about how they play their parents and convince them into fulfilling their wish. Further, parents' indulgence may also occur, as often they themselves are similarly oriented. As discussed in Chap. 1, urban middle classes are striding ahead to acquire a "better" lifestyle symbolized by material acquisitions. Thus, parents too jump into the fray of the "me too" bubble, driven by the desire to be "like the Mehtas next door." Similar messages are transmitted to adolescents who are very aware of parents' own attitude and behavior. Rivaan, 18 years, sarcastically observes, "*My Dad tells me not to chat on WhatsApp all the time, but I see that he is also mostly on his phone after dinner.*"

As described earlier in this chapter, academic performance is the primary focus during this phase, and hence an important domain of social comparison. Adolescents are already anxious regarding their performance in the Xth and XIIth standards. This is only exacerbated by the comparisons that parents and relatives, and sometimes even neighbors, make with the adolescents' peers, cousins, or even neighbors. Anxiety among schoolchildren and adolescents, essentially arising from high parental expectations and pressure, has been well documented in India. A study on mapping anxiety among high school students in Kolkata found that adolescents from the middle class experience the highest amount of anxiety, compared to lower- and higher social-class adolescents. The researchers attribute this to the rising aspirations of the middle class and the pressure that families experience to maintain and enhance their social position, which is defined largely by education and occupation (Deb et al. 2010). Adolescents often protest against such comparisons. Chintan, 17 years angrily retorts, "*I am tired of hearing 'see that boy got 80%, so why can you not try harder'? I feel that if someone has been able to get good marks, it is good for him, but they (parents) do not think that I may have what he does not, so…Also even though I worked hard I was not able to score high marks in my Xth. I get fed up of such comments all the time.*" As Chintan's mother observes, "*My younger son says 'don't compare me with anyone. I am doing well, we are good this way'. He stops me immediately when I give an example of someone. He will argue that their parents are giving this much pocket money, are you going to give me that much? Also, he won't compare himself with others. We often have arguments on studies. Then he will tell us that no one is same or perfect, we are doing this much, be happy with it.*"

Social comparisons thus extend to all aspects of the adolescent's everyday life including material acquisitions, academics, leisure activities, and even physical appearance. The childcentric outlook drives parents to offer their best to the child, often even as a way to compensate for what their own parents could not provide them. Moreover, in the fervor to project their child as a "model child," they make any and every effort to provide everything that will help the child to be at par with the peers, not just adolescents' own peers, but also parents' friends and relatives. This includes academic performance as well as performance in hobbies and extracurricular activities. Parents also harbor fears of the child developing an inferiority complex lest he is not provided what everybody else has. In the words of a school counselor, "*If the parents' friend's child is going to 2 hobby classes, the parent feels my child will go to 4! Or if the friend has a Yamaha bike, then I will get the same one for my child, or perhaps even a better one.*"

Parents' strong desire to fit in and belong to a certain group of friends manifests in increased pressure on the adolescent. Often this aggravates issues that adolescents themselves may be grappling with already. A school counselor proffered a rather disturbing account of a mother pressuring her daughter who was already depressed, to restrict her diet so that she does not become fat. Problems of anorexia nervosa and bulimia that were more prevalent in Western societies are now increasingly observed in India (Singh 2007), possibly as a cumulative effect of macro contextual and micro contextual pressures on the adolescent.

Generation Gap: *So What's New? Or Is There?*

Although generation gap is a recurring phenomenon experienced by each new generation, the rapid pace of change renders this phenomenon more palpable in the present times. The discrepancy between parents' adolescence and adolescence as it unfolds today is rather wide, and reconciling the two inevitably entails insecurity and conflict. The main differences that parents observe are in the domains of adolescent obedience and autonomy. "*Earlier, whenever parents said, we had to sit for studies, when they asked us to stand up, we had to get up, otherwise we got a slap. At present, we cannot slap our children,*" compares a mother. Reflecting on her specific situation and its implications on adolescent socialization, a mother rationalizes, "*In our times, before doing something, we used to ask each and every thing to our parents. Now many a times our children directly come and say that mom I have done this or I have taken this; and they may not have done wrong. But we used to ask our parents first whether it is right or wrong, whereas our children are just doing it. So one way it is good as our children are becoming independent, taking their own decisions. But then it is the other way also, as we used to respect our elders much more than youngsters do now.*"

Adolescents' demand for material items is a significant generational difference that parents express. The globalizing context presents an array of attractive choices, and adolescents are articulate and even insistent upon acquiring certain items to keep up with their peers or with the latest fashion trend. According to parents when they were in their adolescence, they seldom made demands on their parents and often wore hand-me-downs from their older siblings. They complain that adolescents these days seem to have little regard for whether parents will be able to afford a certain item; instead, they are more focused on fulfilling their desires.

The flexibility in career choice that adolescents today enjoy and parents' growing active interest in adolescents' studies emerged as a generational difference. One mother shares, "*When I was young, I wanted to become an interior designer. My parents refused first and then they agreed. But now, people are broad minded. Earlier, they were not allowing us to take fashion designing course also, but now parents are ready. When we were in this stage as adolescents, our father didn't even know that in which standard we are studying. They just gave fees when we asked for it. Even school results they saw once, and let it be. Whereas now parents see results carefully, they ask children why you have scored less or more. They ask in which line (stream) you want to go, and parents will go and search for options for their children. They will also meet teachers if their children have scored less mark in some subjects. Before there was nothing like parent-teacher meetings, but now parents regularly attend these meetings and get all the reports of the child."*

Adolescents' growing desire for independence and assertion of one's own views amidst the widening canvas of choices and opportunities emerge as contentious issues causing intergenerational conflicts.

"Bad" Peer Influence: A Nagging Worry for Parents

A strong source of anxiety for parents is the risk of *"bad influence"* of friends, specifically with regard to substance abuse such as smoking, alcohol, or drugs. A mother worried, *"Main thing I worry is that they don't get into addiction. You see everywhere, youngsters having paan (betel leaf), padiki (tobacco pouch), cigarettes and all. You find small children smoking; it frightens me more. Though I guarantee that my younger son will not do anything like that, I have little more fear for my elder son, because he makes friends very easily. The younger son is little choosy, he has a limited friends circle, not more than that."* Parents fear that friends may encourage such habits and given their immaturity, adolescents may agree to experiment.

Traditionally, the Indian family provided a strong peer network. In a joint family setup, with a number of families residing under one roof, the siblings of the adolescents (who generally fall in the same age group) provided a rich web of peers in the family (Verma and Saraswathi 2002); the outside peer group played a less significant role in the lives of most adolescents. Studies have revealed that the amount of time adolescents spend with parents is more compared to the time spent with peers, especially in middle class Indian families (e.g., Larson et al. 2001). The scenario, however, is somewhat different in the upper middle social class. The upper middle class in our society features a distinctly different lifestyle, expectation, and life course development for children and youth. Due to the distinct and prolonged phase of adolescence in upper middle class, a long period of exposure to the peer group and to alternative lifestyles is emerging. This paves a way for greater relevance and importance of peers and the consequent emergence of a peer culture (Saraswathi 1999). Today, adolescents are spending more time with peers. A typical weekday involves school followed by tuition classes, which keeps them away from home and in the company of friends for most part of the day. Additionally, interactions through social networking sites are constant, not only with local friends, but also global. Adolescents are increasingly inclined to be part of international peer and youth groups and networks, enhancing thereby their acquaintance with other cultural outlooks and practices. The creation of "self-selected cultures" *à la* Arnett (2002, p.777) with like-minded people is on the rise as evidenced in the formation of multiple youth groups that transcend geographical boundaries. According to

Arnett (2002), aligning with global values involves interface with different cultural and national boundaries, and accepting and celebrating diversity. This implies increasing acquaintance with appealing values such as openness to change, freedom of choice, and tolerance of a worldview that does not meet with the majority view. In general, contact and interactions with peers near and far has increased considerably, bringing with it the plausibility of increased influence. For instance, 18-year-old Nikhil shares with a note of pride in his voice, *"I have many friends out of India on Facebook. I do not even remember all their names. But we chat. It is very open there. They post pictures of their girlfriends openly. When I asked if it is ok with their parents, one of them said, they don't care about such things. That's cool."*

Parents feel that as parents they have the right to ask the adolescent questions such as whom he is going out with, where he went, and the nature of their conversation. At the same time, they are aware that adolescents may twist the truth or even tell blatant lies. They tend to keep an eye on the kind of friends that their adolescents form, and even regulate the nature of activities in which they may engage. "Hanging out" with friends, especially if it involves a mixed group, is a contentious issue between parents and adolescents. Anuj's mother asserts, *"I do not allow him to hang out with other boys near the corner of our society, especially late evenings. I put my foot down, as such things cause trouble. Also too much outing with friends is not good. You cannot control his friends too much, so have to regulate our own child."*

In departure from the predominant narrative of the negative influence of peers, Anish's mother highlights the power of positive peer influence and its significance for adolescent success. She explains, *"To become successful, the first thing is you need to have a good friend circle. Good friends give good ideas, because they come from good background. If they get into bad company, their life revolves around them and their 1–2 years are spoiled. Having good friends helps in performance also, as one gets inspiration. It becomes a competition, like he has done this much, I should also do it. When we ask him about his friends, he will say like 'do you want his bio data or what?' So we explain that we should at least know with whom you are going somewhere. If they would have no mobiles, it would be more of a problem for us. At least this way we can call them when they are late."*

The multiple influences of the globalizing context thus filter down to the family and the parent–adolescent relationship, creating challenges, insecurities, and anxieties that were largely unfamiliar up to this time, or perhaps did not assume much significance as these could be dealt with more easily. Further, the greater than ever parental focus on adolescents and their inclination to offer their best to the child leads to concerted involvement in the everyday lives of the adolescents. Despite best intentions and some advantages, such a tendency often introduces further challenges in the parent–adolescent relationship, thereby increasing stress not only for parents, but also adolescents. Although there is much overlap between parents' and adolescents' perspectives as discussed in Chap. 4, yet there are incompatible notions that may be barely visible on the brink, but simmer beneath the surface.

References

Aoki, K., & Downes, E. J. (2003). An analysis of young people's use of and attitudes toward cell phones. *Telematics and Informatics, 20*(4), 349–364.

Arnett, J. J. (2002). The psychology of globalization. *American Psychologist, 57*(10), 774–783. doi:10.1037//0003-066X.57.10.774.

Bourn, D. (2008). Young people, identity and living in a global society. *Policy and Practice: A Development Education Review, 7,* 48–61.

Chan, K. (2013). Development of materialistic values among children and adolescents. *Young Consumers, 14*(3), 244–257. doi:10.1108/yc-01-2013-00339.

David, S. (2013). Urban youth in health and illness: A rights perspective. In P. Prakash (Ed.), *State of the urban youth, India 2013: Employment, livelihoods, skills* (pp. 16–29). Mumbai: IRIS Knowledge Foundation.

Deb, S., Chatterjee, P., & Walsh, K. (2010). Anxiety among high school students in India: Comparisons across gender, school type, social strata and perceptions of quality time with parents. *Australian Journal of Educational and Developmental Psychology, 10,* 18–31.

IPSOS Business Consulting. (2013). *India's mobile phone market.* Mumbai: Author.

India Onward. (2013, July 22). *Indian youth prefers to be constantly connected.* (Web Blog Post) Retrieved from http://www.indiaonward.com/indian-youth-prefers-to-be-constantly-connected/.

Jensen, L. A. (2011). Navigating local and global worlds: Opportunities and risks for adolescent cultural identity development. *Psychological Studies, 56*(1), 62–70. http://doi.org/10.1007/s12646-011-0069-y.

Jensen, L. A., & Arnett, J. J. (2012). Going global: New pathways for adolescents and emerging adults in a changing world. *Journal of Social Issues, 68*(3), 473–492. http://doi.org/10.1111/j.1540-4560.2012.01759.x.

Juthani, N. V. (1992). Immigrant mental health: Conflicts and concerns of Indian immigrants in the USA. *Psychology and Developing Societies, 4*(2), 133–147.

Kapadia, S. (n.d.). *Marriage dilemmas of young women in contemporary India: Negotiating tradition and modernity.* Unpublished manuscript.

Larson, R., Verma, S., & Dworkin, J. (2001). Adolescent's family relationships in India: The daily family lives of Indian middle class teenagers. In J. Arnett (Ed.), *Readings on adolescence and emerging adulthood* (pp. 134–141). Abington, MA: Prentice Hall.

MACRO (Market Research and Consumer Research Organization). (April–May 2004). *A report on study of mobile phone usage among the teenagers and youth in Mumbai.* Retrieved December 18, 2016, from https://www.itu.int/osg/spu/ni/futuremobile/socialaspects/IndiaMacroMobileYouthStudy04.pdf.

Marsella, A. J. (2012). Psychology and globalization: Understanding a complex relationship. *Journal of Social Issues, 68*(3), 454–472. doi:10.1037/e653772011-001.

Pasmantier, D. (2005). Depression and suicide as Indian teenagers dread 'killer exams.' *Epilepsy News.* Retrieved from www.epilepsy.com/newsfeed/pr_1122384638.html.

Saraswathi, T. S. (1999). Adult-child continuity in India: Is adolescence a myth or an emerging reality? In T. S. Saraswathi (Ed.), *Culture, socialization and human development: Theory, research, and application in India* (pp. 213–232). New Delhi: Sage.

Singh, K. (2007, July 18). Anorexia rising at an alarming rate. *Times of India.* Retrieved January 16, 2017, from http://timesofindia.indiatimes.com/city/delhi/Anorexia-rising-at-an-alarming-rate/articleshow/2215626.cms.

Thomas, S. E., & Wilson, P. R. (2012). Youth consumerism and consumption of status products: A study on the prevalence of social pressure among students of professional courses. *IUP Journal of Business Strategy, 9*(2), 44.

Verma, S., & Saraswathi, T. S. (2002). Adolescence in India: Street urchins or Silicon Valley millionaires? In B. B. Brown, R. W. Larson, & T. S. Saraswathi (Eds.), *The world's youth: Adolescence in eight regions of the globe* (pp. 105–140). Cambridge: Cambridge University Press.

Verma, S., Sharma, D., & Larson, R. W. (2002). School stress in India: Effects on time and daily emotions. *International Journal of Behavioral Development, 26*(6), 500–508.

Vogli De, R. (2004). *Change, psychosocial stress and health in an era of globalization.* Working paper. John D. and Catherine T. MacArthur Foundation, Chicago, USA.

Wheeler, L., & Miyake, K. (1992). Social comparison in everyday life. *Journal of Personality and Social Psychology, 62*(5), 760–773.

Chapter 6
Conclusions, Reflections, and Implications

Abstract This chapter recapitulates and discusses the central themes in the social construction of adolescence the stage, the adolescent self, and the parent–adolescent relationship in the urban Indian middle class context. It then reflects on the issue of cultural continuity and change in the context of globalization and discusses the direction of social change. The conceptual framework is revisited, detailing the emerging interplay of cultural and contextual factors that mediate the sociocultural construction of adolescence in the urban Indian middle class. The final section discusses the implications for adolescent development.

Keywords Adolescence · Gender · Parental authority · Self-conception · Cultural continuity · Social change · Positive adolescent development · National youth policy

Adolescents and Parents Amid the Pull and Push of the Globalizing Context

The world is transforming rapidly and people across societies are caught in this vortex of change. Parents and adolescents engage in adaptations, alterations, and adjustments in their attitudes and behaviors with the desire to create a good fit with the contemporary context. The process alternates between leaning on familiar cultural precepts and practices and embracing new ideas and approaches. Unlike technological change, social change is slow to occur, and its manifestations tend to unfold in variable patterns across sociodemographic contexts, life stages, and domains of development. Hence, whereas change may be clearly evident in some settings and domains, it is more variable and nuanced in others. Whatever the case may be, both adolescents and parents are active actors in this phenomenon, simultaneously assimilating and accommodating to the fluctuating landscape in the hope to achieve equilibrium (*à la* Jean Piaget).

The urban Indian middle class is a segment that is in a critical position, setting trends that other groups in the society are likely to follow. As middle class becomes

© Springer (India) Pvt. Ltd. 2017   139
S. Kapadia, *Adolescence in Urban India*,
DOI 10.1007/978-81-322-3733-4_6

a more appealing category of self-identification, people across caste and ethnicity are beginning to identify themselves as such. A popular image of the "new" middle class is that of a group that is open to adopt new practices (Jodhka and Prakash 2016). Consumption, essentially focused on acquisitions that are perceived as status enhancing, is a defining characteristic of the middle class. Money as a marker of status follows closely on the heels, with youth having greater access to disposable income. Aspirations for upward mobility are on the rise, and education is viewed as a primary channel for economic enhancement as well as social status (Fernandes 2016). The lives of parents and adolescents unfold in this context.

Parivartan, Vulnerability, and Academic Achievement: Defining Features of Adolescence in the Urban Indian Middle Class

Adolescence as a distinct stage is evident in the urban middle class and although the terms "adolescence" or "adolescent" or its Indian equivalent "*kishore awastha, yuva awastha*" are not part of the everyday parlance of either the parents or the adolescents, this period is well-recognized as a stage of *parivartan* or transition from childhood to adulthood. The vulnerability of this developmental period is highlighted and situated in adolescents' lack of social and emotional maturity to uphold a balanced outlook and discern "right" from "wrong," especially in the domains of selection of friends, romantic relationships, and education. The latter assumes much importance as the years 16 to 18 coincide with the high school years Xth through XIIth standards, which mark the transition from school to college. More importantly, academic performance during this period circumscribes the arena of choice of major in college, and hence seals one's fate in terms of career. "Studies" and "scoring good percentage" mark the everyday narrative of parents and adolescents, and all activities are programmed around this aspect. Education is a cherished goal in the urban middle class, with much instrumental value for upward social and economic mobility. It thus becomes a collective goal and parents feel greatly responsible to ensure that their adolescent crosses this path successfully. In good faith, therefore, parents take the onus on themselves to lead their child to success. In fact, much of the goal setting also occurs in consultation with each other. "Studies" often becomes a contentious issue creating interpersonal tension related to study habits, regulation of leisure activities, and also choice of major. Guided by the dictum, "*I know what is good for my child*," the role of parents as guide and advisor surfaces rather resolutely in this context.

Decisions regarding career choice are often fraught with confusion. Both adolescents and parents are aware that the decisions taken during this period will have long-term implications that will remain more or less binding. The uncertainty that the global scenario is presenting instills insecurity and in turn difficulty in making decisions. In this context, Blossfeld et al. (2005) highlight three aspects. One is the uncertainty that characterizes the macroenvironment and the looming ambiguity regarding the future scenario, which results in uncertainty in behavioral alternatives. Young individuals find it difficult to compare and rank various educational and career options in terms of future implications. Second, the probability of behavioral outcomes in future is also uncertain. Adolescents do not know if a particular field will be as lucrative in the future. Third is that young individuals are unsure about the amount of information that is necessary to make a particular decision. How much information is adequate to form an opinion to enable a decision is unclear. The societal institutions mediate the flexibility of choice. For instance, the high school education system in India offers one route to enter a particular career. If this route fails, the career path is seriously affected. It is no wonder then that both parents and adolescents are much fretful and insecure about the percentage or marks that the adolescent will secure in the XIIth standard, as this will clinch his or her career choice and path.

The hype around the board exams is all-encompassing with not only the primary family, but also the extended family and other well-wishers jumping into the fray. Much is at stake, not only in terms of the achievement of the adolescent, but also the social reputation of the entire family. The academic performance of the child, especially during the Xth and XIIth standard board exams is associated with the reputation of the family as relatives, friends, and even neighbors are all eager to know the results of the exams. This not only puts pressure on the child but also the parent as well. Comments such as "Make sure to keep our honor" (*Joje, apni ijjat rakhje*) are often voiced by family members. In general, much stress and pressure accompany academic and career aspirations during this period, sometimes resulting in dire consequences such as adolescent suicide from fear of failure to meet parental expectations or from actually meeting with failure in the exam (Gala and Chaudhary 2009). Further, the predominant focus on studying is not only an irritant for the adolescent, but also stress provoking, and hence counter-productive. The time of board exams becomes particularly threatening for the self-esteem of those adolescents who may not be able to perform well. In general, although adolescents recognize the significance of academic achievement during this period and are themselves anxious about it, they wish for lesser pressure from parents.

Amid a climate of anxiety and stress that prevails during the exam period, a positive aspect is that the entire family comes together in supporting the adolescent to deal with this crucial phase. For instance, during the board exams, it is not uncommon for the family to change daily routine activities such as restricting the timing and duration of television viewing, discontinuing cable TV, or postponing recreational outings so as to avoid any distractions for the adolescent. Many parents take time off from their jobs for the entire exam period in order to provide physical and psychological support to the adolescent at all hours of the day and night. The family collective thus makes every effort to ensure the adolescent's success and derives immense pride and satisfaction from it, or disappointment in case of failure. Although unintended, this unfortunately puts more pressure on the adolescent.

Another major domain of adolescent vulnerability relates to the choice of friends, time and activities with friends, and romantic interests. Parents are rather worried about the company that their child keeps, and the anxiety is even greater in case of potentially romantic friendships. Giving attention to romantic interests and relationships is also viewed as a potential distraction from the goal of academic achievement. Parents of both girls and boys are anxious about their adolescent developing romantic relationships that may get them in trouble. Much monitoring occurs in this domain and although parents desire to project a liberal image in showing acceptance about romantic interests and friendships, deep down they wish that their adolescent does not get romantically involved.

Parenting Adolescents: A Mélange of Friend, Guardian, and Guide

Parenting adolescents in urban middle class families in India is interpreted as an overall pleasant experience, albeit challenging in terms of increased responsibilities on the parent, decoded as active inputs and involvement in various domains of the adolescent's everyday life as well as plans for the future. Overall, the perceptions of parents and adolescents regarding parenting indicate a remarkable mutuality and harmony, a telling endorsement of the enduring cohesive and interdependent character of the Indian family (Badrinath 2003). The mutuality occurs in part because of parents' changing outlook comprising a mix of traditional and liberal perspectives.

The image of "parent as friend," implying that the parent is open-minded and understanding, is endorsed by both parents and adolescents. It signifies a more democratic relationship, a departure from the traditional hierarchical authority orientation. The notion of parent as friend is mentioned in the Indian scriptures with reference to modes of disciplining children. As Kakar (1981) has opined, the concept of a child developing through a series of stages, often regarded as a Western notion has always been a part of the Indian folk consciousness and has been expressed through proverbs such as "Treat a son like a king for the first five years, like a slave for the next ten, and like a friend thereafter." Many such advices are ideal prescriptions, and all may not necessarily be reflected in everyday socialization practices through the years. Nevertheless, with the changing macro context, families are revoking some of the traditional, possibly more effective prescriptions.

In the process of coping with the compelling global influences on everyday socialization practices, however, parents often experience tension between their images as friend and guardian, which encompasses the role of disciplinarian. As a mother put it, "*Aisa hai na ki lagaam itni bhi mat kheecho ki lag jaye, aur itni bhi dheeli ho ki bhaag jaye, aisa" (the reins should not be too tight that they hurt and not even be so loose that (the horse) runs away, like that).*" In consonance with traditional roles, parents consider themselves fully responsible for their adolescents' present and future lives and make very conscious efforts to provide a successful and good life for them in material and psychological terms. As indicated in Mascolo et al.'s (2004) study related to self-conceptions in India and USA, Indians more frequently described themselves as "protective" and "responsible" (p. 22), terms that indicate a greater degree of obligation toward others. The adolescents in the present studies have also voiced what may be termed as their responsibilities toward parents through expressions such as "*make my parents proud*", "*treat parents as they have treated me*," "*study well*," and be a "*good daughter or son*." Adolescents are acutely cognizant of all that the parents are doing for them. Although this is perceived as a role-related responsibility and duty of parents, they express the desire to "give back" to their parents, for example, a better life style, yet again a reflection of middle class aspirations. The pattern of generalized need-based reciprocity that is largely characteristic of the Indian orientation toward social support is clearly revealed (Miller et al. in press), alongside the social-moral duty of children toward parents.

Parental Authority: Recasting the Traditional Model

Authority is an essentially relational and dynamic concept, requiring legitimacy. Authority is shaped by the developmental stage, the quality of parent–child relationship, the child's gender and temperament, and cultural factors. It is co-constructed in the process of intergenerational interactions in a specific cultural and socioeconomic context (Kuhar and Reiter 2013). In Western developmental literature, authority is generally discussed in reference to the stage of adolescence, as it is understood to be linked with achievement of autonomy, a key developmental task in Western societies. Of relevance are aspects such as parental control and sanctions, parent–adolescent negotiation, and the extent to which these are perceived as legitimate by adolescents and parents. Parents and adolescents play typical roles in authority negotiation. Parents are occupied with balancing the pros and cons of the extent and nature of authority, and adolescents on their part may resist or accept parental authority, or even recognize it as supportive. In Western societies, the purpose of parental authority during adolescence is to increase adolescent autonomy, with authority gradually fading into the background (Kuhar and Reiter 2013). The instrumental outcome of authority thus conceptualized does not manifest in quite the same manner in the Indian cultural context.

In the Indian context, authority is structured according to hierarchy, which is ingrained in the family system. The theme of authority relations is salient across all social relations in India, but it is particularly relevant in family relationships, especially parent–child relationship. Traditional forms of family authority are fashioned along the patriarchal hierarchical family structure, with age and gender as the defining principles. Greater formal authority generally rests with elders and with men. These tend to be rigid and involve conforming to parents and other elders, with little overt questioning. An ideal form of authority is one wherein the superior acts in a nurturing way demanding strong loyalty and compliance from the subordinate. The subordinate in turn either anticipates the person's wishes or accepts these without questioning (Sinha 1988). This is clearly evident in hierarchical family relationships wherein the superior adopts a nurturing mode and the subordinate demonstrates respect and compliance, within an ethos of mutual attachment (Kakar 1981).

In general, parents are expected to be responsible for guiding children in every major and minor domain, and in fact even beyond adolescence and across the life span, with the corresponding expectation that adolescents will give in return as and when the need may arise. The expectation of active presence in each other's lives and a lifelong relationship of reciprocity between parents and children are characteristic in Indian families. Parental authority is adaptable and flexible, characterized by a collaborative attitude and considerable mutuality. Such authority not only facilitates a democratic family environment, but also makes it possible for adolescents to "anchor" on to parents for safety and security (Omer et al. 2013), reinforcing thereby the traditional role of parents as guardians and guides. The dynamic, co-constructive, and relational elements of parental authority are further observed in the mutuality of parents' and adolescents' expectations from each other. Besides, adolescents expect the parent to make an effort to understand his or her perspective. This kind of expectation corroborates with the image of parent as friend that has been invoked by both adolescent and parent. It implies the diluting of the traditional hierarchical relationship between parent and child, with a shift from parent-centered authority to child-centered outlook. Parents are probably realizing that the traditional hierarchical model of parenting with all its strengths may not work in its existing form; in fact, it may even distance them from their children. A similar trend is observed in middle class adolescents from Chandigarh, Punjab (Larson et al. 2003), thereby suggesting a relaxation of patriarchal hierarchies in educated urban Indian middle class families (Verma and Saraswathi 2002).

The bi-directionality in socialization (Bornstein 2006; Trommsdorff 2006) is evident wherein not only parents influence the child's behavior, but the child also influences and molds parents' behavior. In this context, authority needs to be viewed as a phenomenon that unfolds in a relational context with the active involvement of the child (Kuhar and Reiter 2013). It also implies that parents may not be in total command all the time as children demand adaptations in their parenting style, and parents in turn choose to accommodate to the child's wishes and desire for autonomy (Saraswathi and Pai 1997). To a large extent, the Western focus on autonomy and independence in adolescence has disregarded the reciprocal nature of the relationship wherein parents too need to undergo developmental changes (Trommsdorff 2006). According to Valsiner (2000), this developmental transition may be especially relevant in modern societies where discourse about "how to be a good parent" (p. 273) is emphasized. Such a discourse has not been part of the traditional Indian worldview as reflected in P.N. Kirpal's quote comparing American and Indian childrearing, "You bring up your children, we live with ours" (p. 51) (Kumar 1999), implying the process of enculturation rather than socialization. Socialization presumes an agent, whereas enculturation occurs at a subconscious level wherein individuals absorb cultural beliefs and behaviors (Rentelen 2004). This scenario, however, may be changing in the present times where, in their effort to give the best to their child, urban middle class parents are becoming increasingly conscious of their approach to child rearing and are keen to make every effort to "fit" their goals and practices with the changing context and the changing adolescent. Parental authority is thus reworked to meet the changing context, with the "anchoring" function taking precedence to sustain the parent–child bond and yet retain core features that represent the traditional-moral authority.

The macro contextual changes are demanding a more liberal outlook. Even though the influence of the extended family network continues, the increasing nuclearization of urban families is conducive to a democratic climate that allows for adequate accommodation of the adolescents' opinions and wishes. The anchoring authority is thus reframed along contours that are more flexible, with greater responsiveness to the adolescents' needs and wishes. The traditional dominance-submission framework of parental authority has shifted to a model in which parents are open to consider adolescents' opinions and offer explanations for their views and decisions. Adolescents in turn acknowledge and respect parental authority, and at the same time feel comfortable to voice their views and opinions. The trend of open, friendly, and direct communication in relation to non-sensitive topics such as everyday matters, importance of education, appropriate behaviors and significance of maintaining family reputation, including open disagreements and discussions about problems has also been observed in other regions of India, such as Maharashtra, Andhra Pradesh, and Tamil Nadu (Jejeebhoy and Santhya 2011).

Articulation of adolescents' views is especially observed during instances of interpersonal disagreements. The approach and reasoning used in dealing with disagreements evince the relational and co-constitutive dimensions of authority and also draw attention to the issue of autonomy. In Western societies, parent–adolescent conflicts have been largely regarded as instrumental in the achievement of autonomy, with adolescent's demand for independence from parents viewed as a primary antecedent factor (Branje et al. 2013). Contrarily, as observed in Chap. 4, in the Indian context, parent–adolescent conflict serves a positive function in that it enables the adolescent to develop perspective-taking abilities and empathy, with the interdependent ethos characteristic of Indian families scaffolding this development.

Adolescent Self-conception: Multiplicity of Individual, Relational, and Encompassing Selves

The adolescent self is represented in multiple forms. Individual within-self descriptions focus on adolescents' characteristics and dispositions, as well as activities and interests. Relational conceptions focus upon family, peers, and the larger society. Family-focused qualities such as respecting and obeying parents are primary in the description of an "ideal" adolescent, especially an ideal girl. The relational self is thus accorded primacy. It reflects the Hindu model, in which the worldly self is viewed as evolving in relation to others (Chakkarath 2005). In consonance with this outlook, duties and responsibilities toward significant others, in this case parents, assume significance in developing a sense of self. Reference to parents is a thread that is consistently woven into the descriptions of both adolescents and parents. In fact, the parent–adolescent relationship offers a supportive space for the evolution of the relational self as well as the encompassing self. The encompassing self-construal is embedded in a relationship that extends beyond the self alone, particularly where one feels obligated or responsible for the other, such as in hierarchical relationships (Mascolo et al. 2004). Both parent and adolescent have expressed a moral responsibility and duty toward each other. Performing this duty evokes positive experience and falling short of it arouses guilt. At the present time, parents are responsible for the welfare of the adolescent, and the adolescent has a duty to recognize this and show obedience. Later, the care and support turn around with the adolescent shouldering the responsibility for the parents' welfare. This is observed in the adolescents' articulation of their dreams and wishes as well as parental expectations from the adolescent.

Although the relational and encompassing selves are privileged by both parents and adolescents, and come to the fore consistently, glimpses of the independent or autonomous self are evident in the adolescents' articulation of the need for freedom from parental regulations, expression of one's own views, and the wish for parents to understand their perspective. Whereas adolescents perceive some domains as "personal" and hence in their range of choice and decision, parents think that these require them to exercise authority, mostly arising out of a sense of protection and belief that they are responsible for their children's welfare and that they know better what is in the best interest of the adolescent. At the same time, parents show an inclination to grant autonomy to adolescents in terms of listening to their opinions, allowing them to make decisions in certain domains, and making efforts to understand their perspective. This attitude potentially supports the development of the related-autonomous self.

The Related-Autonomous Self: Waiting in the Wings?

Autonomy is culturally and contextually mediated, not only with reference to the timetable for its development, but also the value and meaning of the concept, and how much and what form of autonomy is encouraged. It is a cultural value involving views on the relation of individual to larger groups, relations of children to family, and developmental expectations for gaining rights and responsibilities (McElhaney and Allen, in press). Autonomy is intrinsically tied to the cultural conception of self as independent or interdependent, collectivistic or relational (Zimmer-Gembeck and Collins 2003). As discussed in Chap. 2, different meanings have been attributed to the construct of autonomy. One is volitional agency, which refers to being subject to one's own rule, and the other meaning refers to distancing oneself from others, being unique and separate. This meaning indicates an individualistic stance and alludes to reduced connection with others. The former is the agency dimension and the latter is the interpersonal distance dimension, and both are likely to co-exist in all societies (Kagitcibasi 2013). The autonomous-related self-construal develops in the family model of psychological interdependence. It is deemed to be high in relatedness and autonomy, with both (order-setting) control and autonomy orientation (Kagitcibasi 1996, 2005).

The nature of autonomy observed among adolescents represents what may be termed as "contextual autonomy" reflecting a mix of "individuating" and "relating" orientations, with either one gaining primacy based on the context and the domain in question. This conceptualization proposes the coexistence of individuating and relating autonomy, with cultural values and family socialization determining the centrality of a particular orientation. Individuating autonomy operates within the intrapsychic domain and leans more toward considering a context as personal, whereas relating autonomy perceives contexts in the interpersonal domain (Yeh et al. 2007). In domains such as choosing a subject of study and career, choice of friends, activities with friends, and dressing style, personal interest is clearly favored. In other domains, however, relating autonomy is evident with adolescents wishing to consider both own interests as well as parents' views, including cognizance of one's duty toward parents. In predominantly interdependent cultures such as India, there is much emphasis on obedience, self-restraint, and social obligation in the interest of relational and family harmony. Corresponding to the family change model of psychological interdependence, the nature of autonomy that is observed in the Indian context tends to align with the agency and not the separation dimension of autonomy (Kagitcibasi 1996). Glimpses of the agency dimension of autonomy are observed in adolescents' capacity to "voice" personal wishes and insecurities, their self-oriented reasoning, and their view that parents too should understand their perspective and accommodate to them in certain situations. Besides, adolescents view their parents as individuals in their own right representing a range of attributes (such as intelligent, polite, fun loving, calm, conservative, short or bad tempered, moody, and irritable). Further, as evident in discussions during situations of disagreement, the recognition that one's opinion differs from parents and the open acknowledgment that parents too can make mistakes are also indicative of autonomy.

Cultural values operate in conjunction with the wider socioeconomic context to influence development (Greenfield 2009; Trommsdorff 2006). The present day Indian society with observable changes in socialization patterns combined with focus on Western-style educational achievement and professional goals holds out an environment for individuals to develop independence and autonomy (Seymour 1999). In the context of widespread social and economic changes, the urban middle class in India is striding toward socioeconomic advancement, which is especially characteristic of progressive cities like Baroda. Individual effort and determination are deemed significant in this process. Autonomy is seen to be instrumental in success in the spheres of education and a lucrative career by way of employment or business, and hence of value. Corresponding to the changing context, parents realize that it is important for their adolescent to become self-reliant and independent in order to stand on one's own in the increasingly competitive environment of education and occupation. In keeping with the developmental stage and the demands of the exceedingly tentative macro context, parents want that their adolescents become independent and self-sufficient, and hence offer support for this dimension of autonomy.

Parental support for autonomy focuses on making the adolescent self-reliant and at the same time socially responsible in the sense of acting not only in one's own interest, but equally in the interest of significant others who may likely be affected by the individual's actions. Further, autonomy support also stems from parents' strong proclivity to hold on to the close-knit nature of the relationship, even if it means adjusting to the changing world of the adolescent. Parents consider it appropriate to grant autonomy within certain boundaries, in select domains and situations. This also influences the nature of authority in its leaning toward an adaptable and co-constructive form which is demonstrated in adolescent-parent conflict resolution. In both hypothetical and real life situations of disagreement, adolescents manifest freedom to voice their views and negotiate with parents in trying to convince them of one's own viewpoint.

At the same time that adolescents articulate self-oriented reasons to negotiate with parents, they tend to be equally uneasy about any hurt that one's actions may cause to the parent, suggesting thereby a leaning toward the relational orientation. Such patterns are observed in ethnic groups in the US (Armenian, Mexican-American, Korean) wherein on the one hand the adolescents expressed strong autonomy in situations that concerned their future, for example, choice of college major and selecting a dating partner, but on the other hand such self-assertive reasoning was tempered by concern for parents or family, thereby suggesting the coexistence of autonomy with relatedness (Phinney et al. 2005).

In interdependent cultures, autonomy granting is circumspect in the interest of upholding the culture of relatedness, even in the face of socioeconomic changes. Adolescents thus seek autonomy without giving up the relatedness with parents as the growing individual views the close family ties as a valuable support. This dynamic is conducive to the development of the related-autonomous self-construal, which may be an optimal model for adolescent self-development not only in terms of satisfaction of two basic human needs of autonomy and relatedness, but also to better adapt to the changing macro context (Kagitcibasi 2013). It is significant to note, however, that a universal balance between autonomy and relatedness may be questionable as the meanings of the two concepts are shaped by the cultural context. In cultures of independence, both can go together; in cultures of interdependence such as India, while the two may co-exist in specific situations, relatedness is likely to undermine autonomy (Trommsdorff 2006). Relational autonomy is thus more likely to take precedence in the Indian context.

Adolescent-Parent Relationship: An Edifice of Faith, Duty, and Care

The adolescent-parent relationship in urban middle class India reflects considerable positive valence orbiting around the core themes of respect for parents, faith in parents, and mutual care and concern. The perceptions of adolescents and parents with regard to expectations from each other correspond for the most part. Parents expect adolescents to fulfill their role-related duties to parents and family, become responsible, study well, prepare to face the competitive world, and make a good career. Adolescents on their part expect parents to understand and guide them, confer love and blessings, and support them in every way. The different dimensions of the adolescent-parent relationship evolve around these fundamental expectations, albeit infused with alterations in select dimensions to better adapt to the changing context.

The multifaceted nature of family relationships and the adolescent's sensitivity to parents' situation and perspective is a phenomenon that research in adolescent development has largely overlooked. The belief that adolescence is a period for gaining autonomy, promoting self-interests, and moving away from parents (especially psychologically) has led to the neglect of adolescent's capacity for empathy and deliberate reflection. Indian adolescents are acutely aware of parents' orientation and demonstrate keen interpersonal sensitivity and insight into their outlook, even when it may be contrasting to one's own. In general, much time is spent together in family activities; and adolescents evaluate this as a largely positive experience evoking feelings of calmness, safety, and relaxation (Larson et al. 2001).

Interpersonal disagreements between adolescents and parents occur across societies, in the Western and non-Western worlds. Disagreements occur mainly on mundane everyday issues such as chores, academics, regulation of behavior and activities, and finance (McElhaney and Allen in press; Schlegel and Barry 1991). In the present research, majority of such disagreements were viewed as minor. The process of resolving a disagreement involved mutual effort to understand the other's point of view and accommodate to it, express one's own perspectives in the process of negotiating the disagreement, and at the same time demonstrate substantial capacity for empathic understanding of parents' perspectives. This is evident from adolescents' opinion that in certain situations parents should not accommodate to the adolescent, instead they should be firm and their (parents') decision should prevail. In the same vein, adolescents also feel that they should accommodate to parents as the latter are experienced, know better, and are aware of what is in the best interest of the child.

During situations of disagreement, family members express their own opinions and adolescents are required to ponder upon differing viewpoints in order to negotiate an issue. Disagreements present opportunities to articulate and reflect upon one's own views, learn how to convince parents about the same, appreciate others' position, and engage in sensitive consideration of parents' views. Adolescents also experience anxiety with ensuing feelings of guilt arising from the possibility of one's actions having brought hurt or unhappiness to the parents. Parents in turn give space to the adolescent to argue and discuss one's perspective. In addition to instilling self-expression, this also creates an opportunity to know the adolescent better and perhaps help him or her to deal with the issue at hand, especially if it is one that the young individual may otherwise hesitate to share (e.g., romantic interest or relationship). This not only strengthens the communication but also reinforces the parents' desire to continue to be an integral part of the adolescent's world. The dynamics that play out in such situations thus become instrumental in strengthening intersubjectivity in the adolescent-parent relationship.

As Trommsdorff (2006) observes, parent–child interaction (including during conflict situations) is sculpted around the generalized cultural script of what is an optimal relationship, which in the Indian context is one of adolescent respect and obedience to parents, and reciprocal support and guidance from parents. Embedded in the approach and perspective is the enduring cultural expectation of maintaining family harmony and affiliation. Given this backdrop, proclivity and effort toward mutual accommodation are sine qua non. The approach to resolution also reflects the internalized Indian psychosocial orientation of opting for a middle path (*madhyam marg; vachlo rasto* or *taru pan nai ane maru pan nai*—meaning neither according to you nor me), which is often the preferred option in situations of conflict since it is perceived as the way to maintain harmony (Panda 2013). Taking the middle path also affords space to dwell upon multiple views and routes of resolution wherein both adolescents and parents express their viewpoints.

A prominent narrative of adolescent development in India is that adolescents develop their identity and gain autonomy with the help of parents rather than by distancing from them. The centrality of family in the Indian psyche is firmly entrenched. The continual interpersonal dynamics lead the adolescents toward a culturally valued social maturity that centers on moral duty and respect for parents, cognizance of parents' care and concern, and unconditional faith in parents' experience and intention. The essential role of parents in scaffolding the adolescent to facilitate a smooth transition in the face of contextual vulnerabilities is well-recognized and accepted, by both the adolescent and the parent. Contrary to the "separate" world that most Western adolescents seem to prefer, the Indian adolescents welcome parents' involvement in their lives. In fact, their intervention is expected and is mostly perceived as springing from care and concern for the adolescent.

Even as the primary pattern of parent–adolescent relationship revolves around mutuality, an alternate pattern also runs parallel. This relates to adolescents' expressed need for greater flexibility in parental regulation and monitoring of their activities and choices, and the perception that parents are perhaps imposing or interfering in the adolescents' affairs a tad too much. The increasing leaning toward child-centeredness combined with anxiety about perceived detrimental influences of the changing environment persuades parents to direct their adolescents' lives as much as possible. Even if adolescents are aware that the parents' intention is to protect them, yet they wish for reprieve from persistent supervision and desire more freedom and flexibility.

Parents as 'Managers' and Adolescents as 'Projects'

Parenting in the present times unfolds in a dynamic landscape. Parents feel responsible to ensure that their children are able to adapt well to the contextual contingencies. Their involvement in the adolescents' lives thus becomes more assertive. In urban Indian upper middle class families in particular, parenting is transforming into a 'project.' Parents are the 'managers' and children are their 'projects' to be polished to perfection, which is defined more from the perspective of parents and less from the viewpoint of adolescents. A school counselor observes, *"Parents look at the child as if they want to give him or her a prize in two areas of competition—school and home. They want to label the child as my model child. Parents want to create 'mini-me's.' So, it is like an image building exercise for parents. And, they say this to the child, 'What you are today we have made you.'"*

Childcentric socialization is gaining ground and parents are eager to participate more actively in their adolescents' lives. The image of parent as friend, and the associated concept of "smart parents" who are "with the times" in appearance and behavior, is gaining momentum in the middle and upper middle class urban settings, evidenced from instances such as the parent and teenage child visiting the gym or beauty salon together. In general, parents are becoming more conscious of their inputs and participation in children's lives; they are keen on spending quality time and involving themselves in many of their adolescents' activities. That this may at all bother the adolescent, causing additional stress and a feeling of being hemmed in seems to be of little concern or is largely ignored. In the present times, middle class parents also have access to technological tools that facilitate their constant contact with adolescents. Contrary to the popular notion that technology is hindering interpersonal interactions, the advent and prolific use of the cell phone is not only instrumental in increased social interactions, but also in fact serves as a useful device that enables parents to stay in touch with children at all times, thereby monitoring them better. Thus, not only does the cell phone function as an instrument of freedom and privacy for the adolescent, but it also facilitates "staying in touch," with family a time-honored imperative in middle class Indian families. Parents realize that the cell phone is a double-edged tool, but its immense potential as a device to stay updated on the adolescent's whereabouts apparently outweighs all other concerns.

Urban middle class parents are caught in a web of escalating material and social aspirations and are keen to instill the same in their adolescents. Competition is pervasive and blatant in all domains. For instance, there is an ever-increasing preoccupation with social status and constant comparisons with the Shahs and Mehtas next door; enthusiastic parents desire to project the achievements of their adolescent child as a trophy to show off. Indians are predisposed to social comparisons (Sinha 1988), amply observed among middle class families. Present day adolescents are thus required to deal with a double-layered phenomenon, which includes self-comparisons with peers and others, as well as comparisons that are induced by parents. The well-ingrained dynamic family and social network in the

Indian society and the inclination to "fit it" with one's primary and secondary social circles perhaps renders the scenario even more favorable to social comparisons. Just as the extended social network provides support, it is equally demanding in its persuasion to involve actively, which entails freedom to advice and judge on a wide range of subjects. There is, however, a "dark side" to it in that frequent social comparisons tend to have negative implications for personal well-being as well as for interpersonal and intergroup relations (White et al. 2006, p. 36). This has serious implications on the adolescents' perception of self in terms of creating self-doubts, insecurity, and even a sense of shame over real or imagined failures. The perceived threats of the globalizing context are driving parents to assume a protective role in order to shield their adolescents from risky influences and ensure a safe and secure path of development. The traditional parental role of guardian and guide is coming into play even more prominently in the present times, with parents perceiving that adolescents' need perpetual support in navigating their vulnerabilities. Parents seem worried that the globalizing world may carry the adolescent on a path that may not only be ill-defined in terms of healthy development, but also steer the child away from valued cultural goals as well as from the family unit. The image of parent as friend hence collides with that of parent as guardian and guide, often resulting in mixed signals and misunderstandings with the adolescent. This also points to a disjunction between the ideal image and the reality of lived experience. To keep abreast with the changing times, parents are keen to adopt an attitude that is more like that of a friend, and adolescents too expect and experience this in some form. Nevertheless, the interactions among the complex contextual factors that require constant balancing of the opportunities and risks, and the imperative to perform one's core cultural role of guardian and guide urge parents to oscillate between these roles as they deem fit.

The notions of freedom that adolescents have are different from what parents experienced in growing up. Both thus feel the "generation gap," and whereas this phenomenon is enacted in each generation, it manifests more compellingly in the extant context of accelerated change. Many issues of dissatisfaction are minor and although some of these may be viewed as integral to the growing up process, their persistent recurrence may lead the adolescent toward dishonesty and manipulation. Will this process take the form of a predicament of parental loss of control and the corollary interpretation of adolescence as a crisis period like in Western societies? (Valsiner 2000). Probably not, as the encircling cultural context of interdependence and family affiliation ensures that parental authority, involvement, and participation in the adolescents' lives will never cease, now and even across later developmental stages, embedded as it is in the hierarchical cultural structure and the deep-rooted conception of parent akin to God. In fact, the anxiety and involvement of middle class parents in the child's academic activities such as homework, schoolwork, board exams, admission to college, and employment may well be paving the way for restoring the traditional adult-child continuity wherein there was little differentiation of the child's world from that of the adults' world (Kumar 1993). As Schelgel (2011) observes, integration of adolescents with adults, a common feature of traditional pre-industrial societies, is beneficial as the latter offers wide ranging support that contributes to adolescent social and emotional development. Notwithstanding such positive aspects, parents may need to work on themselves to strengthen their trust in the adolescents and provide space to enable their choices and perspectives to shape decisions that potentially will have much impact on their lives.

Gender: The Eternal Iceberg

The gender revolution is often heralded as a significant accomplishment of the twentieth century with apparent changes in women's educational achievements, entry into the male-dominated workforce, and political participation (England 2010). Gender is conspicuous in agendas set by international agencies, for example, the United Nations Millennium Development Goals and more recently the Sustainable Development Goals. India is an active partner in such endeavors. The women's movement has been a strong force in the Indian society and its impact is evident in the increased recognition of women's rights and issues of gender equity as well as systematic macro level legal and political inputs (Phadke 2003).

In urban middle class, the positive influence of the women's movement is discernible especially with regard to women's entry into higher education. The value of education in the middle class translates to girls as well, and parents are encouraging of their daughters' educational achievements. Attaining a graduate degree is a norm in middle class families. Education is perceived to have multiple values. It is viewed as a symbol of social status and family pride, adds value in the marriage market as a potential tool for income generation after marriage as well as support for girls in case the marriage fails, and a contributing factor in achieving some independence (Kakar and Kakar 2007). At the same time, the proverbial glass ceiling finds its way into the family context and is particularly evident in the imposition of gender-based boundaries and restrictions in education as well as other domains.

Gender mediates the construction of adolescence. This is evidenced in greater articulation of the concern for protecting a girl from situations that may put her sexuality and reputation at risk, in turn also tarnishing the family reputation. Hence, there is close monitoring and greater imposition of restrictions on girls than boys. The socialization of girls in middle class families reflects a catch-22 like situation. On the one hand, they are raised to become achievement oriented and their aspirations are encouraged. On the other hand, they are persuaded to exercise caution and restraint, lest their aspirations result in any concession of culturally valued gender roles that essentially revolve around marriage, family, and home. Thus, although there is expansion in the repertoire of gender roles in terms of inclusion of education and career, indicators of women's empowerment, the traditional gender norms persist. Education and career choices are mostly weighed against their potential to interfere with the cherished goals of marriage and family life. Any adjustments that need to be made must preferably occur in the former domains.

A strong gender concern of parents pertains to the vulnerability and protection of their daughters' sexuality. Images of what it means to be a "good girl" are transmitted during early socialization, also emphasizing that it is her behavior and demeanor that will shield her against any advances that may blemish her "purity" (Kakar and Kakar 2007, p. 55). Not only do these notions shape girls' pathways to education and career, but also monitor their everyday life in terms of behavior, dress, and interactions with boys. In the middle class, gender discrimination does not occur in obvious ways. In fact, educated middle class families are making every effort to incorporate gender equality in their socialization. However, messages of gender equality are fine-tuned along the guiding narrative that girls are more vulnerable, their sexuality needs to be protected at all costs, and the larger context poses much risk. Hence, the threshold of flexibility accorded to women is confined to an arena that seldom veers beyond the core cultural ideals. Whereas middle class parents pride themselves in being open-minded and in tune with the changing times, compromising on gender ideals appears to be rather problematic for them. Autonomy for girls is thus circumscribed, and the justification for the same is located in the realm of external factors over which the parent or the adolescent has little apparent control.

Evidently, not much has changed since Sharma's (1996) empirical observation about girls from middle socioeconomic strata being caught between meeting the desire for a self-identity and the need to conform to a socially approved identity, which in turn demands a devaluation of individuality. The life space and identity of Indian women revolve largely around social roles and relationships, and the reinforcement or reproach that comes in its wake. Attitude and behavior that may potentially compromise these aspects create conflicts and dilemmas, in turn affecting one's sense of self-worth (Kapadia 1999). Adolescent girls protest against the imposition of "unfair" restrictions on everyday activities as well as long-term choices of career and even marriage. They express much frustration and need for autonomy in such matters, invoking references to "generation gap" and sometimes even rebellion as reflected in the threatening retort of a girl that if parents force her into marriage with someone whom she does not prefer, she will run away from home. The globalizing world is enabling girls to acquaint and engage with alternate forms of being and living, which leads them to question the ways of their parents. As Thapan (2007) observes, "This lived experience of educationally advantaged urban young women remains embedded in a particular social class that shapes their consciousness in many different ways—perhaps critical and liberated in some situations, but limited and oppressive in other social contexts" (p. 43).

Like culture, gender is inherently enmeshed in an individual's psyche. Consistent efforts toward women's emancipation and empowerment by women's movements, non-government organizations, and the government have certainly resulted in improvement in women's situation and status in India. Nonetheless, social, cultural, and religious variables defined by deep-rooted gendered beliefs and practices continue to persist in different degrees and forms. As discussed in Chap. 2, the urban Indian middle class is at the forefront of social change, assuming perhaps even a hegemonic character. The urban upper middle class woman is viewed as an archetype of the modern Indian woman, one who has transcended the domestic sphere to make her mark in the world. Yet, their aspirations and achievements are constantly coordinated with traditional gender norms, even if in new forms (Kapadia, unpublished manuscript). Women are observed to shape their aspirations to evolve a balanced life (Thapan 2007), and the culturally familiar "middle path" is perceived as the best strategy to avoid extreme measures that may lead to contention and relational disharmony. Although women's upward mobility in education and jobs signifies gender egalitarianism, this does not seem to affect belief in essential gender roles. Even among individuals who believe in gender equality, one observes little commitment in addressing gender differentiation for its own sake (England 2010). The resilience of patriarchy and gender bias is evident at all levels of the environment, across all life stages and domains (Philipose 2012).

Interplay of Cultural Continuity and Change

Cultural transformation unfolds unevenly across time and across domains, creating thereby a mosaic of continuity and change. Individuals are active actors in cultural evolution. In general, parents and members of the older generation are more concerned with the transmission of existing cultural values, whereas youth are more inclined to embrace novelty and change. Parent–adolescent relationships and any changes therein function as contributors to cultural change; the dynamic hence offers a glimpse into the interplay of cultural continuity and change.

Adolescents' outlook reflects a mix of both, the perspectives of the family and the large social milieu. The dynamic fluctuations within and across ecocultural contexts and increasing plasticity of boundaries facilitate greater penetration of multiple variable influences, that in turn influence socio-psychological orientation. In the contemporary context in flux, a uniquely Indian tapestry of adolescent development is revealed, comprising a blend of traditional motifs integrated with contemporary ones to create a design more conducive to navigate new horizons. Traditional elements such as family cohesion and relational harmony are preserved, thereby reinforcing the "individual-in-social-world" model of development. Adolescents are aware and appreciative of their parents' concern and support, and at the same time, they expect and demand flexibility from them. Accordingly, parental authority is reframed in a less stringent and more flexible form to accommodate space for adolescents' articulation of self-views. This is in departure from the dominance-compliance orientation assumed to characterize adolescents in Asian societies. In this vein, a new motif of "parent as friend" is invoked to better deal with the spate of contextual influences, lest these disengage the adolescent from the parent. Unlike Western societies, the cultural imperative is not to break away from parents and family (Larson et al. 2003); instead, connection is of essence.

Socialization goals focus on acquiring knowledge and responsibility, with active attention to preserving relational ties, thereby resonating with the traditional framework, although through a different approach. The adolescent self represents a multifaceted construal constituting culturally valued models of the relational and encompassing selves. Concurrently, in response to the demands of the globalizing context, we observe the emergence of yet another new motif—expression of adolescent autonomy. The nature of autonomy, however, assumes a contextual character and unfolds in the relational sphere. Adolescents are voicing self-goals, some of which are encouraged by parents provided these do not interfere with the family and gender-based cultural goals. Parents' focus is on inculcating in adolescents an orientation comprising a mélange of independence and interdependence that involves little compromise with culturally cherished goals.

Whither Blow the Winds of Change?

Cultures are dynamic, and pathways of human development are prone to change in response to changing sociodemographic conditions. Whereas socioeconomic factors influence cultural values, the process entails change as well as resistance (Greenfield 2009). Scholarly discussion of social change and human development often alludes to the modernization assumption and its convergence hypothesis, which assumes that the divergent patterns of family and society across the world will converge over time toward the Western individualistic model. The alternate contention is that change takes different forms and is not bound to follow a single path toward the Western endpoint. The term "transitional societies" is often used to refer to developing countries, implying that these societies are transitioning toward the Western model. Correspondingly, changes in the family are also expected to occur along Western patterns, for example, nucleation and individuation. The counter argument is that although change characterizes all societies, the nature of change may be variable (Kagitcibasi 2007). In a similar vein, Greenfield's (2009) theory of social change contends that different socioeconomic variables can move in different order and at different rates across societies, and not necessarily in the Western direction. At the same time, the theory suggests that movement toward either a more Gemeinschaft value or Gesellschaft value will in turn guide socialization in the corresponding direction. Although glimpses of individual expression and personal choice—Gesellschaft values—are evident among the urban middle class adolescents, the interdependent cultural worldview continues to transmit persuasive influence.

Refuting the modernization hypothesis, the emerging pattern in the adolescent-parent relationship in urban Indian middle class instead highlights strands of cultural resistance and change that is creating a distinctly Indian *avatar*. What is particularly remarkable is that Indians are appropriating global technological advancements such as cell phone and social media to reinforce relationship bonds, not only within a city or country, but across continents as well. Such developments are suggestive of "glocalization," a phenomenon in which the global and the local interact to create a blend or adaptation that is locally suited (Khondker 2004). Facilitating factors are the Indian predisposition toward tolerance of contradictions as well as cultural resilience and tendency for bicultural functioning, the latter being particularly evident in immigration contexts. Recent research with Indian-American and Indian-Canadian adolescents and parents has shown that the overall shared orientation is one that recommends integrating the best of both worlds; for instance, values such as independence from the host societies (America and Canada) along with primary Indian values such as family support, and duty and obligation to parents. A parent termed this as "living like a lotus," such that despite being in the midst of a muddy lake (signifying alien, Western environment), the (Indian) lotus remains untouched and blooms into a beautiful flower (Kapadia 2008, 2009, p. 176, 2013).

Chen (2015) has put forth the "pluralist-constructive" perspective (p. 57) to address the influence of social change on socialization. It argues that whereas new values are likely to affect attitudes and behaviors, these tend to be integrated with existing cultural traditions, in both Western and non-Western societies. He contends that different values have distinct contributions, which will potentially enhance human development. For example, individualistic values facilitate achievement of personal goals whereas collectivistic values would lead to interpersonal responsibility and greater harmony between personal and group goals. Both types of basic human needs—autonomy and connection—would thus be satisfied.

Social change penetrates through the prism of culture. People in a culture welcome some elements and resist others to create a "best fit" in their view. The context-dependent character of the Indian psyche and the proclivity toward the "middle path" or "middle way out" facilitate an adaptation that alternates between assimilation with existing beliefs and values and accommodation to new influences. Interplay of cultural continuity and change is thus revealed, with both adolescent and parent making the effort to retain core cultural values, and yet embrace new ideas so as to render a fusion that is Indian at heart. Apparently, "Culture seems to have two faces, because culture obviously plays a role both when families resist the dissolution of traditional structures as well as when they accommodate to the changed conditions of their lives. It is hard to judge whether these accommodations are successful or not" (Krappmann 2001, p. 15). Only time will tell…

Conceptual Framework Revisited

The understanding of adolescence derived in this book is situated at the interface of culture and context, and its influence on the microsystem of family, specifically on the parent–adolescent relationship. Figure 6.1 revisits the conceptual framework of the study and presents the interplay of cultural and contextual factors involved in mediating the construction of adolescence and parent–adolescent relationship in the urban middle class context in Baroda, Gujarat.

Human development unfolds at the interface of cultural worldview and contextual factors. The Indian cultural worldview is one of connectedness and interdependence, privileging a social-relational script. This fundamental ideology

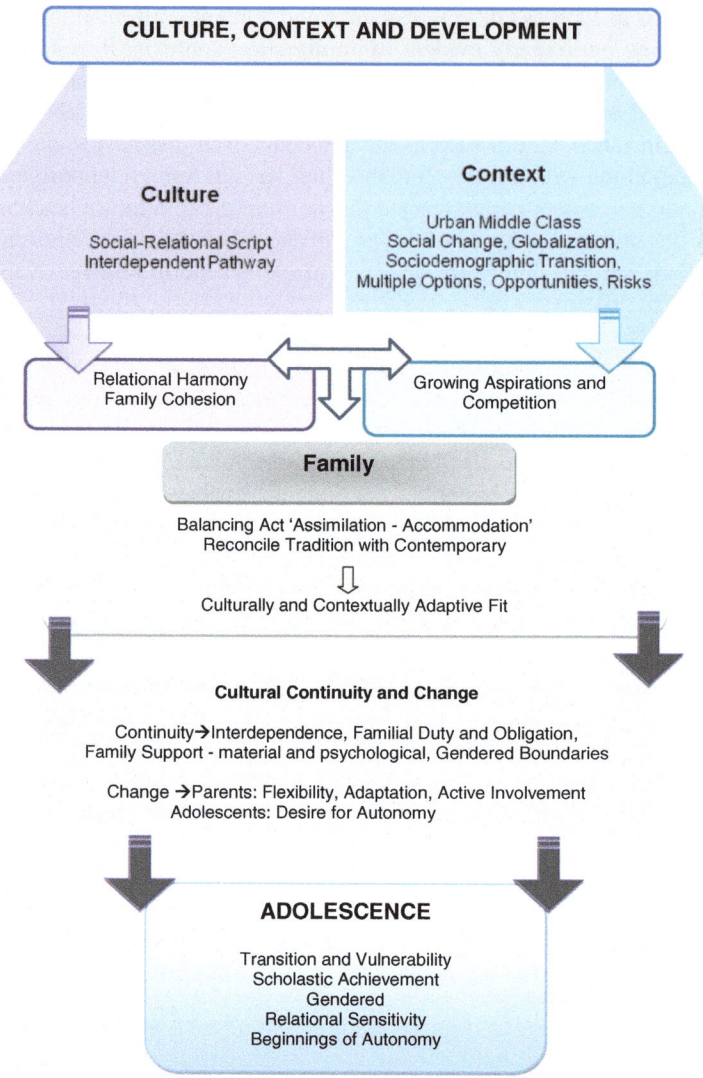

Fig. 6.1 Adolescence in urban middle class India: A cultural-contextual depiction

provides the framework of socialization, guiding notions of self and relationship, and definitions of a "good parent" and a "good child." Familial values of cohesion and harmony are of utmost significance. It is with this central outlook that parents and adolescents meet the phenomena of social change and globalization. The phenomena operate at multiple levels, beginning with sociodemographic changes that permeate the family and individual to influence values and behaviors (Greenfield 2009). Family change in the urban Indian middle class approximates Kagitcibasi's family model of psychological interdependence (2007). With increased economic status, parental dependence on children for material resources is decreasing. Emotional or psychological interdependence, however, continues to be much valued and all effort is made to ensure that it endures.

The Indian middle class is well-poised and eager to embrace the multiple options and opportunities that the macro context is presenting, and the Gujarati middle class is no exception. The cascading demands imposed by the globalizing context are bringing in their wake significant changes at the family and individual levels. Parents and adolescents are drawn into the fold, unwittingly, willingly, or reluctantly. Just as the context offers opportunities, it induces tension and insecurity, essentially stemming from the unfamiliar. A two-fold approach ensues. One is the tendency to assimilate influences to fit with familiar, extant ways of being and living. This approach, however, is not likely to work across all domains and therefore demands adjustment and alteration in idea and practice. Accommodation emerges as the other approach. Middle class Gujarati parents are adjusting their outlook to facilitate adolescents' adaptation to contextual exigencies. For instance, encouragement of independence is observed to the extent that it is perceived as facilitating success in the competitive world of education and work. Baroda offers a fairly broadminded context to young women and men. Gender equality in socialization is evident, with more flexible boundaries, and girls are encouraged for education and career, and also allowed greater mobility. Even so, the core gender ideals and expectations persist.

Increasing contact with non-family influences through media and the Internet is opening up the world of the Barodian adolescent, resulting in greater acquaintance with multiple ways of being and behaving. There is growing awareness of "personal choice" in domains such as selection of friends, style of dressing, and career options. The Indian model of development endorses the relational self during the earlier stages of development and offers scope for the realization of the individual or autonomous self only once the worldly and family responsibilities are fulfilled. Glimpses of change in this model are suggested in adolescents' expression and exercise of personal choice and the frustration with parental restrictions in certain domains. As a response to this, changes in parent–adolescent interactions are observed in terms of openness in communication, parental inclination to be friendly, to try and understand the adolescent, and to make efforts to accommodate to the adolescent's views. Overall, parental authority is relaxed and transpires in a warm and caring environment. With increasing flexibility in the socialization process, the autonomous dimension of self appears to be surfacing earlier, even if in select domains. Whether this is a transitional developmental phenomenon or will likely strengthen as the adolescent moves into emerging adulthood remains an open question.

It is also relevant to note that adolescent autonomy operates within a relational context and that parental encouragement of autonomy does not imply separation or disengagement from parents and family. The inclination is to balance self-goals with family expectations, rather than sacrifice one for the other. Interpersonal responsiveness in the parent–adolescent relationship is mostly experienced as consonant with rather than opposed to self-development. The cultural ideal of interdependence is firmly entrenched and parents especially are strongly committed to preserving it. Whereas adolescents eagerly welcome change, they are equally aware of the value of unconditional family support. It makes them feel secure and supports their navigation of the complexities and uncertainties that are meted out by the globalizing world. More than adolescents, it is the parents who appear apprehensive and insecure about weakening relational bonds. Adolescents seem to take this element for granted as evinced in their expectations that parents are and should always be there to offer material and psychological support.

In general, parents and adolescents are involved in balancing the old with the new, keen on preserving familial values and at the same time adapting to the changing times so that they may march ahead in tandem with each other and with the core cultural ideals. How to generate a workable blend of individual and collective aspirations so as to have the best of both worlds is of primary concern to the adolescent and to the parents as well.

In essence, the traditional constituents of the adolescent-parent relationship sustain, albeit with permeable contours to integrate "newer" forms and facets signifying a cultural integration that will only enable better adaptation to the changing context. Adolescence in the Indian context thus evolves in close alliance with parents involved as active partners in ensuring a successful transition to adulthood. Both parents and adolescents consider parents as indispensable companions in this developmental transition, especially in the present context in flux. Rather than create a "rupture" young individuals prefer to stretch traditional values as a means to realize their dreams (Kakar and Kakar 2007, p. 15). As eloquently observed by Krishna Kumar, "...it is hard to escape the point that in the heart of such alleged symptoms of modernization and social change, the phenomenon of cultural persistence is staring at us if only we would pay attention to it" (1993, p. 72).

Implications for Adolescent Development

Adolescence in the urban middle class largely emerges as a positive experience, facilitated by the support of parents. This highlights the immense strengths that the family and culture offer to ensure that adolescent development proceeds with little tension and anxiety. These positive elements need to be reinforced and nurtured, to enhance development and enable adolescents to live their lives in a constructive way, simultaneously preparing them to embrace social change in a prudent and productive manner. The orientation toward interdependence, positivity and mutuality in parent–adolescent relationship, adolescent reliance on parents' advice and support, and capacity for compromise and empathy combined with parents' flexibility and willingness to adapt to the contemporary changes are elements that potentially contribute to enhancement of family relationships and self-growth. These qualities need to be reinforced and enhanced toward extending compassion to the larger community and society. Importantly, these perspectives shift the lens from a problem-focused conception of adolescence to a positive paradigm that reinforces constructive capacities that will steer the adolescent toward greater well-being.

Even as these positive features are heartening, it is important to take cognizance of aspects that may potentially undermine adolescent development. For instance, while parental involvement and active role in their adolescents' lives are welcoming to the adolescent, are there perhaps times when parents overstep their bounds, inadvertently as it were? The increasing unpredictability in the environment impacts socialization processes, and parents are often confused regarding appropriate practices. The multiple options and challenges of the macro context instill anxiety in parents, which is manifested in different domains for instance, close monitoring of adolescents' activities with friends and putting intense pressure on adolescents to perform well in the high school board exams. Adolescents have shared their frustrations with ambitious and perhaps unrealistic parental expectations, impositions, and interventions in their life choices. In addition to dealing with the vulnerabilities of their developmental stage and the challenges posed by the global context in flux, adolescents feel obligated to attend to the well-meaning mandates of parents. This is most evident in academic performance. On the one hand, the adolescent's preparation and tension in the run up to the board exams are shared with the family collective, thereby dispersing the stress. On the other hand, there is the cultural narrative of respecting and honoring parents' wishes, which creates strain and guilt about letting parents' down. Similar situations occur in the domains of career choice, romantic relationships, and later on in marriage partner selection. Notwithstanding the dominant narrative that parents know better what is good for the child, adolescents have expressed dissatisfactions regarding parents being over protective or imposing their choices on the adolescent. How do these aspects impinge upon adolescent development? What are its implications for growth of independent thinking and creativity? Such questions merit critical consideration.

Augmentation of life style is a collective aspiration that characterizes middle class families in contemporary India, and these aspirations naturally filter down to the adolescent. The aspirational middle class lifestyle is reflected in adolescents' expressions of wishes and notions of success mainly in terms of material acquisitions and comforts. At the same time, the globalizing world has paved the way for increasing acquaintance with other, perhaps more alluring ways of living and being that adolescents tend to covet. Intense desire for material acquisitions along with social peer group comparisons is not only detrimental to development but is also likely to push the adolescent to embark on risky paths that he or she is unable to deal with. This is illustrated in recent reality-based television shows, for example, *Gumrah*—End of Innocence (Channel V) that depicts how a moment of non-judgment could escalate into life damaging consequences for the young individual.

Yet another vital issue is that concerning the implications of parental orientation with regard to gender. Gendered attitudes such as girls being more vulnerable and their primary responsibility being the household and family are consistently observed. Control of female sexuality, although not directly voiced, remains a concern in the Indian society, across social classes. The dominant tendency in middle class families is to maintain cultural continuity in some domains and at the same time incorporate and integrate "progressive" values of education and economic empowerment. While cultural scripts of relatedness and family affiliation offer support for adolescent development, the cultural stereotypes related to gender, tend to interfere in women's long-term career goals and personal growth. How to balance the needs of family with the goal of gender equity and women's personal autonomy is a lingering issue across social class (Seymour 1999). The discrepancy or lag between belief and behavior also plays a role. Educated parents may believe in promoting women's empowerment, nevertheless translating this ideology into practice does not come easy. Adolescents thus receive ambivalent messages regarding the extent and nature of aspirations that they may cultivate. Despite the Indian disposition of living with co-existing contradictions (Sinha and Tripathi 1994), adolescents may find it difficult to reconcile such situations.

In today's multifaceted world, young people require competencies that will facilitate functioning across different circumstances and reconciling diverse value systems (Chen 2015). Indian youth show considerable adeptness in interspersing traditional ideas and behaviors to fit the contemporary context. At the same time, individual differences in attitude and ability are likely, and not all young individuals or parents for that matter, may be successful in transforming variable influences into a functional ensemble. Interventions in this direction would go a long way in preparing young individuals and parents for optimal functioning in the global context (Renner 2014).

As adults, we need to extend our constructive and forward-looking support in order to enable young individuals to stride ahead on the increasingly intricate pathway of development, bearing an optimistic attitude. Along with family, the school and the larger system of formal education need to respond to this context to interweave principles of self-regulation, develop resilience, and inculcate values such as compassion, altruism, gratitude, empathy, and forgiveness. Notwithstanding the difficulties that urban middle class adolescents experience in negotiating the globalizing world, it is necessary to instill in them awareness regarding their privileged positions in comparison with their counterparts in other regions and settings of India. Rural–urban, social class, caste, and gender divides continue across different domains such as age at marriage, literacy and education, and health and nutrition. For instance, at the same time that urban middle class adolescents are occupied with scholastic tasks, adolescents in the lower social class and rural areas, girls especially, are employed in domestic work and home-based industries (Saraswathi and Oke 2013). In the same vein, as these urban adolescents are preparing to enter the portals of higher education, 20% men and 62% women between the ages 18 and 24 in rural areas are already married (Jayaraman 2013). Whereas educational focus on preparing youth for the increasingly competitive world is necessary, we need to be equally cognizant about values that will contribute to a more humane and meaningful life in the long run.

Further, to strengthen positive adolescent development, we need to offer spaces where adolescents can share and discuss freely any and all of their concerns. Parents too are prone to confusion and insecurity, as they may not have the knowledge or means to deal with "new" issues or old issues wrapped in new packages. For example, given the adolescents' inclination toward autonomy, parents may feel even more anxious and fear a disruption in the relationship. They are probably unaware that adolescents appreciate parental flexibility and support for autonomy, which in turn is likely to reinforce positive outlook and contribute to strengthening the relationship. It is necessary to share such perspectives with parents in order to dissipate their anxiety. Discussion and support groups for parents are thus crucial, as they are indispensable central anchors of adolescent development in the Indian context.

With regard to policy, it is critical that we depart from a deficit perspective that views adolescents as an issue to be addressed, and instead regard young people as assets and as active citizens with immense potential for bringing about positive change in society. Drawing attention to the intrinsic and not just instrumental value of policies for youth, Prakash (2013) contends that policies need to acknowledge the ideas and resources that youth bring, allow them to take charge of their lives, and ensure that their voices are heard. The National Youth Policy 2014 manifests a firm commitment to empower youth to achieve their full potential and contribute to the nation's development (National Youth Policy 2014). A critical precondition for this is to create opportunities and spaces for young people and their families to share their hopes, dreams, and concerns. Family will continue to occupy a central place in the lives of young individuals provided it remains responsive to the myriad contextual stimuli and is supportive in enabling the adolescent to express and realize one's unique potential. Safe and neutral spaces are essential to seek guidance when necessary in favor of the goal of enriching the path toward positive development such that adolescents' hopes and dreams flourish in the familiar and caring context of the family collective.

References

Badrinath, C. (2003). The householder, grhastha, in the Mahabharata. In M. Pernau, I. Ahmed, & H. Reifeld (Eds.), *Family and gender: Changing values in Germany and India* (pp. 113–139). New Delhi: Sage.

Blossfeld, H. P., Klijzing, E., Mills, M., & Kurz, K. (Eds.). (2005). *Globalization, uncertainty and youth in society: The losers in a globalizing world*. New York: Routledge.

Bornstein, M. H. (2006). Parenting science and practice. In W. Damon & R. M. Lerner (Chief Eds.), K. Ann Renninger & I. Sigel (Vol. Eds.), *Handbook of child psychology, Vol. 4: Child psychology in practice* (6th ed., pp. 893–949). New York: Wiley.

Branje, S. J. T., Laursen, B., & Collins, W. A. (2013). Parent-child communication during adolescence. In A. L. Vangelisti (Ed.), (2nd ed., pp. 271–286). New York, NY: Routledge.

Chakkarath, P. (2005). What can Western psychology learn from indigenous psychologies? Lessons from Hindu psychology. In W. Friedlmeier, P. Chakkarath, & B. Schwarz (Eds.), *Culture and human development: The importance of cross-cultural research to the social sciences* (pp. 31–51). New York: Psychology Press.

Chen, X. (2015). Exploring the implications of social change for human development: Perspectives, issues and future directions. *International Journal of Psychology, 50*(1), 56–59.

England, P. (2010). The gender revolution: Uneven and stalled. *Gender and Society, 24*(2), 149–166. doi:10.1177/0891243210361475.

Fernandes, L. (2016). India's middle classes in contemporary India. In K. A. Jacobsen (Ed.), *Routledge handbook of contemporary India* (pp. 232–242). London: Routledge.

Gala, J., & Chaudhary, S. (2009). Coping with stress among Indian adolescents belonging to the high income group. In A. K. Tiwari (Ed.), *Psychological perspectives on social issues and human development* (pp. 329–360). New Delhi: Concept Publishing Company.

Greenfield, P. M. (2009). Linking social change and developmental change: Shifting pathways of human development. *Developmental Psychology, 45*(2), 401.

Jayaraman, A. (2013). A demographic overview. In P. Prakash (Ed.), *State of the urban youth, India 2013: Employment, livelihoods, skills* (pp. 8–15). Mumbai: IRIS Knowledge Foundation.

Jejeebhoy, S. J., & Santhya, K. S. (2011). *Parent-child communication on sexual and reproductive health matters: Perspectives of mothers and fathers of youth in India.* New Delhi: Population Council.

Jodhka, S. S., & Prakash, A. (2016). *The Indian middle class.* Delhi: Oxford University Press.

Kagitcibasi, C. (1996). *Family and human development across cultures: A view from the other side.* Hillsdale, NJ: Lawrence Erlbaum.

Kagitcibasi, C. (2005). Autonomy and relatedness in cultural context implications for self and family. *Journal of Cross-Cultural Psychology, 36*(4), 403–422.

Kagitcibasi, C. (2007). *Family, self and human development across cultures: Theory and application* (2nd ed.). New Jersey: Psychology Press.

Kagitcibasi, C. (2013). Adolescent autonomy-relatedness and the family in cultural context: What is optimal? *Journal of Research on Adolescence, 23*(2), 223–235.

Kakar, S. (1981). *The inner world: A psychoanalytic study of childhood in India* (2nd ed.). New Delhi: Oxford University Press.

Kakar, S., & Kakar, K. (2007). *The Indians: Portrait of a people.* New Delhi: Penguin.

Kapadia, S. (n.d.). *Marriage dilemmas of young women in contemporary India: Negotiating tradition and modernity.* Unpublished manuscript.

Kapadia, S. (1999). Self, women and empowerment: A conceptual inquiry. In T. S. Saraswathi (Ed.), *Culture, socialization and human development: Theory, research and applications in India* (pp. 255–277). New Delhi: Sage.

Kapadia, S. (2008). Adolescent- parent relationships in Indian and Indian—immigrant families in US: Intersections and disparities. *Psychology and Developing Societies, 20*(2), 257–275.

Kapadia, S. (2009). Cultural perspectives on parenting in the context of globalization and acculturation: Viewpoints from India and Canada. *International Journal of Interdisciplinary Social Sciences, 3*(10), 171–178.

Kapadia, S. (2013). Adolescents in Indian immigrant families in Canada: Navigating two cultural worlds. *International Journal of Interdisciplinary Global Studies, 7*(3), 7–18.

Khondker, H. H. (2004). Glocalization as globalization: Evolution of a sociological concept. *Bangladesh e-Journal of Sociology, 1*(2), 1–9.

Krappmann, L. (2001). No parenting independent of culture. *Culture and parenting: An overview. ISSBD Newsletter, 38*(1), 15–16.

Kumar, K. (1993). Study of childhood and family. In T. S. Saraswathi & B. Kaur (Eds.), *Human development and family studies in India: An agenda for research and policy* (pp. 67–76). New Delhi: Sage.

Kuhar, M., & Reiter, H. (2013). Toward a concept of parental authority in adolescence. *CEPS Journal: Center for Educational Policy Studies Journal, 3*(2), 135.

Kumar, K. (1999). Children and adults: Reading an autobiography. In T. S. Saraswathi (Ed.), *Culture, socialization & human development. Theory, research and applications in India.* New Delhi: Sage Publications Pvt. Ltd.

Larson, R., Verma, S., & Dworkin, J. (2001). Adolescent's family relationships in India: The daily family lives of Indian middle class teenagers. In J. Arnett (Ed.), *Readings on adolescence and emerging adulthood* (pp. 134–141). Abington, MA: Prentice Hall.

Larson, R., Verma, S., & Dworkin, J. (2003). Adolescence without family disengagement: The daily family lives of Indian middle class teenagers. In T. S. Saraswathi (Ed.), *Cross-cultural perspectives in human development theory, research and application* (pp. 258–286). New Delhi: Sage.

Mascolo, M. F., Misra, G., & Rapisardi, C. (2004). Individual and relational conceptions of self in India and the United States. *New Directions for Child and Adolescent Development, 104,* 9–26.

McElhaney, K. B., & Allen, J. P. (in press). Sociocultural perspectives on adolescent autonomy. In P. Kerig, M. Schulz, & S. T. Hauser (Eds.), *Adolescence and beyond.* Oxford University Press.

Miller, J., Akiyama, H., & Kapadia, S. (in press). Cultural variation in communal vs. exchange norms: Implications for social support. *Journal of Personality and Social Psychology.*

National Youth Policy. (2014). *Ministry of Youth Affairs and Sports, Government of India.*

Omer, H., Steinmetz, S. G., Carthy, T., & Schlippe, A. (2013). The anchoring function: Parental authority and the parent-child bond. *Family Process, 52*(2), 193–206. doi:10.1111/famp.12019.

Panda, M. (2013). Madhyam Marg: How it constitutes Indian mind? *Psychology and Developing Societies, 25*(1), 77–107. doi:10.1177/0971333613477317.

Phadke, S. (2003). Thirty years on women's studies reflects on the women's movement. *Economic and Political Weekly, 38*(43), 4567–4576.

Philipose, P. (2012). The resilience of patriarchy. *Infochange Agenda,* (25), 2. Retrieved from http://infochangeindia.org/downloads/agenda_25.pdf.

Phinney, J. S., Kim-Jo, T., Osorio, S., & Vilhjalmsdottir, P. (2005). Autonomy and relatedness in adolescent-parent disagreements ethnic and developmental factors. *Journal of Adolescent Research, 20*(1), 8–39.

Prakash, P. (2013). Towards a youth agenda in policy and practice. In P. Prakash (Ed.), *State of the urban youth, India 2013: Employment, livelihoods, skills* (pp. 2–7). Mumbai: IRIS Knowledge Foundation.

Renner, W. (2014, December). Globalization and Indian youth: Findings from moral foundations theory. In *Current issues of science and research in the global world: Proceedings of the International Conference on Current Issues of Science and Research in the Global World, Vienna, Austria; 27–28 May 2014* (p. 7). CRC Press.

Rentelen, A. D. (2004). *The cultural defense.* London, Oxford: Oxford University Press.

Saraswathi, T. S., & Pai, S. (1997). Socialization in the Indian context. In D. Sinha & H. S. R. Kao (Eds.), *Asian perspectives on psychology* (pp. 74–92). New Delhi: Sage.

Saraswathi, T. S., & Oke, M. (2013). Ecology of adolescence in India: Implications for policy and practice. *Psychological Studies, 58*(4), 353–364.

Schlegel, A. (2011). Human development and cultural transmission. *Anthropologischer Anzeiger, 68*(4), 457–470. doi:10.1127/0003-5548/2011/0155.

Schlegel, A., & Barry, H., III. (1991). *Adolescence: An anthropological inquiry.* New York: Free Press.

Seymour, S. C. (1999). *Women, family, and child care in India: A world in transition.* Cambridge University Press.

Sharma, N. (1996). *Identity of the adolescent girl.* New Delhi: Discovery Publishing House.

Sinha, D. (1988). Basic Indian values and behavior dispositions in the context of national development: An appraisal. In D. Sinha & H. S. Kao (Eds.), *Social values and development: Asian perspectives* (pp. 31–55). New Delhi: Sage.

Sinha, D., & Tripathi, R. C. (1994). Individualism in a collectivist culture: A case of coexistence of opposites. In U. Kim, H. C. Triandis, C. Kagitcibasi, S. Chin-Choi, & G. Yoon (Eds.), *Individualism and collectivism: Theory, research and methodology series* (pp. 123–136). ND: Sage.

Thapan, M. (2007). Adolescence, embodiment and gender identity: Elite women in a changing society. In R. Ghadially (Ed.), *Urban women in contemporary India*. New Delhi: Sage.

Trommsdorff, G. (2006). Parent-child relations over the life-span. A cross-cultural perspective. In K. H. Rubin & O. B. Chung (Eds.). (2013). *Parenting beliefs, behaviors, and parent-child relations: A cross-cultural perspective* (pp. 143–183). New York: Psychology Press, Taylor & Francis Group.

Valsiner, J. (2000). *Culture and human development: An introduction*. London: Sage.

Verma, S., & Saraswathi, T. S. (2002). Adolescence in India: Street urchins or Silicon Valley millionaires? In B. B. Brown, R. W. Larson, & T. S. Saraswathi (Eds.), *The world's youth: Adolescence in eight regions of the globe* (pp. 105–140). Cambridge: Cambridge University Press.

White, J. B., Langer, E. J., Yariv, L., & Welch, J. C., IV. (2006). Frequent social comparisons and destructive emotions and behaviors: The dark side of social comparisons. *Journal of Adult Development, 13*(1), 36–44.

Yeh, K. H., Liu, Y. L., Huang, H. S., & Yang, Y. J. (2007). Individuating and relating autonomy in culturally Chinese adolescents. In J. Liu, C. Ward, A. Bernardo, M. Karasawa, & R. Fischer (Eds.), *Casting the individual in societal and cultural contexts* (pp. 123–146). Korea: Kyoyook-Kwahak-Sa Publishing.

Zimmer-Gembeck, M. J., & Collins, W. A. (2003). Autonomy development during adolescence. In G. R. Adams & M. D. Berzonsky (Eds.), *Blackwell handbook of adolescence* (pp. 175–204). Malden, MA: Blackwell.

Appendix A
Survey Questionnaire

Survey Questionnaire for Adolescents

Section I

Background Information

1. Name:
2. Address:
3. Tel. No.:
4. Sex:
   (a) Female ☐
   (b) Male ☐
5. Age:
6. Name of School:
7. Class:
8. Mother Tongue:
9. Religion:
10. Type of Family (Please tick one box)
    (a) Nuclear ☐
    (b) Joint ☐
11. Education of Mother:
12. Occupation of Mother:

13. Education of Father:
14. Occupation of Father:

© Springer (India) Pvt. Ltd. 2017
S. Kapadia, *Adolescence in Urban India*,
DOI 10.1007/978-81-322-3733-4

Section II

1. According to you in which phase/stage of life are you in?
2. List all the terms/phrases you know that describes the phase/stage of life in which you are at present.
3. What are the common characteristics of girls and boys of your age? (Please answer for both (a) and (b)

    (a) Common characteristics of girls (at least 3)

        (i)
        (ii)
        (iii)
        (iv)
        (v)

    (b) Common characteristics of boys (at least 3)

        (i)
        (ii)
        (iii)
        (iv)
        (v)

4. Does the age in which you are hold any special importance in your life?

    (a) If yes, why?
    (b) If no, why not?

5. List the qualities you like the most in yourself (at least 3).

    (a)
    (b)
    (c)
    (d)
    (e)

6. List the qualities you dislike the most in yourself (at least 3).

    (a)
    (b)
    (c)
    (d)
    (e)

7. List the qualities of an ideal girl and an ideal boy (at least 3). (Please answer for both (a) and (b))

    (a) An ideal girl

        (i)

        (ii)

        (iii)

        (iv)

        (v)

    (b) An ideal boy

        (i)

        (ii)

        (iii)

        (iv)

        (v)

8. What are your expectations from yourself?

9. What do your parents expect from you?

10. What are your expectations from your parents?

Checklist for areas of disagreement/conflict

Areas of disagreement/conflict	Frequency				With whom			Intensity	
	Everyday	Once a week	Once a month		Mother	Father	Both	Serious	Not serious
1. Sleeping habits (e.g., sleeping late in the night, waking up late)									
2. Eating habits (e.g., does not eat on times of meals, eats a lot of junk food, very fussy about food)									
3. Being disorganized with one's things (e.g., books, clothes, sports kit, shoes in their place/keeping the room disorganized)									
4. Wasting time by watching movies, television and roaming around									
5. Wasting money (e.g., on clothes, personal grooming, buying CD's, buying or maintenance of vehicle)									
6. Emphasizing too much on physical appearance/looks (e.g., style of dressing, make up, hair style)									
7. Not helping with household chores (e.g., cooking, shopping for home)									
8. Driving/riding the vehicle too fast									

(continued)

(continued)

Areas of disagreement/conflict	Frequency			With whom			Intensity	
	Everyday	Once a week	Once a month	Mother	Father	Both	Serious	Not serious
9. Talking too much on the phone								
10. Choosing subjects/stream (e.g., commerce/arts/science)								
11. When child scores less marks								
12. Emphasizing too much on extra-curricular activities (e.g., sports, dance, drama, music)								
13. Not concentrating/spending enough time on studies								
14. Spending too much time on the Internet/computer/video game								
15. Spending too much time listening to music								
16. Spending too much time with friends								
17. Going out with a mixed group of boys and girls								
18. Having a girlfriend/boyfriend								
19. Going out for late night parties								
20. Going for overnight stay at friend's place								

(continued)

(continued)

Areas of disagreement/conflict	Frequency				With whom			Intensity	
	Everyday	Once a week	Once a month		Mother	Father	Both	Serious	Not serious
21. Expecting/demanding more freedom from parents									
22. Instead of seeking permission the child just informs parents while going out with friends									
23. Parents disliking child's friend/friends									
24. Parents beating the child									
25. Parents favoring one child over the other									
26. Child disrespecting parents									
27. Child disobeying parents									
28. Parents scolding the child									
29. Parents do not/are not able to fulfill child's expectations/demand									
30. Child does not/is not able to fulfill parents expectations/demands									
31. Child is very talkative									
32. Child does not want to visit relatives									
33. Child does not wish to attend family/social functions									

(continued)

(continued)

Areas of disagreement/conflict	Frequency				With whom			Intensity	
	Everyday	Once a week	Once a month		Mother	Father	Both	Serious	Not serious
34. Child does not behave in a socially desirable manner (e.g., talking loudly, interfering when adults talk)									
35. Choosing a marriage partner									
36. Choosing a career									
37. Showing disrespect toward teachers (e.g., making fun of teachers, talking bad about them)									
38. Any other, please specify									

Thank you for your cooperation

Survey Questionnaire for Parents

Section I

Background Information

1. Name:
2. Address:
   Tel. No.:
4. Sex:
   (a) Female ☐
   (b) Male ☐
5. Age:
6. Mother Tongue:
7. Religion:
8. Type of Family (Please tick one box):
   Nuclear ☐
   Joint ☐
9. Your Education:
10. Your Occupation:
11. Education of Spouse:
12. Occupation of Spouse:
13. No. of Children:

Sr. No	Age	Sex
a.		
b.		
c.		
d.		

Section II

1. According to you, your daughter/son is in which phase of life?
2. List all the terms/phrases you know that describe the present phase of life of your daughter/son.
3. What are the common characteristics of the girls/boys in the age group in which your daughter/son is at present? (Please answer for both (a) & (b))

(a) Common Characteristics of girls (at least 3)

    (i)

    (ii)

    (iii)

    (iv)

    (v)

(b) Common characteristics of boys (at least 3)

    (i)

    (ii)

    (iii)

    (iv)

    (v)

4. Does the age/stage in which your daughter/son is, holds any importance in her/his life?

    (a) If yes, why?

    (b) If no, why not?

5. List the qualities of your daughter/son, which you like the most (at least 3).

    (a)

    (b)

    (c)

    (d)

    (e)

6. List the qualities of your daughter/son, which you dislike the most (at least 3).

    (a)

    (b)

    (c)

    (d)

    (e)

7. List the qualities of an ideal girl and an ideal boy (at least 3). (Please answer for both (a) and (b)

    (a) An ideal girl

        (i)

        (ii)

        (iii)

        (iv)

        (v)

(b) An ideal boy

   (i)
   (ii)
   (iii)
   (iv)
   (v)

8. What do you expect your daughter/son to do for herself/himself?
9. What do you expect your daughter/son to do for you?
10. What does your daughter/son expect from you?

Checklist for areas of disagreement/conflict

Areas of disagreement/conflict	Frequency			With whom			Intensity	
	Everyday	Once a week	Once a month	Mother	Father	Both	Serious	Not serious
1. Sleeping habits (e.g., sleeping late in the night, waking up late)								
2. Eating habits (e.g., does not eat on times of meals, eats a lot of junk food, very fussy about food)								
3. Being disorganized with one's things (e.g., books, clothes, sports kit, shoes in their place/keeping the room disorganized)								
4. Wasting time by watching movies, television and roaming around								
5. Wasting money (e.g., on clothes, personal grooming, buying CD's, buying or maintenance of vehicle)								
6. Emphasizing too much on physical appearance/looks (e.g., style of dressing, make up, hair style)								
7. Not helping with household chores (e.g., cooking, shopping for home)								
8. Driving/riding the vehicle too fast								
9. Talking too much on the phone								
10. Choosing subjects/stream (e.g., commerce/arts/science)								
11. When child scores less marks								
12. Emphasizing too much on extra-curricular activities (e.g., sports, dance, drama, music)								
13. Not concentrating/spending enough time on studies								
14. Spending too much time on the Internet/computer/video game								
15. Spending too much time listening to music								
16. Spending too much time with friends								
17. Going out with a mixed group of boys and girls								
18. Having a girlfriend/boyfriend								
19. Going out for late night parties								
20. Going for overnight stay at friend's place								
21. Expecting/demanding more freedom from parents								

(continued)

(continued)

Areas of disagreement/conflict	Frequency			With whom			Intensity	
	Everyday	Once a week	Once a month	Mother	Father	Both	Serious	Not serious
22. Instead of seeking permission the child just informs parents while going out with friends								
23. Parents disliking child's friend/friends								
24. Parents beating the child								
25. Parents favoring one child over the other								
26. Child disrespecting parents								
27. Child disobeying parents								
28. Parents scolding the child								
29. Parents do not/are not able to fulfill child's expectations/demand								
30. Child does not/is not able to fulfill parents expectations/demands								
31. Child is very talkative								
32. Child does not want to visit relatives								
33. Child does not wish to attend family/social functions								
34. Child does not behave in a socially desirable manner (e.g., talking loudly, interfering when adults talk)								
35. Choosing a marriage partner								
36. Choosing a career								
37. Showing disrespect toward teachers (e.g., making fun of teachers, talking bad about them)								
38. Any other, please specify								

Thank you for your cooperation

Appendix B
Interview Form: Real Life Disagreements

Opening Questions:

A. Thinking about your relationship with your mother, what are some of the sources of satisfaction that you have experienced? *Explain why you find that satisfying.*
B. Now, thinking about your relationship with your father, what are some of the sources of satisfaction that you have experienced? Explain *why you find that satisfying.*
C. Now, can you think of any dissatisfactions that you may have experienced in your relationship with your mother? Explain *why you find that dissatisfying.*
D. Thinking about your relationship with your father, can you think of any dissatisfactions that you may have experienced? Explain *why you find that dissatisfying.*

Most young people have shared with us that even when they get along well with their parents, there are occasional times when differences of opinion occur between them. These may be about everyday matters or about major issues. I would like you to talk about the kinds of things that come up in your family. Can you think of a specific disagreement or difference of opinion that you have had recently with your parents?

(Note: If respondent mentions a conflict that involves both of his parents, identify, if possible, which parent was most centrally involved and phrase probes below asking about that parent only).

1. Please describe the situation. With whom did the difference of opinion/ disagreement occur? What happened?

   (a)What were your views/reactions?
   (b)Why did you react in this way?

2. (a) What were the views/reactions of your parent?
   (b) Why did he/she react in this way?

© Springer (India) Pvt. Ltd. 2017
S. Kapadia, *Adolescence in Urban India*,
DOI 10.1007/978-81-322-3733-4

3. (a) How was the difference of opinion/disagreement resolved? What was the outcome?

(b) Using the scale below, rate how the disagreement was resolved:

0	1	2	3	4	5
not at all	a little	somewhat	a lot	much	totally

(i) I ended up accommodating or giving into my parent's initial concerns or outlook.

(ii) My parent ended up accommodating or giving into my initial concerns or outlook.

Explain your ratings:

(c) Rate how important each of the considerations below was in <u>why YOU responded</u> in the way that you did:

0	1	2	3	4	5
not at all	a little	somewhat	a lot	much	totally

I was trying to be sensitive to my parent's concerns and wishes

My parents' views made sense and were in my best interest.

In my opinion, what I wanted to do to in this situation was in my own best interest

It was my responsibility as their son/daughter to accommodate to what they wanted

I felt that what I did in this situation should be my own business.

My parents were pressuring me to do this.

(d) Rate how important each of the considerations below was in <u>why YOUR MOTHER/FATHER responded</u> in the way that he/she did

0	1	2	3	4	5
not at all	a little	somewhat	a lot	much	totally

He/she was trying to be sensitive to my concerns and wishes

He/she felt that his/her own views on this were in my best interest

In my parents' opinion, what I wanted to do in this situation was in my own best interest

It is his/her responsibility as a parent to act in this way

He/she felt that what I did in this situation should be my own personal decision

He/she was trying to control what I did.

4. (a) Were YOU satisfied with the way the disagreement/issue was resolved?
Why or why not? How did you feel?
(b) Rate how satisfied you felt on the scale below:

-5	-4	-3	-2	-1	0	1	2	3	4	5
extremely dissatisfied					neutral			extremely satisfied		

5. (a) Do you think YOUR MOTHER/FATHER was satisfied with the way it was
resolved? Why or why not? How did He/she feel?
(b) Rate how satisfied your mother/father felt on the scale below:

-5	-4	-3	-2	-1	0	1	2	3	4	5
Extremely dissatisfied					neutral			extremely satisfied		

6. (a) Do you feel that there is a responsibility or obligation to accommodate in
some way to what your parents wanted you to do in this situation or do you
consider it your own business whether or not to _____? Explain.
6. (b) Do you feel that your parents have a responsibility or obligation to
accommodate in some way to what you wanted to do in this situation? Explain.
7. (a) In your opinion, how important was the incident that we just talked about:

0	1	2	3	4	5
not at all	a little	somewhat	a lot	very	extremely important

(b) Do you consider it a MINOR or a MAJOR disagreement? Explain:
Note. Questions 1–7 to be repeated in relation to a second disagreement narrated
by the adolescent.

Appendix C
Interview Form: Adolescence Stage and Self

Adolescents

1. **How would you describe your present stage of life?**
   (Probe/Sub questions)

   - Think of a boy/girl your age, what are the typical characteristics/qualities that the person would have?
   - What characteristics/qualities do you like in boys/girls your age?
   - What characteristics/qualities do you not like in boys/girls your age?

2. **How would you describe yourself?** (Please state and share at least 3 descriptions/explanations).

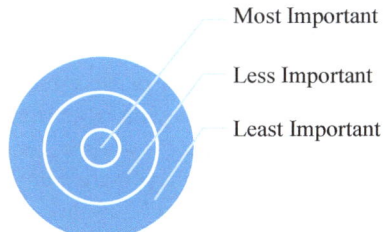

Most Important

Less Important

Least Important

- The innermost circle is for the self-descriptions that are considered as "most important" to you.
- The next layer is for "less important" attributes.
- The most outer circle is for attributes viewed as "least important".

   - With reference to self-descriptions/explanations and qualities/attributes/characteristics you just shared above, would you able to put them into categories from most important to least important?

© Springer (India) Pvt. Ltd. 2017
S. Kapadia, *Adolescence in Urban India*,
DOI 10.1007/978-81-322-3733-4

3. **According to you what are the major concerns of this stage? Give reasons/explain with example**.
   (Probe)

   - What are the main concerns people of your age generally have?
   - Being a girl/boy, what are some special concerns that you may have?

4. **What do you dream about in life? What do you need for your dreams to come true?**

5. **Please share your three important wishes (in order of priority)**.

   - Give reasons/Explain with examples. (Probe: wishes related to self, family, other wishes)
   - What are your parents' wishes for you?

6. **What are your parents' expectations from you?**

   - Do you think your parents expect some things from you especially because you are a boy/girl? What are these?

7. **In order of priority, please share your three major insecurities/concerns/worries/anxieties**.

   - Give reasons/Explain with examples.

8. **Who is your role model? Why?**

9. **Who are you closest to? Who would you approach to discuss any problem that you may have?**

10. **How would you describe your relationship with your parents? (Mother? father?)**

    - In every relationship, there are differences of opinion or disagreements. What are the common disagreements that you have with your mother? Father? How are these resolved?
    - Are there any special things that parents tell you because you are a boy/girl?

11. **What is your most cherished/favorite/memory till date?**

    - If you had a magic wand and could change any 3 things about your life/yourself/your parents or family, what would these be and why?
    - What brings you most joy?/what makes you happy?
    - What brings you sadness?/what makes you sad?

12. **What is success according to you? How do you define success?**

13. **Where/How do you see yourself five years from now? Ten years from now?**

Parents

1. According to you, your daughter/son is in which phase/stage of life? OR What phase of life would you say your son/daughter is in?
2. List all the terms/phrases you know that describe the present phase of life of your daughter/son.
3. What are the common characteristics of the girls/boys in the age group in which your daughter/son is at present? Please answer for both (a) and (b).

   (a) Common Characteristics of girls (at least 3)
   (b) Common characteristics of boys (at least 3)

4. Does the age/stage in which your daughter/son is, hold any importance in her/his life?

   (a) If yes, why?
   (b) If no, why not?

5. List the characteristics/qualities of your daughter/son, which you like the most (at least 3).
6. List the characteristics/qualities of your daughter/son, which you dislike the most (at least 3).
7. List the characteristics/qualities of an ideal girl and an ideal boy (at least 3). Please answer for both "(a)" and "(b)".

   (a) An ideal girl
   (b) An ideal boy

8. What do you expect your daughter/son to do/become in life?
9. What do you expect your daughter/son to do for you?
10. What does your daughter/son expect from you?
11. Please share three important wishes that you have for your son/daughter?
12. What are your concerns or worries for your son/daughter? (share at least three)
13. According to you, what characteristics would be ideal for a parent of a child in this age (phase of life) to have? Why? Give reasons for your response.
14. What are the challenges in raising a child of this age in the present day context?
15. What kind of parenting practices would be most effective in this context? Why? Give reasons for your response.
16. What are your goals for your son/daughter? Where do you expect to see your son/daughter five years from now? Ten years from now?
17. (a) Raising a son and daughter involves similar and different opportunities and challenges in the present day context. What are these? (Request separate responses for girl and boy). How does one deal with the challenges?

    (b) What are your concerns as a parent of a teenage/adolescent boy/son or girl/daughter? How do you deal with these?

Appendix D
Focus Group Discussion Guidelines

Adolescents

Stage Description and Concerns

How would you describe your present stage of life?
According to you what are the major concerns of this stage? Give reasons/explain with example.

Authority

Every family has some rules for children. What are the rules in your family?
What will your parents simply not allow you to do?
How would you describe your parents? Strict? Not so strict? Not at all strict
Strict in what aspects? Why do you think so? Examples?
To what extent and in what aspects do your parents allow you to make choices?
To what extent and in what aspects are your parents willing to consider your point of view?

If you do not agree with something your parents are asking you to do or not to do, what do you do? Why? Example.

As there are a lot of situations where the views of parents and children sometimes match and sometimes doesn't. How do you think these misunderstanding between the children and parents can be reduced? Can you share two such recent incidents?

Comment on the following statements:
There are some things about me that my parents don't know

My parents know everything there is to know about me
When I become a parent, I'm going to treat my children in exactly the same way that my parents have treated me
There are things that I will do differently from my mother and father when I become a parent

---

(continued)

© Springer (India) Pvt. Ltd. 2017
S. Kapadia, *Adolescence in Urban India*,
DOI 10.1007/978-81-322-3733-4

(continued)

For each domain below, select any one statement of the following two:

Marriage

– In matters of marriage, boys and girls must be consulted. However, final decision should be taken by parents
– In matters of marriage, parents must be consulted. However, final decision should be taken by the boy or girl

Girl-Boy Friendships

– In our societies, meeting of girls and boys before marriage must be restricted
– There should be no restriction in meeting of girls and boys
– What are your views regarding girl-boy friendships/relationships? Describe any situation in where your parents supported you or had conflicting views about it?

Gender

– Girls and boys are different and hence need different treatment. What is your opinion?
– Do you think boys and girls have different roles to play?
– Do you think parents should restrict mobility of girls more than boys?

Privacy Issues

Parents have a right to know everything that goes on with you/in your life?
– Agree/disagree
– Reasons/explain (ask for examples)

Use of cell phones and computers is very common today, especially among young people.
Do you have any rules regarding this in your family? (e.g., amount of time, nature of use?)
Do your parents have access to your phone? Computer? Do they check it? How do you feel about it?
What is your idea of having privacy? Is it necessary or good to have privacy? Yes/no —give reasons.
What are the one or two things that upset you about your parents very much? Why?

Social Comparisons

Sometimes we are all envious or jealous of our friends for some reason or the other. Arun/Anita is often envious/jealous of his/her friends on one or more of the following aspects:
– He/she appearance is better than his/hers
– He/she always scores high marks
– He/she has a popular brand in a bike
– The family owns an expensive car
– He/she wears only branded clothes
– He/she has regular holidays abroad
– He/she has an Iphone
– He/she can spend any amount of money that he/she wishes

(continued)

(continued)

What do you think about this?

Have you experienced any of this?

What is it that you wish you had that your friends already have? (Probe—physical appearance—fat, slim, fair, dark, well built, Iphone, car, a certain brand of bike, nice clothes, holidays abroad, more money to spend)

General

We all get worried, anxious, or insecure sometimes. What makes you anxious? Why? Share any three matters (order of priority).

What makes your parents anxious about you?

According to you what are the major concerns of this stage? Give reasons/explain with example.

(Probes)

– What are the main concerns people of your age generally have?
– Being a girl/boy, what are some special concerns that you may have?

What is success according to you? How do you define success? What is needed to be successful in today's world?

Where/How do you see yourself five years from now? Ten years from now?

If you had a magic wand and could change any three things about your life/yourself/your parents or family, what would these be and why?

What is your idea of being independent? (or what is your idea of freedom?) How do your parents feel about it? Are there any issues with regard to this? Please give examples.

There are some things about our parents that bother us. If you could bring a change in your parents, what would it be? Why?

Parents

Son _____   Daughter _____
Age _____   Age   _____

I am doing a study on adolescents in urban Indian settings—about their lives, what they think about themselves, their hopes, aspirations, and insecurities and worries. I would like to understand this from parents as well.

According to you, your daughter/son is in which phase/stage of life? OR What phase of life would you say your son/daughter is in? What is the significance of this stage?

List the characteristics/qualities of an ideal girl and an ideal boy (at least 3).

An ideal girl
An ideal boy

Please share three important wishes that you have for your son/daughter?

What are your goals for your son/daughter? Where do you expect to see your son/daughter five years from now? Ten years from now?

What kind of parenting practices would be most effective during this period? Why? Give reasons for your response.

Raising a son and daughter involves similar and different opportunities and challenges in the present day context. What are these? (Request separate responses for girl and boy). How does one deal with the challenges?

What are the challenges in raising a child of this age in the present day context?

What are some aspects or characteristics of young people today that are better/not as good as earlier times (When you were an adolescent for example)?

We all get worried or anxious sometimes concerning our children. What makes you anxious? Why? (probe for at least three)

How do you teach your child about the societal values? How did you find the process of teaching your child these values?

All of us many times face a lot of competition and we sometimes fail to keep up with the pressure. How do you encourage your children in such situation and do you find it difficult sometimes to motivate your child?

There are many situations where the views of parents and children sometimes match and sometimes do not. What are some of these? How do you think these misunderstandings between children and parents can be reduced?

Hypothetical Vignettes

Mixed Group Weekend Picnic

"Samir/Reena has an invitation to go out for a weekend picnic with a group of boys and girls. However, the parents are not giving permission to go as they are not in favor of heterosexual friendships."
What is your opinion? Why?

Career Choice

"Vikram/Pooja wants to pursue a career of his/her own choice. However, the parents have thought of another career which they think will be the best for him/her".
What is your opinion? Why?

Marriage Partner Selection

"Arun and Nisha want to get married to each other. But their parents are opposed to this marriage because they both belong to different castes. The parents feel that their children should get married within their own caste and to someone who their parents choose for them".

What is your opinion? Why?

Marriage

Select any one statement and explain:

- In matters of marriage, boys and girls must be consulted. However, final decision should be taken by parents.
- In matters of marriage, parents must be consulted. However, final decision should be taken by the boy or girl.

Girl-Boy Friendships

Select any one statement and explain:

- In our societies, meeting of girls and boys before marriage must be restricted.
- There should be no restriction in meeting of girls and boys.

Gender

- Girls and boys are different and hence need different treatment. What is your opinion?

Technology Use

- How is technology influencing young people today? Cell phone? Computer? Internet?
- As a parent, how do you deal with this?

Privacy Issues

Use of cell phones and computers is very common today, especially among young people.

- Do you have any rules regarding this in your family? (e.g., amount of time, nature of use?)
- Do you have access to your adolescent's phone? Computer? Do you check it? Does he/she know? How does he/she feel about it?
- What is your idea of giving privacy to your adolescent? Is it necessary or good to do so? Yes/No. Give reasons.

Independence

- What is your idea of being independent? (or what is your idea of freedom?) Are there any issues with regard to this with your adolescent? Please give examples.
- What are some aspects/areas where you will put your foot down?

Success

- What is your idea of success (of your adolescent?) What is needed for this?

Worries, Anxieties

– What are the one or two things that worry you most regarding your adolescent? Explain.

Social Comparisons

– In this age, social comparisons are rather common, for example, comparing with friends regarding material items or even physical appearance. Please share any such instances regarding your adolescent.

Overall comment on the parental role today.

Appendix E
Select Quantitative Results

Expectations of Parents and Adolescents

See Tables E.1 and E.2.

Table E.1 Expectations of parents from adolescents (percentage)

Themes	Parent	Adolescent
Academic/career	20	43
Good person and work habits	13	18
Parents/family related	42	16
No expectations	12	2
No response/NA	13	4

Table E.2 Expectations of adolescents from parents (percentage)

Themes	Parent	Adolescent
Understanding and guidance	36	51
Love and blessings	22	16
Academic/career	12	11
Material support	13	3
No expectations	3	10
No response/NA	14	9

Themes of Interpersonal Disagreements

See Table E.3

© Springer (India) Pvt. Ltd. 2017
S. Kapadia, *Adolescence in Urban India*,
DOI 10.1007/978-81-322-3733-4

Table E.3 Themes of interpersonal disagreements (percentage)

Theme	Early adolescents (n = 60)						Mid-Adolescents (n = 60)					
	Girls (n = 30)		Boys (n = 30)		Total		Girls (n = 30)		Boys (n = 30)		Total	
	With mother	With father	With mother	With father			With mother	With father	With mother	With father		
Chores	2 (4.35)	–	–	–	2 (1.77)		1 (3.85)	1 (3.45)	1 (2.70)	–	3 (2.63)	
Academics	8 (17.39)	2 (16.67)	15 (48.39)	3 (12.5)	28 (24.78)		3 (11.54)	7 (24.14)	11 (29.73)	4 (18.18)	25 (21.93)	
Regulation interpersonal activities	9 (19.57)	1 (8.33)	–	–	10 (8.85)		4 (15.38)	4 (13.79)	5 (13.51)	3 (13.64)	16 (14.04)	
Regulation behavior/activities	24 (52.17)	8 (66.67)	14 (45.16)	19 (79.17)	65 (57.52)		15 (57.69)	14 (48.28)	15 (40.54)	13 (59.09)	57 (50)	
Finance	–	–	1 (3.23)	2 (8.33)	3 (2.65)		2 (7.69)	2 (6.90)	3 (8.11)	2 (9.09)	9 (7.89)	
Physical appearance	3 (6.52)	1 (8.33)	–	–	4 (3.54)		1 (3.85)	–	2 (5.41)	–	3 (2.63)	
Other (Partiality to sibling)	–	–	1 (3.23)	–	1 (0.88)		–	1 (3.45)	–	–	1 (0.88)	
Total	46 (100)	12 (100)	31 (100)	24 (100)	113 (100)		26 (100)	29 (100)	37 (100)	22 (100)	114 (100)	

Note 13 respondents gave one disagreement. Dashes indicate information not applicable

Adolescent and Parent Accommodation in Disagreement Situations

See Tables E.4 and E.5.

Table E.4 Means, standard deviations, and *t*-values of accommodation by adolescents and parents (early adolescents and mid-adolescents)

Accommodation	Early adolescent (*n* = 60)		Mid-adolescent (*n* = 60)		*t*-value
	M	SD	M	SD	
Adolescent accommodates	2.90	1.11	2.63	1.16	1.32
Parent accommodates	2.09	1.20	2.16	1.27	−0.33

Table E.5 Means, standard deviations, and *t*-values of accommodation by adolescents and parents (boys and girls)

Accommodation	Early adolescents (*n* = 60)					Mid-adolescents (*n* = 60)				
	Boys (*n* = 30)		Girls (*n* = 30)		*t*-value	Boys (*n* = 30)		Girls (*n* = 30)		*t*-value
	M	SD	M	SD		M	SD	M	SD	
Adolescent accommodates	2.76	1.19	3.05	1.02	−0.98	2.70	1.14	2.56	1.20	0.44
Parent accommodates	2.25	1.27	1.93	1.11	1.02	2.10	1.17	2.23	1.38	−0.40

Considerations Important for Adolescents and Parents in Resolving Disagreements

See Tables E.6, E.7, E.8 and E.9.

Table E.6 Means, standard deviations, and *t*-values of considerations important for adolescents in resolving the disagreements (early adolescents and mid-adolescents)

Considerations	Early adolescents (*n* = 60)		Mid-adolescents (*n* = 60)		*t*-value
	M	SD	M	SD	
Adolescent is being sensitive to parents' concern and wishes	2.19	1.24	2.12	1.09	0.35
Adolescent thinks parents' views are in her/his best interest	3.08	1.34	3.02	1.33	0.27
Adolescent thinks her/his decision is in own best interest	2.68	1.28	2.64	1.32	0.18

(continued)

Table E.6 (continued)

Considerations	Early adolescents ($n = 60$)		Mid-adolescents ($n = 60$)		t-value
	M	SD	M	SD	
Adolescent feels it is her/his responsibility to accommodate to parents	3.18	1.34	2.67	1.20	2.19*
Adolescent feels it is her/his own business	1.93	1.56	1.69	1.38	0.87
Adolescent feels parents are pressuring him/her	1.41	1.24	1.57	1.40	−0.66

*$p < 0.05$

Table E.7 Means, standard deviations, and t-values of considerations important for adolescents in resolving the disagreements (boys and girls)

Considerations	Early adolescents ($n = 60$)					Mid-adolescents ($n = 60$)				
	Girls ($n = 30$)		Boys ($n = 30$)		t-value	Girls ($n = 30$)		Boys ($n = 30$)		t-value
	M	SD	M	SD		M	SD	M	SD	
Adolescent is being sensitive to parents' concern and wishes	1.82	1.34	2.57	1.03	2.43*	2.30	1.11	1.93	1.06	−1.31
Adolescent thinks parents' views are in her/his best interest	2.90	1.42	3.27	1.26	1.06	2.97	1.44	3.07	1.23	0.29
Adolescent thinks her/his decision is in own best interest	2.58	1.28	2.78	1.28	0.60	2.65	1.19	2.63	1.46	−0.05
Adolescent feels it is her/his responsibility to accommodate to parents	3.03	1.47	3.32	1.21	0.82	2.95	1.11	2.38	1.24	−1.87
Adolescent feels it is her/his own business	1.62	1.62	2.23	1.47	1.54	1.45	1.26	1.93	1.48	1.36
Adolescent feels parents are pressuring her/him	1.27	1.10	1.55	1.37	0.88	1.31	1.24	1.82	1.53	1.39

*$p < 0.05$

Table E.8 Means, standard deviations, and t-values of considerations important for parents in resolving the disagreements (early adolescents and mid-adolescents)

Considerations	Early adolescents ($n = 60$)		Mid-adolescents ($n = 60$)		t-value
	M	SD	M	SD	
Parent is being sensitive to adolescent's concerns	2.21	1.27	2.16	1.10	0.23
Parent thinks own views are in adolescent's best interest	3.48	1.43	3.43	1.06	0.18
Parent thinks adolescent is acting in own best interest	2.15	1.44	1.98	1.35	0.69
Parent feels it is his/her responsibility as a parent to act this way	3.57	1.31	3.38	1.19	0.84
Parent feels this is adolescent's own business	1.15	0.96	1.32	1.13	−0.87
Parent is trying to control child's behavior	2.43	1.42	2.11	1.30	1.30

Table E.9 Means, standard deviations, and t-values of considerations important for parents in resolving the disagreements (boys and girls)

Considerations	Early adolescents ($n = 60$)					Mid-adolescents ($n = 60$)				
	Girls ($n = 30$)		Boys ($n = 30$)		t-value	Girls ($n = 30$)		Boys ($n = 30$)		t-value
	M	SD	M	SD		M	SD	M	SD	
Parent being sensitive to adolescent's concerns	2.00	1.35	2.42	1.18	1.27	2.47	1.08	1.85	1.06	−2.23*
Parent thinks own views are in adolescent's best interest	3.57	1.41	3.38	1.47	−0.49	3.17	1.25	3.70	0.75	2.01*
Parent thinks adolescent is acting in own best interest	2.00	1.50	2.30	1.38	0.81	2.13	1.31	1.82	1.40	−0.90
Parent feels it is his/her responsibility as a parent to act this way	3.47	1.48	3.67	1.13	0.59	3.32	1.39	3.43	0.97	0.38
Parent feels this is adolescent's own business	1.12	0.91	1.18	1.02	0.27	1.45	1.18	1.18	1.07	−0.92
Parent is trying to control child's behavior	2.45	1.58	2.42	1.28	−0.09	1.85	1.27	2.37	1.29	1.56

*$p < 0.05$

Printed by Printforce, the Netherlands